The Constitution of Religious Freedom

The Constitution of Religious Freedom

God, Politics, and the First Amendment

Dennis J. Goldford

BAYLOR UNIVERSITY PRESS

Cover Design by Stephanie Blumenthal
Cover Image courtesy of the U.S. National Archives and Records Administration, http://www.archives.gov/exhibits/charters/.

Library of Congress Cataloging-in-Publication Data

Goldford, Dennis J., 1948–
The constitution of religious freedom : God, politics, and the First Amendment / Dennis J. Goldford.
276 p. cm.
Includes bibliographical references and index.
ISBN 978-1-60258-419-8 (hardback : alk. paper)
1. Freedom of religion--United States. 2. Church and state--United States. 3. Religion and politics--United States. I. Title.
KF4783.G654 2012
342.7308'52--dc23

2011032292

BAYLOR
UNIVERSITY

Printed in the United States of America on acid-free paper with a minimum of 30% PCW recycled content.

For Sharon

Contents

Preface

According to an old cautionary maxim, the two things we should never discuss in polite company are politics and religion. This book, either bravely or brazenly—or perhaps both—proposes to discuss both. As an American political scientist, I have been interested for a long time in the connections between politics and religion in the United States, and particularly interested in the rise of religion as an American political phenomenon in the latter part of the twentieth century in the form of religious conservatism and its accompanying constitutional theory. Despite, or perhaps even because of, the lack of an officially established church in the United States, religion has always been a factor in American politics. Many political scientists deal with the connection between politics and religion in behavioral terms of religious affiliation as an important factor in partisan identification, voting behavior, and policy preferences along the lines of factors like race, gender, ethnicity, education, income, and so on.

My approach in this book, by contrast, is one of political and constitutional theory rather than the conventional behavioral perspective on politics and religion. At first I conceptualized my interest in terms of the question of whether it is possible to have a secular society, but as I pursued that question I came to see that such a conceptualization was a faulty way to get at what I found especially important to understand about the connections between politics and religion. I came to see that the issue that concerns me was not the religious characteristics of the American people but, instead, the religious character, if any, of the American political order established by the American Constitution. Religion, we might say, is like electricity—overall, it is a force for good, but at the same time it is potentially dangerous, necessitating that we deal with it carefully. This book offers an account of how the Constitution requires and enables the

American political order to negotiate that task. As a work of political and constitutional theory, its principal concern is the question of whether, as the argument goes, any political order is and must be—and cannot not be—the establishment of a set of religious values and beliefs. My project here is to address that question in terms of the political and constitutional theory that explains, makes sense of, the religion clauses of the American Constitution.[1] What does the presence of those clauses indicate about the answer to that question provided by the American Constitution?

With its focus on the political- and constitutional-theoretical underpinnings of the religion clauses, this book does not attempt to address its central issue in terms of abstract political theory. At the same time, its focus on the political meaning of the religion clauses is more theoretical than an approach that seeks a narrower, more concrete and technical legal meaning of the religion clauses. This book thus differs, for example, from two recent companion works by Kent Greenawalt that devote many chapters to a wide range of religion-clause issues.[2] While I will turn to particular Supreme Court cases and law review articles to support the claim I will make as to the fundamental constitutional meaning of the religion clauses in general and the Establishment Clause in particular, my concern is to return to first principles rather than to create an adjudicative calculus that one can use to decide particular religion-clause cases. Constitutional adjudication takes place in terms of the constitutional text and the underlying principles expressed by the text. This book focuses on those principles, the principles that make sense out of having the religion clauses in the constitutional text. My purpose is to look "beneath" or "behind" the religion-clause cases to discover the principles of political and constitutional theory that best explain what it means to the American political order to have these clauses in the Constitution.

In particular, because the Establishment Clause goes to the question of the official or public status of religion, I will offer what I believe is the best statement of the principle embodied in that clause. Controversial for more than a half-century now, the Establishment Clause, more than the Free Exercise Clause, is central to my project, for it ultimately concerns

[1] Found in the First Amendment, the religion clauses are the following: "Congress shall make no law respecting an establishment of religion, or prohibiting the free exercise thereof." The former clause is the Establishment Clause, and the latter is the Free Exercise Clause.

[2] Kent Greenawalt, *Religion and the Constitution*, Vol. 1: *Free Exercise and Fairness* (Princeton, N.J.: Princeton University Press, 2006), and *Religion and the Constitution*, Vol. 2: *Establishment and Fairness* (Princeton, N.J.: Princeton University Press, 2008). With respect to the Establishment Clause, I will challenge the contention advanced by Greenawalt and others that "[n]either free exercise nor nonestablishment is reducible to any single value; many values count" (*Religion and the Constitution*, Vol. 2, 1).

both the public, political character of the religious dimension and the religious character of the public, political dimension of life in the United States. A segment of the American population, certainly a substantial and vocal minority with tremendous political and legal influence even if it is not a majority, holds that law and politics are essentially religious in nature. Does the Constitution presuppose or imply this proposition? Can we make sense of the religion clauses in general, and the Establishment Clause in particular, only on the basis of this proposition, or only on the basis of a rejection of this proposition?

Finally, one more maxim helps frame the following discussion, a maxim I encountered in German. *Jedes Ding hat Drei Seiten: Meine, Deine und die Richtige—also doch meine.* In other words, "Everything has three sides: my side, your side, and the right side—in other words, my side." That is precisely the problem with my subject matter here. In the arena of political and intellectual conflict over contentious, often intense, views of the relationship between politics and religion, even from the more philosophical perspective of political and constitutional theory, our task is to try to maintain the distinction between my side and the right side, striving always to aim at the latter as a way of correcting the former. If politics, at bottom, is the activity through which we negotiate our differences, enabling people of diverse values and beliefs to live together in the same society, can we have a viable political order if some fundamental values and beliefs are irreconcilable? Politics has to do with negotiating our differences, but are there some differences so fundamental that we cannot agree to disagree? Religion is certainly a prime candidate for that concern, and, in the last analysis, we have to understand the religion clauses of the American Constitution as an attempt to address that concern.

The intellectual debts of this book are numerous. My teaching responsibilities at Drake University generate research questions even as they make the pursuit of those questions take longer than one might wish. I created a course titled "Law, Politics, and Religion" several years ago to give me an opportunity to begin to think about the issues of political and constitutional theory I address in this book, and I am grateful to my students in the various iterations of that course for raising good questions that helped me develop, think through, and improve my ideas. Originating in that course, this project developed over the course of several years as I presented conference papers that began in their diversity to manifest a unitary underlying argument. Panel discussants frequently offered words of encouragement and, more significantly, helpful comments. I am grateful to the Drake University College of Arts and Sciences for inviting me to deliver the annual Stalnaker Lecture, which provided the opportunity for me to make myself find and elucidate publicly the argument underlying those papers in a broad, coherent form. The Drake University Center for the Humanities kindly awarded me a summer stipend that supported the project at a critical stage.

I am especially grateful to Carey Newman, Director of Baylor University Press, for his initial interest in those conference papers and subsequent support of and confidence in this project throughout the lengthy process of bringing it to fruition. Carey and the outside reviewers provided constructive suggestions and criticism that improved the substance of the argument of the book, and the Baylor editorial staff helped polish the manuscript and prepare it to see the light of day. Any remaining errors are, of course, my own responsibility.

Last in order but first in importance, my wife, Sharon, makes every day and every project worthwhile. I am grateful for her patience and understanding as I wrestled with the issues I explore here.

Introduction

Despite, or perhaps even because of, the prohibition of an officially established church in the United States, religion has always been a factor in American politics. Political scientists, for example, for years have studied the correlation of party identification and voting behavior with religious affiliation.[1] If we start with the premise that the Constitution establishes a particular kind of political order, however, we can distinguish between questions regarding the activities and agendas of religious groups in the American political order, and questions regarding the religious nature, if any, of the American political order. Questions of the former type take that political order for granted in order to explore certain political phenomena within it, whereas questions of the latter type take the overall character of that political order itself as their object of investigation. This book is not a work of political science concerned with questions of the political behavior of religious groups, but rather a work of political and constitutional theory, grounded in attention to religion-clause jurisprudence, concerned with questions regarding the nature of the political order established by the American Constitution. Specifically, it is an investigation of what the existence of the religion clauses of the Constitution, and

[1] Two standard textbooks on the general topic of politics and religion, but including discussions of religion-clause jurisprudence, are Robert Booth Fowler, Allen D. Hertzke, Laura R. Olson, and Kevin R. den Dulk, *Religion and Politics in America: Faith, Culture, and Strategic Choices*, 4th ed. (Boulder, Colo.: Westview, 2010), and Kenneth D. Wald and Allison Calhoun-Brown, *Religion and Politics in the United States*, 6th ed. (Lanham, Md.: Rowman & Littlefield, 2010). The Religion and Politics organized section of the American Political Science Association (http://www.apsa-section-religion-and-politics.org/) publishes a journal, *Politics and Religion*, which focuses on "the impact of religion on political attitudes, decision-making, and public policy development" (http://www.apsa-section-religion-and-politics.org/journal.html).

of the Establishment Clause in particular, signifies about the religious nature of the political order established by the American Constitution.

Conflict over this theoretical and jurisprudential question has become, over the past half-century since *Engel v. Vitale* and *Abington v. Schempp*,[2] a central issue itself in everyday, practical politics, both between the Democratic and Republican parties and within the Republican Party itself. Beyond specific issues in religion-clause case law, arguments about the religious character of the American political order stand behind the more explicitly political conflicts over what we can call a de facto religious test for office and the Christian-nation debate. The Constitution of the United States prohibits any official, de jure religious test for public office. The last paragraph of Article VI requires all government officials, both federal and state, to support the Constitution, but adds the stipulation for federal office that "no religious test shall ever be required as a qualification to any office or public trust under the United States." As for state office, the Supreme Court held in *Torcaso v. Watkins* (1961) that

> neither a State nor the Federal Government can constitutionally force a person "to profess a belief or disbelief in any religion." Neither can constitutionally pass laws or impose requirements which aid all religions as against non-believers, and neither can aid those religions based on a belief in the existence of God as against those religions founded on different beliefs.[3]

Nevertheless, it is not unusual to encounter in American electoral politics an unofficial, de facto religious test for public office. According to an August 2010 poll sponsored by the Pew Forum on Religion & Public Life, 67 percent of Americans say that religion is losing its influence on public life, and 53 percent say that this is a bad thing. Additionally, "Fully 61% say it is important that members of Congress have strong religious beliefs; just 34% disagree."[4] During the 2008 presidential-election cycle, former Massachusetts governor Mitt Romney found it necessary during his run for the Republican presidential nomination to give a speech titled "Faith in America" in late 2007 in order to deal with concern in some

[2] *Engel v. Vitale*, 370 U.S. 421 (1962), and *Abington School District v. Schempp*, 374 U.S. 203 (1963).

[3] *Torcaso v. Watkins*, 367 U.S. 488 (1961), at 495 (footnotes omitted). The Court overturned that part of Article 37 of the Declaration of Rights of the Maryland Constitution stating that "no religious test ought ever to be required as a qualification for any office of profit or trust in this State, other than a declaration of belief in the existence of God" (http://www.msa.md.gov/msa/mdmanual/43const/html/00dec.html, retrieved 6-23-10).

[4] Pew Forum on Religion & Public Life, "Growing Number of Americans Say Obama Is a Muslim" (http://pewforum.org/Politics-and-Elections/Growing-Number-of-Americans-Say-Obama-is-a-Muslim.aspx, retrieved 8-20-10).

circles about his Mormon religion. Implicit in that concern was a de facto religious disqualification for office, the view on the part of some people that they might not or would not be able to vote for a Mormon for the presidency.[5]

Three examples of more common occurrences of a de facto religious qualification for office occurred in the 2010 election cycle. First, South Carolina state representative Nikki Haley, an Indian-American, won the 2010 Republican nomination for governor but had to deal with questions as to her religious faith. The daughter of Indian immigrants, Haley told *The State* after her election to the South Carolina House in 2004 that she attended both Methodist and Sikh services but said in 2010 that "since her 1997 conversion to Christianity, she consistently has attended a Methodist church and occasionally attended Sikh services at her parents' request."[6] *The State* noted that "some voters were confused by Haley's campaign Web site, thinking she may be both Sikh and Methodist and were unclear which 'Almighty God' Haley was referencing on the site," and the Haley campaign found it necessary during the 2010 campaign to change her website to read, " 'My faith in Christ has a profound impact on my daily life and I look to Him for guidance with every decision I make.' "[7] Despite the official prohibition of religious tests for office, these religious matters were clearly politically relevant to at least some South Carolina Republican voters.

A second example of a de facto religious qualification for office in 2010 occurred in the Iowa Republican gubernatorial primary. After the Iowa Supreme Court in 2009 declared a state statute forbidding same-sex marriage contrary to the equal-protection clause of the state constitution,[8] Iowa religious conservatives made a commitment to overturn the decision a fundamental—even *the* fundamental—criterion in their evaluation of candidates for election to state office. Because former governor Terry Branstad had welcomed the support of his former lieutenant governor, Joy Corning, who supported same-sex marriage, the Iowa Family Policy Center (IFPC), a social-conservative organization, pledged in January 2010 not to support Branstad in his quest to win the 2010 Republican gubernatorial nomination and retake the governor's mansion.[9] Once

[5] See chapter 2 *infra*.

[6] Gina Smith, "Will Religion Become a Weapon?" *The State*, June 16, 2010.

[7] Smith, "Will Religion Become a Weapon?" According to the same story in *The State*, Haley's 2010 Democratic opponent, Vincent Sheheen, was told that his Catholicism caused some people to doubt "his Christian credentials," and, previously, two 1988 candidates "were targets of a 1988 flier that referred to the two as 'anti-Christian Jewish Democrats' and urged voters to support their Christian opponents."

[8] *Varnum v. Brien*, No. 07-1499 (April 3, 2009).

[9] "Marriage Activists Back Vander Plaats," *Cedar Rapids Gazette*, January 13, 2010

Branstad won the nomination in the June primary, IFPC Chairman Danny Carroll said,

> Our commitment to Biblical principles and the constitutional rule of law is not the result of any political affiliation, nor is it something that changes depending on the names on a ballot. If a candidate or their political party would like our support, they will need to offer a plan for promoting public policy that honors both God and the constitution.[10]

A candidate seeking IFPC support, Carroll continued, must, among other things, "commit to uphold the Biblical principle of individual responsibility" and stand "in the mold of the Founding Fathers who were guided by their respect for the laws of nature and of nature's God." Finally, Carroll stated, "Our organization desires to honor God. We are looking for candidates who we can support, not for candidates who aren't quite as bad as their opponent. In our opinion, to abandon God's calling for our ministry and civic involvement is what would truly be unacceptable."

As in the case of South Carolina, these religious criteria—above and beyond the reference to "the Laws of Nature and of Nature's God" from the Declaration of Independence—were clearly relevant to social-conservative voters in Iowa.[11] The third example comes from the opening sentences of a letter to the editor of the *Des Moines Register* during the 2008 election campaign, published with the headline, "Palin's Beliefs Make Her a Perfect Choice":

> Here are some well-known facts about Gov. Sarah Palin. She believes the Bible to be the revealed word of God. She believes in biblical morality. She believes in the biblical definition of marriage and family. She believes in God's abhorrence of sodomy and killing womb children.
>
> What more could America's believers or decent American voters want in a leader?[12]

(http://gazetteonline.com/local-news/2010/01/13/marriage-activists-back-vander-plaats, retrieved 6-23-10).

[10] Iowa Family PAC press release: "We Will Keep Our Word, Because the Alternative Is Unacceptable," June 14, 2010 (http://www.iowapolitics.com/index.iml?Article=199768, retrieved 6-22-10). All subsequent quotations in this paragraph come from this source.

[11] Additionally, during the 2008 election season in Iowa a yard sign reading "Vote God's Word and Your Conscious [*sic*]" appeared in a Des Moines suburb, and as late as November 2009 a sign on U.S. 163 near Monroe, Iowa, read, "Faith Still Matters: One Nation Under God. Vote Republican."

[12] Maxine Bechtel, letter to the editor, *Des Moines Register*, September 11, 2008. This approach to presidential politics continued in 2011. See Paul Waldman, "The God Squad. The Republican Frontrunners: Christian Superstars," *The American Prospect,* June 14, 2011 (http://prospect.org/cs/articles?article=the_god_squad3, retrieved 6-16-11).

By raising overtly religious notions such as "biblical morality," "Biblical principles," "faith in Christ," "Almighty God," "Christian credentials," and "public policy that honors God" as relevant to their evaluation of political candidates, public officials, and public policy, social conservatives in these states and others are in effect employing an unofficial, de facto religious test for office and for government in general. To do so implies, as a condition of the intelligibility of employing such a test, the assumption that there is some religious dimension to government and, indeed, law itself that makes relevant and requires a de facto, if not de jure, religious test.[13] The idea captured in the phrase "religious dimension to government and law itself" is what is at stake in the contemporary political debate over the public role of religion in the United States.

Nevertheless, though arguments about the public role of religion in the United States are usually taken to be a question about the legitimacy and constitutionality of the public expression of religion, the issue is more fundamental than that. To speak of a religious dimension to government and law itself is to raise the question whether "We the People," as citizens of the nation or citizens of a state, constitute a religious community. The individual is or can be the locus of religious identity, and the political order too can be a locus of religious identity, as it is in some countries with an established religion. Individuals have a religious identity, in the positive sense of affirming and adhering to the one in which they were raised or choosing to adopt a new one, or in the negative sense of choosing to reject a particular religion or a religious orientation in general.

Against that background, the question is, do "We the People" collectively have a religious identity? That is, does the American political order established by the Constitution have a religious identity constituted and affirmed by the Constitution? Groups dedicated to the proposition that Christians founded the United States on Christian principles as a Christian nation answer in the affirmative, and the de facto religious tests for office imply the proposition that the United States is a religious community with a religious identity. According to Isaac Kramnick and Laurence Moore, "Being a religious person is what constitutes for many the common experience of being an American. Newt Gingrich defined this civic religion

[13] According to the June 11, 2010, *Newsweek* cover story, "Saint Sarah," many women consider Sarah Palin "a prophet, ordained by God for a special role in the cosmic battle against the forces of evil. A 2009 profile in the Christian magazine *Charisma* compared Palin to the Old Testament's Queen Esther, who saved her people, in this case the Jews, from annihilation." The story by Lisa Miller describes Palin supporter Vicki Garza as believing, "like many evangelicals, . . . that a great cosmic battle is underway for the soul of America and that Palin has been singled out by God for leadership: 'The anointing on her is so strong,' she says" (http://www.newsweek.com/2010/06/11/saint-sarah.html, retrieved 6-23-10).

best when, in introducing his proposal for a school-prayer amendment, he argued that it would produce 'an America in which a belief in the Creator is once again at the center of being an American.'"[14] Wallbuilders, to take a second example, founded by David Barton, "is an organization dedicated to presenting America's forgotten history and heroes, with an emphasis on the moral, religious, and constitutional foundation on which America was built—a foundation which, in recent years, has been seriously attacked and undermined."[15] That foundation, Wallbuilders claims, was laid in a time when "laws and policies were firmly rooted in Biblical principles."[16] The organization seeks to "(1) educat[e] the nation concerning the Godly foundation of our country; (2) provid[e] information to federal, state, and local officials as they develop public policies which reflect Biblical values; and (3) encourag[e] Christians to be involved in the civic arena."[17]

The claim that "We the People" collectively have a religious identity in that the United States is a Christian nation, however, involves at least two propositions that are often conflated but that must be distinguished carefully. The first proposition is simply descriptive: it is a matter of empirical fact, although we will see that it is a fact more complicated than normally assumed, that most Americans, both contemporarily and throughout American history, self-identify as Christian in some sense or another. The second proposition is a normative one and as such is controversial: Americans, on this view, are Christian not merely in the sense that aggregating individuals one by one we find that the majority are Christian, but, additionally and more importantly, the United States

[14] Isaac Kramnick and R. Laurence Moore, *The Godless Constitution: The Case against Religious Correctness*, 2nd ed. (New York: Norton, 1997), 196. In the race for the 2012 Republican presidential nomination, former Minnesota Governor Tim Pawlenty stated at the Iowa Faith and Freedom Coalition Forum in Des Moines, Iowa, on March 7, 2011, "We need to be a country that turns toward God, not a country that turns away from God." Dana Milbank, "With Pawlenty's Iowa Speech, a Side of Syrup," *Washington Post*, March 9, 2011 (http://www.washingtonpost.com/wp-dyn/content/article/2011/03/08/AR2011030805530.html?wpisrc=nl_politics, retrieved 3-9-11).

[15] Wallbuilders: Presenting America's Forgotten History and Heroes with An Emphasis on Our Moral, Religious, and Constitutional Heritage (http://www.wallbuilders.com/ABTOverview.asp, retrieved 6-22-10).

[16] Wallbuilders. In publicity for a video by David Barton titled "The Myth of the Separation of Church and State: American's [*sic*] Founding Fathers: Deists or Christians," Gary Martin, website administrator for the Young Earth Creation Club, is even more direct about a religious mission for America: "The majority of the founding fathers and American's [*sic*] in general were Christians. . . . [T]he main reason this country was founded was so that those Christians could spread the gospel of salvation through Jesus Christ (http://www.creationists.org/myth-of-the-seperation-of-church-and-state.html [*sic*], retrieved 6-28-10).

[17] Wallbuilders.

is a Christian nation in a corporate sense.[18] Here the nation as a nation self-identifies as Christian—or, to use a term commonly understood to be ecumenical but which, we will see, is itself essentially Christian, as Judeo-Christian—which is qualitatively different from individuals self-identifying as Christian. For those who argue in favor of the idea of a Christian America, the empirical proposition necessarily translates into the normative proposition. In order to clarify what this might mean, I would suggest a parallel that we can draw between the character of a political order and that of three different types of colleges or universities in the United States.

First, consider the Catholic character of the University of Notre Dame. Notre Dame's mission statement includes the following points: "The University of Notre Dame is a Catholic academic community of higher learning, animated from its origins by the Congregation of Holy Cross"; "The Catholic identity of the University depends upon, and is nurtured by, the continuing presence of a predominant number of Catholic intellectuals"; "The University encourages a way of living consonant with a Christian community and manifest in prayer, liturgy and service"; and "In all dimensions of the University, Notre Dame pursues its objectives through the formation of an authentic human community graced by the Spirit of Christ."[19] This mission statement also includes a wide range of goals admirable from any religious or secular point of view,[20] but in its affirmation of academic freedom it notes, just after the statement cited above about Catholic intellectuals, that "[w]hat the University asks of all its scholars and students, however, is not a particular creedal affiliation,

[18] In other words, to speak of whether the status of religion in the United States is public or private is not to ask a question about public knowledge or secrecy, but rather to ask a question about government. Individual citizens certainly have the right to express their religious beliefs, values, and commitments in public—i.e., to publicize them or make them public—but the issue here is whether the American political order itself has a religious identity and mission in some sense. To argue that religion is essentially private, therefore, is to argue not that people may practice it only in the privacy of their own homes, but that the political order itself has no religious identity or mission.

[19] University of Notre Dame mission statement (http://www.nd.edu/aboutnd/mission-statement/, retrieved 4-14-10).

[20] For example, "The University prides itself on being an environment of teaching and learning that fosters the development in its students of those disciplined habits of mind, body, and spirit that characterize educated, skilled, and free human beings. In addition, the University seeks to cultivate in its students not only an appreciation for the great achievements of human beings but also a disciplined sensibility to the poverty, injustice and oppression that burden the lives of so many. The aim is to create a sense of human solidarity and concern for the common good that will bear fruit as learning becomes service to justice." University of Notre Dame mission statement.

but a respect for the objectives of Notre Dame and a willingness to enter into the conversation that gives it life and character."[21] The significance of this point is that while Notre Dame welcomes students and faculty (and presumably staff) of diverse religious and nonreligious orientations, they are obligated to respect the essentially Catholic nature and mission of the institution.[22] Thus, while individual student, faculty, and staff members of the Notre Dame community have their own individual religious identity, the university itself has *its* own religious identity and mission above and beyond those individual identities even as it welcomes people of diverse religious identities.

Second, consider the religious character of evangelically oriented Patrick Henry College.[23] According to its website, the mission of Patrick Henry College is "to prepare Christian men and women who will lead our nation and shape our culture with timeless biblical values and fidelity to the spirit of the American founding."[24] The mission statement goes on to define the college community in terms of a specific religious commitment: "Patrick Henry College welcomes all people who have a personal relationship with Jesus Christ and who take seriously the claims of the inerrant Word of God."[25] Significantly, the college states, "We choose to limit our student body, board, and staff to those who are committed to our statement of faith," and "Each and every faculty member is pledged by contract to undergird all of his teaching with a biblical worldview."[26]

Like other similar colleges or universities, then, Patrick Henry College has an institutional religious identity and mission of it own. What makes it different from Notre Dame, however, is that its website states explicitly that all individual student, faculty, and staff members of its community are expected to accept and subscribe to that religious identity

[21] University of Notre Dame mission statement.

[22] It was just this issue that arose in conservative Catholics' protest against the university's invitation to President Obama, prochoice on the matter of abortion, to deliver the commencement speech at Notre Dame on May 17, 2009. "Bishops, advocates on each side and students complained that it was inappropriate to have him deliver the address and receive an honorary degree since he diverges so profoundly from the church's teachings." Peter Baker and Susan Saulny, "At Notre Dame, Obama Calls for Civil Tone in Abortion Debate," *The New York Times*, May 18, 2009 (http://www.nytimes.com/2009/05/18/us/politics/18obama.html, retrieved 6-28-10).

[23] We could take a look at Liberty University (www.liberty.edu) or Calvin College (www.calvin.edu) as well.

[24] Patrick Henry College (http://www.phc.edu/mission.php, retrieved 6-22-10).

[25] Patrick Henry College. The college website includes a prominent "Biblical Foundations Statement" that includes what it calls its "Statement of Faith" and "Statement of Biblical Worldview" (Patrick Henry College, http://www.phc.edu/Biblical_Foundations_Statement.php, retrieved 6-22-10).

[26] Patrick Henry College (http://www.phc.edu/distinctives.php, retrieved 6-22-10).

as a condition of membership. At Notre Dame, individuals, whatever their particular religious orientation, must respect the university's institutional religious identity and mission; at Patrick Henry, it appears that individuals must not only respect but also affirm and endorse the institution's religious identity and mission. As we see in the quotation above, it welcomes not people of any and all theological orientations, but "all people who have a personal relationship with Jesus Christ and who take seriously the claims of the inerrant Word of God." While the college welcomes people of "many doctrinal and denominational traditions," it claims to be neutral not on all doctrinal matters, but "on the doctrinal distinctives *which go beyond the points covered in our Statement of Faith and are outside the mission of the College*" (emphasis added).[27] To be sure, the students, faculty, and staff of Patrick Henry are highly likely to be self-selecting, but in any case the college clearly has an institutional religious identity that appears to merge with the individual religious identity of members of its community.

Third, consider the mission statements of a public institution like the University of Michigan and private institutions like Amherst College and Drake University. At Michigan, the mission is "to serve the people of Michigan and the world through preeminence in creating, communicating, preserving and applying knowledge, art, and academic values, and in developing leaders and citizens who will challenge the present and enrich the future."[28] Additionally, the university claims to "celebrate and promote diversity in all its forms, seeking the understanding and perspective that distinct life experiences bring. We proclaim ourselves a scholarly community in which ideas may be freely expressed and challenged, and all people are welcomed, respected and nurtured in their academic and social development."[29] On the private side, Amherst states that it "educates men and women of exceptional potential from all backgrounds so that they may seek, value, and advance knowledge, engage the world around them, and lead principled lives of consequence,"[30] and Drake states, in part, "Drake's mission is to provide an exceptional learning environment that prepares students for meaningful personal lives, professional accomplishments, and responsible global citizenship."[31]

[27] Patrick Henry College.

[28] University of Michigan (http://www.umich.edu/pres/mission.php, retrieved, 6-28-10).

[29] University of Michigan.

[30] Amherst College (https://www.amherst.edu/aboutamherst/mission, retrieved 6-28-10).

[31] Drake University (http://www.drake.edu/about/, retrieved 4-14-10, emphases omitted).

If in the first case—Notre Dame—we find an institutional religious identity and mission that a diverse university community must respect but not necessarily affirm and endorse and in the second case—Patrick Henry College—we find an institutional religious identity and mission, including fairly lengthy and detailed doctrinal statements, that a university community apparently must not only respect but also affirm and endorse as a condition of membership, then in the third case—the public University of Michigan and the private Amherst College and Drake University—there is no institutional religious identity and mission. While a majority of students, faculty, and staff at Michigan, Amherst, and Drake are likely to have an individual religious identity that is Christian in some sense of that term, the institutions themselves do not. With regard to religious orientation, students, faculty, and staff are members of those communities on equal terms regardless of their individual religious identities; affirmation and endorsement of a particular religious identity are not a precondition of full membership and participation in each community.

The parallel at issue, then, is that those who say that America is a Christian nation are saying that we are, in the foregoing terms, at least like Notre Dame, if not like Patrick Henry College. Indeed, the loudest voices in favor of the idea of a Christian America in this corporate sense conceive that idea along the lines of the latter. Rod Parsley, senior pastor of World Harvest Church in Columbus, Ohio, and host of Breakthrough on the Trinity Broadcasting Network, established the Center for Moral Clarity. "CMC believes public policy serves the nation and its citizens well only when it draws from the truth of God's Word. So we advocate for the biblical position on matters of life, faith, marriage, family, religious liberties, social justice and citizenship." The Reverend Lou Sheldon established the Traditional Values Coalition, which defines such values as follows:

> A moral code and behavior based upon the Old and New Testaments. We believe that Jesus Christ is the Son of God and that the Lord has given us a rule book to live by: The Bible. We are committed to living, as far as it is possible, by the moral precepts taught by Jesus Christ and by the whole counsel of God as revealed in the Bible.[32]

This organization "focuses on such issues as religious liberties, marriage, the right to life, the homosexual agenda, pornography, family tax relief and education" and, through its sister organization, the Traditional Values Coalition Education & Legal Institute, is "dedicated to educating and supporting churches in their efforts to restore America's cultural heritage."[33]

[32] Traditional Values Coalition (http://www.traditionalvalues.org/defined.php, retrieved 6-22-10, original emphasis omitted).

[33] Traditional Values Coalition. See also the website of Oklahoma-based Hobby

Lest one consider the foregoing organizations straw men, a position that does not take their advocacy seriously, we often can find statements of a similar nature in state political-party platforms and state constitutions. The 2008 Texas Republican Party platform included these two planks:

> Traditional Principles in Education—We support school subjects with emphasis on Judeo-Christian principles upon which America was founded and which form the basis of America's legal, political and economic systems.
>
> Judeo-Christian Nation—As America is a nation under God founded on Judeo-Christian principles, we affirm the constitutional right of all individuals to worship in the religion of their choice.[34]

Next, the 2008 Iowa Republican platform stated in part, "[W]e are endowed by our Creator with certain inalienable rights, and . . . our nation's foundation and subsequent blessings flow from adherence to and respect for the Judeo-Christian ethic."[35] Third, consider this statement from the 2008 Missouri Republican platform:

> WE BELIEVE that all of us are endowed by our Creator with certain unalienable rights including life, liberty and the pursuit of happiness. It is our fundamental belief that our morals, our values and our culture are derived from Almighty God, and we are committed to keeping it that way. To quote the Psalmist, "Blessed is the nation whose God is the Lord." Psalm 33:12[36]

State constitutions, for their part, were drafted and ratified prior to the contemporary culture-war concerns reflected in recent party platforms, but quite a few contain in their preamble an expression of "gratitude to Almighty God" for the blessings of liberty or an appeal to divine guidance and support.[37] California's preamble states, "We, the People of the State of California, grateful to Almighty God for our freedom, in order to secure and perpetuate its blessings, do establish this Constitution." Massachusetts' preamble goes further:

Lobby, which published a July 4, 2010, newspaper advertisement that celebrated Independence Day as not just a national holiday but also an essentially religious and, indeed, Christian holiday. After citing various Founders and President Ronald Reagan on the importance of God and religion to the United States, the ad concludes with the statement, "If you would like to know Jesus as Lord and Savior, call Need Him Ministry at 1-888-NEED-HIM" (http://www.hobbylobby.com/assets/pdf/holiday_messages/current_message.pdf, retrieved 7-5-10).

[34] 2008 Texas Republican Party platform (www.texasgop.org, retrieved 01-11-09).

[35] 2008 Iowa Republican Party platform (www.iowagop.net, retrieved 01-11-09).

[36] 2008 Missouri Republican Party platform (www.mogop.org, retrieved 01-11-09).

[37] "God in the State Constitutions," in "The U.S. Constitution Online" (http://www.usconstitution.net/states_god.html, retrieved 6-11-10). This is the source of the next two citations and one reference in this paragraph.

> We, therefore, the people of Massachusetts, acknowledging, with grateful hearts, the goodness of the great Legislator of the universe, in affording us, in the course of His providence, an opportunity, deliberately and peaceably, without fraud, violence or surprise, of entering into an original, explicit, and solemn compact with each other; and of forming a new constitution of civil government, for ourselves and posterity; and devoutly imploring His direction in so interesting a design, do agree upon, ordain and establish the following Declaration of Rights, and Frame of Government, as the Constitution of the Commonwealth of Massachusetts.

Almost all of the state constitutions contain similar language in their preambles, excepting those of Oregon and Tennessee; the New Hampshire, Vermont, and Virginia constitutions have no preamble.

The argument presented in popular and political form in these examples, then, is that We the People do collectively have a religious identity; that the American political order established by the Constitution has a religious identity constituted and affirmed by the Constitution, one that is in fact Christian or, as some advocates attempt to be ecumenical, Judeo-Christian. The purpose of this book, however, is to contend, based upon an argument about the core meaning of the Establishment Clause, that the United States is like Michigan, Amherst, and Drake, and not like Patrick Henry College or even Notre Dame. The American Constitution allows for the existence of particular religious communities with their own particular religious identity and mission, and in fact, by virtue of the religion clauses of the First Amendment—"Congress shall make no law respecting an establishment of religion, or prohibiting the free exercise thereof"—encourages the existence of such communities. Nevertheless, I argue, as a nation the United States is not itself a religious community with a religious identity and religious mission.

Specifically, what is at issue here is the question of American identity: what is it to be an American? Is it a commitment to the ideals embodied in the Declaration of Independence and the Constitution, or is it also a commitment to certain religious beliefs and values? Furthermore, is a commitment to the ideals embodied in the Declaration of Independence and the Constitution itself a commitment to certain religious beliefs and values? The argument of this book is that the existence of the religion clauses in the Constitution indicates (1) that the basic decisions as to religious orientation rest with the individual and not the majority, and (2) that the United States as a corporate body, as a political order, has itself neither a religious identity nor a religious mission.[38] We would have

[38] I should add that an American state, too, as a corporate body, as a political order, has itself neither a religious identity nor a religious mission.

an entirely different political order without the religion clauses,[39] but what it means for them to be in the Constitution is that we are a country, not a congregation; we are a nation composed of various particular religious communities, but we are not, as a nation, a religious community itself.[40] The United States, according to the logic of the religion clauses, is a nation—not a church or religious community—and it is not divinely ordained—the Declaration of Independence says that government derives

[39] There is currently a website entitled Christian-America.com (copyright 2008–2010), that proposes what it calls the Christian America Constitutional Amendment: "The United States is a Christian Nation. Congress shall make no law abridging the free exercise of all Christian religions, nor make law giving preference of one Christian denomination over another Christian denomination, nor giving preference of one Christian sect over another Christian sect. This amendment replaces the religion clause of the first amendment and supersedes all treaties as relevant to this amendment" (http://www.christian-america.com/, retrieved 6-22-10).

Replacing the religion clauses in this manner would indeed fundamentally change the character of the American political order. The proposal, however, raises an interesting question. If the Christian America Constitutional Amendment is necessary, then in its current form the United States in fact must not be a Christian America, thus validating the argument I want to make in this book. The best response amendment supporters could make would be to say that the United States originally was indeed a Christian America, that the country has drifted or been pushed away from that character, and that consequently the amendment is necessary in order to get us back to what we were designed to be.

[40] According to the U.S. Citizenship and Immigration Services, this is the official oath of allegiance for naturalized citizens:

> I hereby declare, on oath, that I absolutely and entirely renounce and abjure all allegiance and fidelity to any foreign prince, potentate, state, or sovereignty of whom or which I have heretofore been a subject or citizen; that I will support and defend the Constitution and laws of the United States of America against all enemies, foreign and domestic; that I will bear true faith and allegiance to the same; that I will bear arms on behalf of the United States when required by the law; that I will perform noncombatant service in the Armed Forces of the United States when required by the law; that I will perform work of national importance under civilian direction when required by the law; and that I take this obligation freely without any mental reservation or purpose of evasion; so help me God. (http://www.uscis.gov/portal/site/uscis/menuitem.5af9bb95919f35e66f614176543f6d1a/?vgnextoid=931696981298d010VgnVCM10000048f3d6a1RCRD [retrieved 7-29-08])

Two points are worth noting here. First, unlike the case with many creedal religions, there is no element of this oath that requires the applicant to affirm or reject any religious or theological belief in order to become a citizen in good standing. Second, despite the requirement of an oath signified by the phrase "so help me God," an applicant is entitled to have that requirement waived in the case of his or her religious objections. "If USCIS finds that you are unable to swear the Oath using the words 'on oath,' you may replace these words with 'and solemnly affirm.' Finally, if USCIS finds that you are unable to use the words 'so help me God' because of your religious training or beliefs, you are not required to say these words" (http://www.immihelp.com/citizenship/naturalization-oath-ceremony.html, retrieved 7-21-10).

its just powers not from God, but from the consent of the governed. I say this not out of hostility toward *religion*, but out of the greatest respect for each and every citizen's *equal right to religious freedom*, and out of the greatest respect for the democratic idea of consent of the people.

The central argument of this book, then, is that the political order established by the American Constitution is a secular rather than religious order, with "secular" a concept I will distinguish from "secularist" and the philosophical position of secularism. The political meaning of the religion clauses in general, and of the Establishment Clause in particular, is that while the individual is certainly free to talk to people about his or her religious beliefs and even try to convince them to accept those beliefs, the individual must respect their decision to reject his or her views; he or she is *not* free to attempt to use government, the machinery of the state, to assist him or her in either a coercive or even a noncoercive way. One cannot use government to support and advance one's own religious beliefs (Establishment Clause), and one cannot use government to oppose and undermine the religious beliefs of others (Free Exercise Clause). The religious clauses determine this character of the American political order by the fact that they protect not religion, but religious freedom. Indeed, although protecting religion and protecting religious freedom are often conflated, we cannot understand the meaning of the religion clauses in the Constitution and their place in American political order unless we grasp the distinction between the two. To say that the religion clauses protect religious freedom rather than religion is to say that they protect individual religious choices rather than religious belief systems and the specifically religious institutional dimensions of those religious belief systems. Therefore, the function of the religion clauses of the Constitution is to constitute us as a political order in which the locus of religious identity is the individual and not the political order itself. It follows that law and politics, particularly in a liberal democracy, are simply not about God, and the attempt to make them so is an attempt, witting or unwitting, to change radically the character of the American constitutional order.

The goal of this book, then, is to conduct a theoretical and jurisprudential examination of the way the American Constitution, through the religion clauses, constitutes a political order of religious freedom. I seek to do so through an investigation of the political and constitutional theory that underlies the religion clauses and that is capable of explaining the competing tests and principles that form the content of conventional religion-clause, and especially Establishment Clause, jurisprudence.[41]

[41] The literature on the religion clauses is, as one would expect, simply enormous. As of August 2010 LexisNexis, which is not a complete list, warns the researcher that there are over 3,000 law-review articles with the word religion or the words religion

The political significance of the religion clauses comes into play most directly with the Establishment Clause. The Free Exercise clause is most important principally regarding the individual, having to do with the individual's liberty in matters of private religious belief and practice. The Establishment Clause, however, raises the issue of the public—i.e., official—place, role, and status of religion, which goes to the heart of the question as to the meaning of the religion clauses to the nature of the American political order. I will argue that what the Establishment Clause ultimately expresses is what I will call the secularity principle: the principle—again, different from a substantive philosophy of secularism—that government shall not take a position, nor do anything that amounts to taking a position, on the truth or worth of religion, religious belief and values, or religious practices—and that this secularity principle makes the most sense of our Establishment Clause jurisprudence. The concept of secularity is at the heart of even the most bare-bones meaning of the Establishment Clause, namely, the idea that it is possible for Congress to make no law respecting an establishment of religion.

Thus, in brief, chapter 1 explores religion and the religion clauses in terms of the tension between majority rule and individual rights that preoccupied American political and constitutional theory in the Federalist Papers, and then argues that we must understand the meaning of the religion clauses in terms of political and constitutional theory rather than political and constitutional history. Chapter 2 sets out a distinction between religion and religious freedom, and then explores the remarkable

---

clauses anywhere in the text and 1,537 articles with religion in the title. Prominent recent book-length treatments of the religion clauses include Donald L. Drakeman, *Church, State, and Original Intent* (New York: Cambridge University Press, 2010); Charles W. Dunn, ed., *The Future of Religion in American Politics* (Lexington: University Press of Kentucky, 2009); Christopher L. Eisgruber and Lawrence G. Sager, *Religious Freedom and the Constitution* (Cambridge, Mass.: Harvard University Press, 2007); Noah Feldman, *Divided by God: America's Church-State Problem—and What We Should Do about It* (New York: Farrar, Straus & Giroux, 2005); Kent Greenawalt, *Religion and the Constitution*, Vol. 1: *Free Exercise and Fairness* (Princeton, N.J.: Princeton University Press, 2006), and Vol. 2: *Establishment and Fairness* (Princeton, N.J.: Princeton University Press, 2008); Philip Hamburger, *Separation of Church and State* (Cambridge, Mass.: Harvard University Press, 2002); Martha C. Nussbaum, *Liberty of Conscience: In Defense of America's Tradition of Religious Equality* (New York: Basic Books, 2008); and Vincent Phillip Muñoz, *God and the Founders: Madison, Washington, and Jefferson* (New York: Cambridge University Press, 2009). Three somewhat older works are Leonard W. Levy, *The Establishment Clause: Religion and the First Amendment*, 2nd ed., revised (Chapel Hill: University of North Carolina Press, 1994); Frederick Mark Gedicks, *The Rhetoric of Church and State: A Critical Analysis of Religion Clause Jurisprudence* (Durham, N.C.: Duke University Press, 1995); and Steven D. Smith, *Foreordained Failure: The Quest for a Constitutional Principle of Religious Freedom* (New York: Oxford University Press, 1995).

religious diversity in the United States in order to argue that we can make sense of the religion clauses only if we bear in mind the fact that we all are members of actual or potential religious minorities. The religion clauses, we will see, do not present the unpleasant alternative of tyranny of the majority vs. tyranny of the minority, but instead defend We the People against a majority religious faction. Chapter 3 distinguishes between conventional and radical Establishment Clause jurisprudence and explores the latter in the form of certain Christian Right theorists who exemplify the broader argument that any political order necessarily and inevitably embodies some set of religious beliefs and values. Chapter 4 examines the work of two legal scholars who make a similar argument, and then contends that while any political order represents a certain orthodoxy, the logic of the religion clauses suggests that not all orthodoxies are necessarily religious. The chapter concludes with an argument that there is at best a prudential rather than theoretical solution to the problem of orthodoxy.

With chapters 5, 6, and 7 we move to the heart of the book, a theory of the fundamental meaning of the Establishment Clause. Chapter 5 introduces the concept of coercion as it has been used by the Supreme Court to distinguish free-exercise cases from establishment cases. If the purpose of both religion clauses is to protect religious freedom, then we must understand that both clauses protect religious freedom from religious coercion. Thus, against the majority of the Court the chapter argues that the concept of coercion is central to an understanding of an Establishment Clause violation, but, as against justices Scalia and Kennedy, it introduces a concept of coercion much thicker than the one they advocate to narrow the scope of Establishment Clause protection. Chapter 6, in turn, sets forth an account of what I first call the concept of position taking, part of the central principle at the core of the Establishment Clause, and it shows how that concept has appeared, sometimes overtly and sometimes implicitly, in classic Establishment Clause cases as well as in scholarly literature on the clause. Finally, chapter 7 presents the concept of coercion developed in chapter 5 and the concept of position taking developed in chapter 6 as in fact the two components of what, in the end, I identify as the fundamental principle that underlies the Establishment Clause—the secularity principle, a concept that I distinguish and, I believe, the logic of the religion clauses requires that we distinguish, from any substantive philosophy or doctrine of what is usually understood as secularism. Thus, by virtue of the religion clauses themselves, the Constitution establishes a political order that is distinct from and independent of religious values, beliefs, and commitments. That is the necessary theoretical presupposition—the condition of the meaningfulness—of the mandate that "Congress shall make no law respecting an establishment of religion or prohibiting the free exercise thereof."

Given the religious diversity of the United States, the oft-recited phrase "One Nation under God" cannot help but provoke the question, one nation under whose God? As a matter of political and constitutional theory, the meaning of the religion clauses of the First Amendment, and especially that of the Establishment Clause—that is, what their existence in the Constitution means to the American political order—is that we are one nation under no one's God. The Declaration of Independence does not constitute the United States as a religious community, even when we recall the famous passage declaring that all men "are endowed by their Creator with certain unalienable Rights." One can argue that human or natural rights are God given but that individuals are responsible to God for their actions as individuals rather than as a nation.[42] And, more important, the Constitution does not constitute the United States as a religious community. Recognizing that the United States is one nation under no one's God is not an official endorsement of atheism or opposition to religion, but rather the constitutional means of ensuring the freedom of the individual to stand under whatever *he or she* conceives to be *his or her* God. The Constitution creates a political order that is not itself a religious community, but instead allows for and supports the existence of a tremendous diversity of religious communities. By doing so, the Constitution creates a political order that attempts to solve the most fundamental task of politics broadly conceived: the need to provide a process that enables us to live together peacefully with people who differ from us about what we hold to be the most important truths and values in our lives.

[42] Declaration of Independence (http://www.ushistory.org/declaration/document/, retrieved 7-24-10). While many people pay the most attention to the statement that all men "are endowed by their Creator with certain unalienable Rights," we must not forget the equally important contention that "Governments are instituted among Men, deriving their just powers from the consent of the governed,—That whenever any Form of Government becomes destructive of these ends, it is the Right of the People to alter or to abolish it, and to institute new Government." Government, according to the Declaration, does not derive its just powers from God and thus cannot be answerable to God; it derives its just powers from, and is answerable to, the people.

Chapter 1

Constitutional Fundamentals

People differ. As individuals, we differ from each other in matters ranging from the mundane to the significant. Beyond such mundane differences as being right-handed or left-handed, we differ from each other in regard to such naturally based characteristics as our age, sex, sexual orientation, race, and ethnicity and such socially based characteristics as how much and what kind of education we have, the state of our economic and financial condition, where we grew up and live, what kind of occupation we pursue, what leisure activities we choose, and others. Related to these and other differences, we develop our own particular traditions, interests, values, beliefs, and opinions, differences we share with some people and not others, but which are likely to be enduring. Indeed, as James Madison famously said in Federalist 10, "As long as the reason of man continues fallible, and he is at liberty to exercise it, different opinions will be formed."[1] The result is that, looking at almost any society, we see the simultaneous existence of different individuals and groups, and thus different traditions, interests, values, and beliefs, within a territorial unit under a common rule. We are confronted, that is, by the fact of *diversity*. In the United States we attempt to cope with our differences by living according to the motto *E Pluribus Unum*, whereby hyphenated Americans—e.g., Italian-Americans, Irish-Americans, African-Americans, etc.—are and strive to be at the same time simply Americans.[2] Additionally, even the seemingly

[1] Federalist 10, in Alexander Hamilton, James Madison, and John Jay, *The Federalist Papers*, ed. Clinton Rossiter, with a new introduction and notes by Charles R. Kesler (New York: New American Library, 1961 and 1999), 46.

[2] This is not uncontroversial, for "Out of many, one" incorporates a tension that seeks to avoid reducing the many to the one and the one to the many. The former reduction appears when some argue that in practice being "simply American" has meant or even should mean aspiring to a white, Anglo-Saxon, Protestant (WASP)

most homogeneous nations elsewhere have their own differences to negotiate. In Germany one should never confuse a Bavarian with a Prussian or a Rhinelander, and in Great Britain one should never, ever call a Welshman or a Scotsman—not to mention an Irishman—an Englishman.

Diversity, then, whether understood in regard to physical, sociological, economic, geographic, or intellectual differences, is universal and ubiquitous, but diversity creates a major problem. While there are some spheres of human activity in which individuals may safely pursue their diverse interests as they see fit, there are other areas or issues that affect the entire society and thus cannot be safely left to individual choice and discretion. For example, as we drive down the highway in our car, the decision as to which radio station we listen to, if to any at all, remains in American society with the individual.[3] What is not left to individual decision, on the other hand, is the question of on which side of the road we may drive, for our physical and financial well-being requires that we have reasonable grounds to trust that no one will be heading directly at us as we drive down the road and around a blind curve. Thus, some decisions are individual decisions, while other decisions must be social or what we call collective decisions. That is, in some areas of life the individual may be safely left to make his or her own choices, while in other areas of life he or she cannot be left to make his or her own choices—he or she, along with everyone else, must be bound by the same rule. Different societies draw this line in different places, and we normally consider those who attempt to maximize the domain of individual choice to be the freest.

The major problem, however, is that the combination of diversity and the need for certain collective decisions creates conflict. If people cannot be left to choose as they see fit, if one rule must be chosen to be binding on everyone regardless of individual values and preferences to the contrary, then which rule—whose values and preferences—do we choose? Conflict arises because different rules affect people in different ways—some people are benefited and advantaged, and some are burdened and disadvantaged. In the United States, to continue our traffic example, the rules of the road mandate that we drive our cars and trucks on the right-hand side of the road, with the driver sitting behind the steering wheel on the left-hand side of the vehicle, whereas the reverse holds in Great Britain. Given those rules of the road, the gearshift in American cars, whether manual or automatic, is designed for the driver to operate with his or her right hand, and the consequence of that choice is that our driving system benefits right-handed people and burdens left-handed people. So too, the

norm. The latter reduction appears when some argue that we should speak of the American *peoples* rather than the American *people*.

[3] For purposes of this example, I assume the driver has no passengers.

rules of the road in Great Britain lead to a gearshift design that benefits the left-handed driver. Choices, then, have differential consequences, even when they are made without malicious intent, and thus people have an interest, sometimes weak and sometimes strong, in which choice is made. Of course, my solution is to support the choices that advantage me or at least do not disadvantage me, but everyone else will propose the same solution centered upon his or her own advantage and disadvantage. Hence, our diversity of values and interests leads, in the areas of life that require one single rule binding upon everyone equally, to conflict.

What are the possible solutions to such conflict? Broadly speaking, there are typically three. First, there is the use of force, a tried and true method with a long and often bloody history. Through the use or even just the threat of force, Smith compels Jones to accede to the rule that advantages Smith or disadvantages Jones. The question, of course, is how long Jones will accept this situation, raising the issues of stability and justice. The second, also with a long history, is what sociologists call exit—emigration. Most of us are here in the United States because someone in our family's past left the old country (voluntarily or involuntarily) to come to America. Nowadays, however, emigration is often quite difficult—we usually have to make the case that we will not take a job away from a natural-born citizen who could do it—and immigration has become a highly contested issue in many countries around the world. The only alternative we have for solving the conflicts that arise from our differences that does not involve force or exit, then, is the process of negotiation and compromise. A society can hold together in its diversity only if conflict is channeled into institutions and processes that can resolve it peacefully. That, in the broadest sense, is what we call politics: it is the process through which we negotiate our differences, in order to live together with people with whom we have substantial differences.[4]

[4] In this broad sense of the term, politics is a potential solution to the problem of diversity-induced conflict but itself is also an aspect of the problem of diversity-induced conflict. The differences we negotiate through politics are, in the United States at least, of two types that themselves constitute political diversity. First, our diversity of values and interests leads us to differ as to whether we need a collectively decided rule in a particular domain or can allow individuals to decide as they please. The conflict over the legitimacy of abortion rights is one such example: prolife advocates argue that we must have a single, binding rule that makes one decision for everyone, whereas prochoice advocates argue that individual women can and should make their own decisions about abortion. Second, once we agree that we must have a collectively decided rule binding on everyone, our diversity of values and interests leads us to differ as to precisely what that single rule should be. We ordinarily agree, for example, that we must have a speed limit—that is, we cannot allow individuals to decide for themselves how fast to drive—but we can differ as to whether urban traffic patterns and road conditions require a speed limit of thirty-five or thirty miles per hour.

Perhaps in no area of human life are our possible differences more important than religion, which is among the most fundamental causes of social conflict. Religion is one of the most difficult kinds of difference that politics has to negotiate. The contemporary politics of religion centers less on questions of individual religious practice that implicate the Free Exercise Clause than on the Establishment Clause question of the public role of religion, a fact that derives from the so-called culture wars of the past thirty years. From an analytical perspective (and with due regard for the perils that attend the drawing of historical parallels), we can understand those "wars" as a conflict between a peculiarly American Reformation and Counter-Reformation. If we can say that the political and cultural thrust of the 1960s was a general liberalization that emphasized individual autonomy over against traditional authorities and orthodoxies, then the conservative political reaction that arose in the 1970s has been an attempt to reassert those traditional authorities and orthodoxies. The ongoing conservative political focus on "traditional values" and the conservative constitutional focus on originalism—the "intentions of the Framers"—are elements of this attempt at reassertion. At the forefront of that reaction has been the movement of religious conservatives aiming at reclaiming a public role for religion in American life, itself a controversial notion. Cases like *Engel v. Vitale* and *Abington v. Schempp*,[5] which ruled unconstitutional the traditional practices of organized prayer and Bible reading in the public schools, fueled the outbreak of the culture war over the place of religion in the public domain.

Beyond the particular politics of contemporary times and issues, however, religion is always constitutionally problematic in a political order because its centrality to the life of the individual and its assertion of a higher source of loyalty and obligation create the potential for competition with the demands of loyalty and obligation attached to the political order itself. Both government and religion are systems of authority, and each is an alternative, possibly competing authority to the other. As Thomas Hobbes wrote long ago, "The most frequent praetext of Sedition, and Civil Warre, in Christian Common-wealths hath a long time proceeded from a difficulty, not yet sufficiently resolved, of obeying at once, both God, and Man, then when their Commandements are one contrary to the other."[6] This problem appears even in popular culture—in the words of renowned folk and protest singer Bob Dylan:

[5] *Engel v. Vitale*, 370 U.S. 421 (1962), and *Abington School District v. Schempp*, 374 U.S. 203 (1963).

[6] Thomas Hobbes, *Hobbes's Leviathan* (Oxford: Oxford University Press, 1967), 457.

> Oh God said to Abraham, "Kill me a son"
> Abe says, "Man, you must be puttin' me on"
> God say, "No." Abe say, "What?"
> God say, "You can do what you want Abe, but
> The next time you see me comin' you better run"
> Well Abe says, "Where do you want this killin' done?"
> God says. "Out on Highway 61."[7]

The commands of men and human institutions, on this view, pale in comparison to the commands of God, which makes religion more powerful and potentially incendiary than an individual's purely personal philosophy or worldview.[8] Furthermore, both politics and religion are matters of great and intense concern to most people because they deal with the disparate and contentious beliefs and opinions people hold about

[7] Bob Dylan, "Highway 61 Revisited" (http://www.seeklyrics.com/lyrics/Bob-Dylan/Highway-61-Revisited.html, retrieved 3-9-08).

[8] In *The Myth of Religious Violence: Secular Ideology and the Roots of Modern Conflict* (New York: Oxford University Press, 2009), William T. Cavanaugh challenges this distinction between religion and nonreligion with regard to what I label as potentially incendiary. "What I call the 'myth of religious violence,'" he writes, "is the idea that religion is a transhistorical and transcultural feature of human life, essentially distinct from 'secular' features such as politics and economics, which has a peculiarly dangerous inclination to promote violence" (3). Specifically, he states, "The arguments I examine attempt to separate a category called religion, which is prone to violence because it is absolutist, divisive, and nonrational, from a secular, or nonreligious, reality that is less prone to violence, presumably because it is less absolutist, more unitive, and more rational. As we shall see, such arguments do not stand up to scrutiny, because they cannot find any coherent way to separate religious from secular violence" (16). Consequently, he argues, "so-called secular ideologies and institutions like nationalism and liberalism can be just as absolutist, divisive, and irrational as those called religious" (8).

Cavanaugh makes a valid point here, but in the context of the argument of this book the key issue at stake may be less "religion" than what we might call the broader idea of absolutes. As Cavanaugh recognizes, secular belief systems can be absolutist in their claims and demands just as much as religious belief systems. Richard John Neuhaus, whom I begin to discuss later in this chapter and then in chapter 3, argues in *The Naked Public Square*, 2nd ed. (Grand Rapids: Eerdmans, 1986) that secular doctrines will constitute an "*ersatz* religion" in a supposedly naked public square, which I take to mean that there are always absolutes in any political order. However, when I refer to religion as more powerful and potentially incendiary than an individual's purely personal philosophy or worldview, I reflect the Founders' position, embodied in the religion clauses, that religion must be approached with caution as well as respect. My argument is not that religion and religious disagreement necessarily cause violence whereas secular belief systems and disagreement do not, but that religious disagreement potentially causes an extremely difficult problem to the extent that religious beliefs call upon an absolute mandate but at the same time, by virtue of the religion clauses, have a constitutional protection that, beyond free-speech dimensions, nonreligious belief systems do not.

the fundamental questions of human life.[9] Politics ultimately involves the emotionally charged issues of order, liberty, equality, and justice, while religion ultimately involves the emotionally charged issue, put most broadly, of the meaning of human life itself. Daniel Conkle, for example, describes well the centrality of religion to human identity:

> Religious beliefs, by their very nature, form a central part of a person's belief structure, his inner self. They define a person's very being—his sense of who he is, why he exists, and how he should relate to the world around

[9] There is of course an enormous literature on the nature of religion and an entire academic discipline of religious studies, which potentially opens up a not uncontroversial line of inquiry far beyond the scope of this book. According to Cavanaugh, "There is nothing close to agreement among scholars on what defines religion; the inability to define religion has been described as 'almost an article of methodological dogma' in the field of religious studies" (*The Myth of Religious Violence*, 57, citing Brian C. Wilson, "From the Lexical to the Polythetic: A Brief History of the Definition of Religion," in Thomas A. Idinopulos and Brian C. Wilson, eds., *What Is Religion? Origins, Definitions, and Explanations* [Leiden: Brill, 1998], 141–62). As a result, as Winnifred Fallers Sullivan argues in *The Impossibility of Religious Freedom* (Princeton, N.J.: Princeton University Press, 2005), "Courts, legislatures, and other government agencies judge the activities of persons as religious or not, as protected or not, based on models of religion that often make a poor fit with religion as it is lived" (10).

Nevertheless, in the context of my analysis of the constitutional and political significance of the religion clauses, we may content ourselves with this definition by Franklin Gamwell of the University of Chicago Divinity School: "In its strict sense, a religion is a cultural system of concepts and symbols and associated communal practices in terms of which or through which adherents express a set of beliefs about the ultimate context of human worth and, thereby, seek to inform all of their lives, all they are and do, with a certain comprehensive commitment or orientation. In sum, a religion is a cultural system with which adherents cultivate or mediate a comprehensive self-understanding." Franklin I. Gamwell, "The Question of Democracy," *DePaul Law Review* 57 (2008): 997, at 1004. This definition, particularly with its reference to the idea of an "ultimate context of human worth" and a "comprehensive commitment or orientation," reflects the attempt of the Supreme Court in cases like the draft-exemption case of *United States v. Seeger*, 380 U.S. 163 (1965), to navigate the tricky task of defining religion independently of a sectarian religious or theological perspective. In *Seeger* the Court struggled to define religion by focusing on the structure and sincerity rather than the content of belief, with the key question being whether there is some sort of authority that transcends the private moral calculus of the individual and imposes obligations.

The singling out of religion in the Constitution suggests that some things are not religion, and *Seeger* tries to distinguish between religion, which is protectable, and nonreligious beliefs and practices, which are not (beyond possible freedom of speech and association). Whatever the difficulties in defining religion from the standpoint of the field of religious studies and in practical terms in particular court cases, the presence of the religion clauses suggests that there is something identifiable about religion and distinguishable from other, nonreligious types of beliefs and practices. If not, then the inclusion of the religion clauses in the Constitution makes no sense.

> him. A person's religious beliefs cannot meaningfully be separated from the person himself; they are who he is. The essential identity of a person and his religious beliefs means that these beliefs often will be grounded on intense convictions.[10]

When combined with the demographic diversity of American society, this centrality of religion to human identity creates the potential for intense and bitter conflict:

> In a religiously pluralistic society such as ours, [challenges to a person's religious beliefs] are not uncommon; religious believers frequently attempt to persuade and convert those with differing views. These efforts at persuasion and conversion are inoffensive if they are premised on a basic respect for the existing belief structure of the person whose beliefs are being challenged. Otherwise, however, the efforts may be deeply offensive to that person. Attacks on a person's religious beliefs are attacks on his conception of himself as a human being; if the challengers suggest that the person's existing beliefs are deeply flawed and not entitled to respect, they therefore are suggesting that the person himself is deeply flawed and not entitled to respect.[11]

At the same time, it is difficult if not impossible to isolate politics and religion from each other to avoid such conflict, because they overlap and intersect with each other insofar as each deals with the question of how we are to live with one another and by what moral standards. We thus come into conflict with friends, family, and fellow citizens not only with regard to our opinions on politics and religion as distinct and separate matters, but also with regard to our opinions on the proper relation between politics and religion. These conflicts generate the politics of religion, and, as

[10] Daniel O. Conkle, "Toward a General Theory of the Establishment Clause," *Northwestern University Law Review* 82 (1988): 1115, at 1164–65 (footnotes omitted). Despite coincidentally having a title that points toward a central concern of this book, this article, written at the time of the reemergence of the originalism debate around the bicentennial of the Constitution, explores "the relationship between the Supreme Court's establishment clause doctrine and various theoretical models of judicial review" (1117). Those models he calls originalism and the "process-based" and "common values" models of nonoriginalist review. The article argues that the Court's Establishment-Clause doctrine can and should be justified on a theory of political-moral reasoning. Its perspective is thus somewhat different from my own.

[11] Conkle, "General Theory," at 1165. There is no significant difference, Conkle adds at 1166, for those who are nonreligious: "Although perhaps not to the same extent as religious beliefs, irreligious beliefs also form a central part of a person's belief structure and constitute a type of self-definition. Like religious beliefs, they tend to be intensely felt, and they are both strong and fragile in the same way. As a result, attacks on irreligious beliefs also may affront the individual who holds them, causing anguish, alienation, and resentment, and damaging his relationship with those who have affronted him."

do so many other conflicts in American society, the politics of religion raises arguments of principle that the antagonists in our political order ultimately translate into the form of constitutional debate.

It is centrally important to note, however, that while the politics of religion in the United States involves cases of nonreligion versus religion, it more often involves cases of religion X versus religion Y. As reported in 2010 by *The Ledger* of Lakeland, Florida, for example, an organization called Atheists of Florida filed a suit in U.S. District Court in Tampa charging that the Lakeland City Commission's practice of opening its meetings with prayer is unconstitutional.[12] More famously, the 2004 case of *Elk Grove Unified Sch. Dist. v. Newdow* involved a challenge to the constitutionality of the phrase "under God" in the Pledge of Allegiance.[13] Michael Newdow was an atheist who objected to his daughter's public elementary school's practice of having teachers lead their classes in a recitation of the Pledge to start each day.[14] Nevertheless, despite cases like these and others, as well as the existence of organizations like American Atheists,[15] the Secular Coalition for America,[16] and the American Humanist Association,[17] much if not most religious conflict in America has to do with one religious group's disagreement with another religious group. Thus, according to Marci Hamilton and Rachel Steamer, "In truth, the United States' debate over the separation of church and state is not between believers and nonbelievers. Rather, it is a debate between believers/nonbelievers and believers/nonbelievers."[18] Examples of religion X versus religion Y are not uncommon.

First, the Interfaith Alliance of Iowa, according to its website, "is made up of people of faith and goodwill from across Iowa who believe in protecting religious freedom, respecting individual rights and uniting the diverse voices across our state for the common good. We are Christians, Unitarians, Jews, Muslims, Sikhs, Hindus, Buddhists, atheist, agnostics

[12] Cary McMullen, "Atheist Group Sues Lakeland for Prayers," *The Ledger.com*, July 12, 2010 (http://www.theledger.com/apps/pbcs.dll/article?AID=/20100712/NEWS/7125028&template=printart, retrieved 7-12-10).

[13] *Elk Grove Unified Sch. Dist. v. Newdow*, 542 U.S. 1 (2004).

[14] The Court held that Newdow lacked standing to sue, reversing the Court of Appeals' decision that Newdow had standing and that the practice violated the Establishment Clause. Justice Stevens' opinion for the Court did not reach the merits of the claim, though Chief Justice Rehnquist and Justices O'Connor and Thomas did so in their opinions concurring in the judgment.

[15] See http://www.atheists.org/.

[16] See http://www.secular.org/.

[17] See http://www.americanhumanist.org/.

[18] Marci A. Hamilton and Rachel Steamer, "The Religious Origins of Disestablishment Principles," *Notre Dame Law Review* 81 (2006): 1755, at 1790.

and more."[19] After 167 clergy signed and presented to Iowa legislators a February 16, 2010, Alliance letter in support of same-sex marriage,[20] Chuck Hurley, president of the Iowa Family Policy Center, an organization opposing same-sex marriage, called those who signed the letter "pseudo pastors." Referring to the pastors, he said, "They are sacrificing the eternal souls of those who follow them by seeking the approval of men rather than the approval of God (John 12:43-48). Let there be no confusion, the people who signed the Interfaith Alliance petition are defying the Word of God. They are confused at best and blatantly evil at worst."[21]

A second example of religion X versus religion Y appears in a 2008 controversy over religious billboards in Indiana. The "Florida-based Eternal Gospel Church Formed in 1992 by Seventh-Day Adventist Believers" paid for billboards along Interstate 65 in Jeffersonville, Indiana, proclaiming that Saturday rather than Sunday was the true Sabbath, and that the antichrist changed the Sabbath to Sunday.[22] The Catholic League protested, calling such statements "bigoted." A third example appears in the 2010 ruling by a federal judge in Wisconsin that the National Day of Prayer, a statute enacted by Congress in 1952, was unconstitutional. Though the case was brought by the Freedom from Religion Foundation, suggesting an instance of religion versus nonreligion, the opinion by Federal District Judge Barbara B. Crabb included a lengthy list of interreligious conflicts she attributed to the statute:

- In 2008 a national Jewish organization complained that the National Day of Prayer has been "hijacked by Christian conservatives," who are "excluding and dividing us on religious lines."
- In Plano, Texas, a multicultural group and a group of Christians held "dueling prayer services" on the National Day of Prayer after fighting over the right to hold their events at the city council building and threatening to file a lawsuit.
- In San Antonio, Texas, a local resident threatened to file a lawsuit over the mayor's involvement in National Day of Prayer events.
- In Richmond, Virginia, a Jewish organization criticized a National Day of Prayer event attended by various state officials at the state capitol because the event's sponsor excluded non-Christians.

[19] The Interfaith Alliance of Iowa (http://www.interfaithallianceiowa.org/index.php?option=com_content&view=article&id=47&Itemid=62, retrieved 7-22-10).

[20] See http://www.interfaithallianceiowa.org/attachments/084_Interfaith%20clergy%20letter%20signatures%202_16_10.pdf.

[21] file:///Religion%20Book/Inter-religious%20conflict/Hurley.webarchive (retrieved 6-6-10).

[22] David Mann, "Religious Billboards along I-65 Pulled after Protests," *Evening News and Tribune*, February 8, 2007 (http://newsandtribune.com/local/x519362641/Religious-billboards-along-I-65-pulled-after-protests, retrieved 10-28-08).

- In Anniston, Alabama, a church pastor complained that the National Day of Prayer has been "hijacked by evangelical Christians" because the National Day of Prayer Task Force has "establish[ed] a policy of excluding not only those of other faiths but also moderate and mainline Christians."
- In Bakersfield, California, a Christian group created controversy when its coordinator stated that "[t]he National Day of Prayer is actually all about the Lord. So we're representing the Christian community." A local rabbi stated that "I think the National Day of Prayer, if it was ever inclusive—which I'm not sure it ever was entirely—has morphed into something else."
- In Buffalo, New York, Jewish and Muslim groups complained that the local National Day of Prayer events are "more about politics than prayer" and that the day is more accurately called the "Christian National Day of Prayer."
- In Memphis, Tennessee, local groups complained that the National Day of Prayer "mak[es] members of minority religions feel that unless they adhere to Christianity they are unpatriotic" and that "[p]eople of minority faiths are very alarmed by" the exclusively Christian nature of the events.
- In Victorville, California, local residents complained that "Hindus, Buddhists, Muslims and Sikhs are being excluded" from the National Day of Prayer event at the town hall. The organizer responded, "this entire nation was founded on Christian faith. The reason we are a great county is because we're Christian. In the Muslim countries, you can get shot if you're Christian."
- In Springfield, Illinois, organizers of a National Day of Prayer event at the state capitol were criticized after saying that event is "only about Jesus and Jesus the Savior alone"; they had "no problem having [members of other religions] participate, though not in speaking roles."
- In Troy, Michigan, a Christian group and an interfaith group fought over access to city hall to hold an event on the National Day of Prayer, both sides threatening law suits. When the mayor announced that she would attend the interfaith event, she was accused of promoting "witches and Satanists." An effort to recall the mayor was started later.
- In 2004 religious leaders and nonprofit groups accused the "White House of using prayer for political purposes" after the President broadcast National Day of Prayer remarks "over several Christian and television and radio networks as part of an evangelical concert."
- In Salt Lake City, Utah, Mormons were excluded from National Day of Prayer of events because they are not "in accordance with the evangelical principles [of] the task force," including a belief in the "Holy Trinity" and that the Bible is the "only written word of God."

- In Muncie, Indiana, the organizer of a National Day of Prayer event denied requests to speak by Unitarian, Muslim, and Jewish leaders, "sharply divid[ing]" city residents.[23]

Judge Crabb's general point was the divisiveness illustrated by these examples; my point is that these examples illustrate the fact that religious conflicts—and especially the bitterest religious conflicts—often are not between religion and nonreligion but between religion X and religion Y.[24]

This is not a new or merely a contemporary phenomenon, of course. According to Steven Gey,

> With regard to the country's history of respecting religious diversity, the sad fact is that the history of relations between dominant and minority religious groups in this country is not a terribly happy one. In pre-revolutionary times, religious groups who came to American seeking religious freedom for themselves quickly fell into the habit of oppressing members of other faiths when they became the dominant religious group in their new home. The history of the American colonies is riddled with examples of religious oppression.[25]

Religion thus can become a source of what Madison called faction or, in today's terms, special interest: "By a faction," he wrote, "I understand a number of citizens, whether amounting to a majority or a minority of the whole, who are united and actuated by some common impulse of passion, or of interest, adverse to the rights of other citizens, or to the permanent and aggregate interests of the community."[26] The central point in this well-known definition is the idea that not only a minority but a majority too can be a faction; the interest of the majority is not by definition equivalent to the common good but in fact can be adverse to the interests of other

[23] *Freedom from Religion Foundation et al. v. Obama*, Case 3:08-cv-00588-bbc, U.S. District Court for the Western District of Wisconsin, April 15, 2010, at 57–59 (references omitted). The Obama Department of Justice filed a notice of appeal on April 22, 2010 (Leah Nylen, "DOJ to Appeal in National Day of Prayer Case," http://www.mainjustice.com/2010/04/22/doj-to-appeal-in-national-day-of-prayer-case/, retrieved 7-22-10).

[24] On a lighter but nonetheless relevant note, consider Tom Lehrer's famous satire of National Brotherhood Week:

> Oh, the Protestants hate the Catholics
> And the Catholics hate the Protestants,
> And the Hindus hate the Moslems,
> And everybody hates the Jews.

Tom Lehrer, "National Brotherhood Week" (http://members.aol.com/quentncree/lehrer/natbroth.htm, retrieved 3-09-08).

[25] Steven G. Gey, "Vestiges of the Establishment Clause," *First Amendment Law Review* 5 (2006): 1, at 43.

[26] Federalist 10, 46.

citizens or to that common good. Madison claimed that "the most common and durable source of factions has been the various and unequal distribution of property," but it is significant that the very first of the various sources of faction he cited was "[a] zeal for different opinions concerning religion."[27] Religion is potentially the ultimate or über-faction: by its nature, it is not just a competing interest but also an alternative system of authority, obligation, and obedience. Factions constituted in terms of the pursuit of material interests operate within, rather than challenge, the existing system of authority, obligation, and obedience; and, as material, these interests are subject to compromise, however difficult that may be in practice. If Smith wants government to spend $2 billion and Jones wants government to spend $1 billion, a compromise is not impossible to find.

On the other hand, religion itself, to the extent that it involves a commitment to a set of absolute principles, is much more difficult to compromise, because an absolute that can be compromised is by definition not an absolute. Pastor Rick Warren, at his Saddleback Civic Forum during the 2008 presidential campaign, said, "We believe in the separation of church and state, but we do not believe in the separation of faith and politics, because faith is just a world view and everybody has some kind of world view and it's important to know what they are."[28] Yet faith is not "just" a worldview—for many if not most faith traditions, it involves divine commands and sanctions. We are familiar with the temptation for a president to "wrap himself in the flag," according to which he fends off challenges to and criticism of his policies with the claim, "You're not attacking me; you're attacking the United States of America." Since faith involves divine commands and sanctions, there is a similar temptation in the heat of argument to "wrap oneself in God" and say, "You're not attacking me; you're attacking God." The central importance of religion and the accompanying passions that so often attach to it, in other words, mean that religion lends itself all too easily to demagoguery, a danger against which both Madison and Hamilton warned in the Federalist Papers.[29]

[27] Federalist 10, 47.

[28] Pastor Rick Warren, welcoming remarks, Saddleback Civic Forum, August 16, 2008 (http://www.clipsandcomment.com/2008/08/17/full-transcript-saddleback-presidential-forum-sen-barack-obama-john-mccain-moderated-by-rick-warren/, retrieved 6-21-10).

[29] Justifying the Senate in Federalist 63, Madison wrote, "As the cool and deliberate sense of the community ought, in all governments, and actually will, in all free governments, ultimately prevail over the views of its rulers; so there are particular moments in public affairs when the people, stimulated by some irregular passion, or some illicit advantage, or misled by the artful misrepresentations of interested men, may call for measures which they themselves will afterwards be the most ready to lament and condemn" (Federalist 63, 352). Hamilton, explaining the relative independence of the president, wrote in Federalist 71, "The republican principle demands that the

To be sure, some argue that religion can be a, or even the only, source of unity in a political order. Richard John Neuhaus claimed years ago that the American experiment "is not only derived from religiously grounded belief, it continues to depend upon such belief."[30] Specifically, he wrote, "[W]hether it is called the Judeo-Christian ethic, or Christianity, or the operative social values, or a civil religion, it is the dynamic of religion that holds the promise of binding together (*religare*) a nation in a way that may more nearly approximate *civitas*."[31] American Protestantism, he said, always had the confidence that America is a "sacred enterprise" and "had a meaning within the larger purposes of God in world-historical change."[32] Indeed, for Neuhaus, liberal democracy itself depends upon a religious foundation.[33] In response to such an argument, Gey argues that religion, by its very nature, can never be a source of unity: "[I]n a religiously pluralistic country, no one religion will be capable of mustering the necessary support among the country's diverse population around a common set of ultimate goals or ideals. The quest for religious unity therefore will inevitably degenerate into sectarian factionalism and political ostracism for those who refuse to climb onto the majority's religious bandwagon."[34]

---

deliberate sense of the community should govern the conduct of those to whom they intrust the management of their affairs; but it does not require an unqualified complaisance to every sudden breeze of passion, or to every transient impulse which the people may receive from the arts of men, who flatter their prejudices to betray their interests. It is a just observation, that the people commonly *intend* the PUBLIC GOOD. This often applies to their very errors. But their good sense would despise the adulator who should pretend that they always *reason right* about the *means* of promoting it. They know from experience that they sometimes err; and the wonder is that they so seldom err as they do, beset, as they continually are, by the wiles of parasites and sycophants, by the snares of the ambitious, the avaricious, the desperate, by the artifices of men who possess their confidence more than they deserve it, and of those who seek to possess rather than to deserve it" (Federalist 71, 400, emphasis in original).

[30] Neuhaus, *Naked Public Square*, 95.

[31] Neuhaus, *Naked Public Square*, 60.

[32] Neuhaus, *Naked Public Square*, 7, 61.

[33] "First, democratic government is premised upon the acknowledgement of transcendent truth to which the political order is held accountable. Second, democracy assumes the lively interaction among people who are acting from values that are, in most instances, grounded in specific religious belief." Neuhaus, *Naked Public Square*, 120.

[34] Steven G. Gey, "Unity of the Graveyard and the Attack on Constitutional Secularism," *Brigham Young University Law Review* (2004): 1005, at 1006–7. "In fact," he continues, "the religious framework is peculiarly unsuited to the quest for unity because the very design of that framework is configured around notions of inclusion and exclusion. The religious framework is designed to thwart efforts at unity by making demands on believers that are specifically intended to ensure their inclusion into the holy precincts of the faith. But those same standards for inclusion are also standards

Thus, given the intractability of religious differences and the constant potential for conflict that stems from those differences, the distinction between areas of life in which the individual may be safely left to make his or her own choices and areas of life in which he or she cannot be left to make his or her own choices takes on fundamental importance. The American emphasis on that distinction is what makes the United States a liberal democracy. A liberal democracy is at bottom an institutionalized disagreement to disagree: we allow popular majorities to decide some things, which is what makes our political order a democracy, but not others, which is what makes that order a *liberal* democracy.[35] In other words, majorities rule, but not over everything: there is a domain of individual decision making, and there is a domain of social or collective decision making. Robert Bork has properly called this dual character of our liberal democracy Madisonian:

---

for exclusion of nonadherents, and any religion of substance will define itself in part by reference to those who do not meet the standards of the creed." Gey, "Unity," at 1011.

On the other hand, Robert D. Putnam and David E. Campbell argue in *American Grace: How Religion Divides and Unites Us* (New York: Simon & Schuster, 2010) that "[f]or many Americans, religion serves as a sort of civic glue, uniting rather than dividing" (517). The key, they say, is that "rather than cocooning into isolated religious communities, Americans have become increasingly likely to work with, live alongside, and marry people of other religions—or accept people with no religion at all. In doing so, they have come to accept people with a religious background different from theirs" (6).

Assuming with Putnam and Campbell that this sociological solution works, my argument is that one of the principal reasons for this is the constitutional framework created by the religion clauses. Indeed, they mention the Bill of Rights as early as page 4 of their book, and toward the end of their analysis they write, "The constitutional framework for religion in America does not guarantee this degree of interfaith mingling, mixing, and matching, but it has enabled the religious fluidity that we have described throughout this book. This fluidity, in turn, facilitates interpersonal connections across religious lines" (523). Concluding their discussion of religious pluralism, they state further, "we acknowledge the important role of the nation's constitutional infrastructure. The U.S. Constitution's prohibitions on both an established religion—which eventually came to mean any public support for religious entities by government at any level—and religious tests for public office helped to create a flourishing religious ecosphere" (550). To the extent that we do have the ability to agree to disagree about the claims of religious belief, that ability rests on the religion clauses. In other words, it is not the case that religion is not a polarizing factor and thus the religion clauses are relatively unimportant; rather, it is because the religion clauses are of fundamental importance in the political order created by the constitutional framework that religion can be less polarizing than it might otherwise be.

[35] In this regard, I should note the political question that lurks uneasily under the analysis this book seeks to provide: if politics is the activity that enables us to live together peacefully with people with whom we have major differences, are there some differences so fundamental that we cannot agree to disagree about them?

> The United States was founded as a Madisonian system, which means that it contains two opposing principles that must be continually reconciled. The first principle is self-government, which means that in wide areas of life majorities are entitled to rule, if they wish, simply because they are majorities. The second is that there are nonetheless some things majorities must not do to minorities, some areas of life in which the individual must be free of majority rule.[36]

The problem peculiar to popular government, according to Madison, is the need to control majority faction in a society governed by majority rule:

> If a faction consists of less than a majority, relief is supplied by the republican principle, which enables the majority to defeat its sinister views by regular vote. It may clog the administration, it may convulse the society; but it will be unable to execute and mask its violence under the forms of the Constitution. When a majority is included in a faction, the form of popular government, on the other hand, enables it to sacrifice to its ruling passion or interest both the public good and the rights of other citizens. To secure the public good and private rights against the danger of such a faction, and at the same time to preserve the spirit and the form of popular government, is then the great object to which our inquiries are directed.[37]

Madison's solution to this problem, famously, was institutional and sociological: institutionally, design the government according to the principles of federalism and separation of powers so that even if a majority wanted to act oppressively, it would be institutionally unable to do so; and, sociologically, design an extended republic so that there would be so many different interests in society that there never could be any "natural" majority—any majority could be at best artificial, that is, nothing more permanent than a shifting coalition of minority interests.[38]

Hence, according to Madison himself, "A religious sect may degenerate into a political faction in a part of the Confederacy; but the variety of sects dispersed over the entire face of it must secure the national councils against any danger from that source."[39] The logic of this argument can be sketched as follows:

[36] Robert H. Bork, *The Tempting of America: The Political Seduction of the Law* (New York: Simon & Schuster, 1990), 139.

[37] Federalist 10, 46.

[38] See Federalist 51, 288–93.

[39] Federalist 10, 52.

Issue	*Groups (Minorities)*						
1	**A**	**B**	**C**	**D**	**E**	F	G
2	A	**B**	**C**	**D**	**E**	**F**	G
3	**A**	B	**C**	**D**	E	**F**	G
4	A	B	**C**	**D**	**E**	**F**	G

Assuming for present purposes that each group itself—A, B, C, etc.—is numerically the same size and, by itself, only a minority and not a natural majority, then any functioning majority will always be an artificial majority—an alliance or coalition of minorities (the boldface letters above). Madison's argument, first, is that we tell A through E not to abuse their majority power over F and G on issue 1 because they—A through E—may well be in the minority on other issues (such as issue 2 here). Second, we tell F not to despair, feel threatened, or resort to drastic measures due to their loss on issue 1, because on other issues they may well be part of a majority coalition (such as issue 2 here).

However, there are two problems with Madison's argument. First, of course, is the existence of G, a group unlikely to be part of any majority coalition because it is a permanent "discrete and insular minority."[40] G's reliance on the political process is only a precarious protection, a fact that Justice Scalia acknowledged but accepted in *Employment Division v. Smith*.[41] The second is the temptation of a majority coalition to exercise

[40] See the famous footnote 4 in *United States v. Carolene Products Company*, 304 U.S. 144 (1938), at 152, which suggested the particular importance of "a more exacting judicial scrutiny" of legislation in cases, among others, where "prejudice against discrete and insular minorities may be a special condition, which tends seriously to curtail the operation of those political processes ordinarily to be relied upon to protect minorities, and which may call for a correspondingly more searching judicial inquiry."

[41] "Values that are protected against government interference through enshrinement in the Bill of Rights are not thereby banished from the political process. Just as a society that believes in the negative protection accorded to the press by the First Amendment is likely to enact laws that affirmatively foster the dissemination of the printed word, so also a society that believes in the negative protection accorded to religious belief can be expected to be solicitous of that value in its legislation as well. . . . It may fairly be said that leaving accommodation to the political process will place at a relative disadvantage those religious practices that are not widely engaged in; but that unavoidable consequence of democratic government must be preferred to a system in which each conscience is a law unto itself or in which judges weigh the social importance of all laws against the centrality of all religious beliefs." *Opinion of the Court, Employment Division, Oregon Department of Human Resources v. Smith*, 494 U.S. 872 (1990), at 890.

what power it can over an issue and not fear what it might consider the unlikely threat of potential retaliation. As Gey notes with regard to religion, "The larger the religious majority, the less likely that religious diversity can serve as an adequate political check on sectarian self-dealing; a judicially enforced Establishment Clause exists to prevent powerful religious majorities from using the political system to consolidate their dominance."[42] Despite the extensive and ineradicable diversity of religious commitments, beliefs, and practices in the United States, therefore, the very existence of the religion clauses is thus evidence of the principle that religious matters are reserved to the individual and protected against majority intrusion. The structural and sociological check, in other words, might not suffice. Were it not for the religion clauses, the Constitution in effect would say, in Bork's words above, that religion is one of those "wide areas of life [in which] majorities are entitled to rule, if they wish, simply because they are majorities." Religious matters would be subject to majority rule, like tax policy and speed limits.

The purpose of a liberal democracy, then, is to allow, but put limits on, the range of majority rule in order to control the effects of faction by distinguishing those matters to be reserved to individual decision making and shielded against majority intrusion. The particular form of liberal democracy we have is that of a constitutional democracy, in which we limit the power of government—i.e., the representatives of popular majorities—and safeguard the domain of individual decision making, by anchoring that distinction in a written constitution with the status of fundamental law that cannot be overridden by ordinary law.[43] In the words of Justice Robert Jackson,

> The very purpose of a Bill of Rights was to withdraw certain subjects from the vicissitudes of political controversy, to place them beyond the reach of majorities and officials and to establish them as legal principles to be applied by the courts. One's right to life, liberty, and property, to free speech, a free press, freedom of worship and assembly, and other fundamental rights may not be submitted to vote; they depend on the outcome of no elections.[44]

[42] Gey, "Vestiges of the Establishment Clause," at 34.

[43] The purpose of constitutional guarantees of individual rights, Justice Scalia has written, "is precisely to prevent the law from reflecting certain changes in original values that the society adopting the Constitution thinks fundamentally undesirable. Or, more precisely, to require the society to devote to the subject the long and hard consideration required for a constitutional amendment before those particular values can be cast aside." Antonin Scalia, "Originalism: The Lesser Evil," *University of Cincinnati Law Review* 57 (1989): 849, at 862.

[44] *West Virginia v. Barnette*, 319 U.S. 624 (1943), at 638.

Religion *is* different; we do not find in the Constitution a clause that states, "Congress shall make no law respecting the establishment of political, moral, or philosophical worldviews, or prohibiting the free exercise thereof." From the standpoint of American political and constitutional theory, therefore, the purpose of the religion clauses of the First Amendment is to enable us to agree to disagree about religious matters by taking them out of the domain of majority rule and placing them in the domain of individual rights.[45] Regarding government, the religion clauses stand for the proposition, as Justice Jackson put it, that "[i]f there is any fixed star in our constitutional constellation, it is that no official, high or petty, can prescribe what shall be orthodox in politics, nationalism, religion, or other matters of opinion or force citizens to confess by word or act their faith therein."[46] This emphasis on freedom means that religious matters are matters for individuals, singly or in communities, to decide, and not for government to decide for and on behalf of the entire political order, be it the nation or a state. Regarding the individual, the classic religion-clause cases suggest that, put abstractly, the religion clauses stand for the proposition that the affirmation of a particular religion, religious belief, or religious practice cannot be a condition of full participation in American citizenship (Establishment Clause), and the rejection of a particular religion, religious belief, or religious practice cannot be a condition of full participation in American citizenship (Free Exercise Clause).

Many people maintain, of course, that to ascertain the meaning of the religion clauses requires that we ask what the Founders had in mind when they wrote and ratified the clauses. This question arises in particular from the foregoing references to Madison and the Federalist Papers. It is therefore fundamentally important to note that the analysis here of what the religion clauses mean for the nature of the American political order is not a question of political and constitutional history, but rather a question of political and constitutional theory. This is so for three principal reasons. First, even if we grant the contested assumption that the Founders were

[45] Speaking not specifically of the religion clauses but of the Constitution in general, Amartya Sen has argued that the "constitutional motivation" of the Framers was "to make it possible for people with different interests and divergent views to live and prosper together." See his 2010 H. L. A. Hart Memorial Lecture at the Faculty of Law in Oxford University, published as "Rights, Words, and Laws: Constitutions and Their Motivation," *The New Republic*, October 28, 2010, 24–29, at 26. Twice elsewhere in this lecture Sen refers to this idea: he attributes to the Framers "a social vision of constitutional appropriateness, which would make room for people with divergent interests and values to live together" (27) and refers to "a democratic and participatory constitution that tries to create a legitimate space for different types of people with varying preoccupations and circumstances in a diverse society" (27).

[46] *West Virginia v. Barnette*, at 642.

orthodox Christians as opposed to Deists, secularists, or the like,[47] we cannot say that because the Founders were overwhelmingly Christian the United States is an essentially Christian nation. The Founders—those who wrote and ratified the Constitution—were also entirely or almost entirely male and white, and yet we would be hard pressed to find anyone within the bounds of conventional political discourse who would want to claim that the United States therefore is an essentially male and white nation. Likewise, the people who created baseball, football, and basketball were most probably Christian, but that fact does not make baseball, football, and basketball essentially Christian sports. Granting the premise that the Founders were Christian does not lead, by itself, to the conclusion that the United States is an essentially Christian nation. There are at least two missing premises in the transition from that first premise to the conclusion: first, that the Founders intended to create the United States as an essentially Christian nation, and, second, that they succeeded in doing so—that is, that the Constitution they wrote and ratified actually made the United States an essentially Christian nation. All three such premises are subject to debate.

Second, leaving aside the huge issue of the validity of originalism,[48] the possibility of resolving the meaning of the religion clauses through the approach of historical analysis is based upon an historical consensus that serious constitutional scholars and commentators argue simply does not exist. There are enough conflicting statements in the historical record that it is too easy simply to "cherry-pick" historical evidence to support whatever position one favors. On the one hand, for example, leaving aside contemporary pronouncements, in the 1892 case of *Church of the Holy Trinity v. United States*, the Supreme Court stated, drawing on a New York state blasphemy case, "[T]his is a Christian nation."[49] On the other hand, as early as 1796, Article 11 of the Treaty of Tripoli stated,

> As the government of the United States of America is not in any sense founded on the Christian Religion,—as it has in itself no character of enmity against the laws, religion or tranquility of Musselmen,—and as the said States never have entered into any war or act of hostility against any Mehomitan nation, it is declared by the parties that no pretext arising from

[47] See, for example, the argument traced, from a partisan standpoint, in Isaac Kramnick and R. Laurence Moore, *The Godless Constitution: The Case against Religious Correctness*, 2nd ed. (New York: Norton, 1997), chaps. 1–2, 11–45.

[48] See my earlier book, *The American Constitution and the Debate over Originalism* (New York: Cambridge University Press, 2005).

[49] *Church of the Holy Trinity v. United States*, 143 U.S. 457 (1892), at 471. The New York case was *People v. Ruggles*, 8 Johns. 290 (1811).

> religious opinions shall ever produce an interruption of the harmony existing between the two countries.[50]

Again, on the one hand, in his Farewell Address President George Washington wrote of the essential connection between religion and morality:

> Of all the dispositions and habits which lead to political prosperity, Religion and morality are indispensable supports. In vain would that man claim the tribute of Patriotism, who should labour to subvert these great Pillars of human happiness, these firmest props of the duties of Men & citizens. The mere Politician, equally with the pious man ought to respect & to cherish them. A volume could not trace all their connections with private & public felicity. Let it simply be asked where is the security for property, for reputation, for life, if the sense of religious obligation *desert* the Oaths, which are the instruments of investigation in Courts of Justice? And let us with caution indulge the supposition, that morality can be maintained without religion. Whatever may be conceded to the influence of refined education on minds of peculiar structure—reason & experience both forbid us to expect that National morality can prevail in exclusion of religious principle.[51]

Yet, on the other hand, the proposed Constitution encountered substantial opposition because of its prohibition on a religious test for office and its silence about any religious character of the nation. According to Isaac Kramnick and R. Laurence Moore, "[T]he Constitution was bitterly attacked for its failure to mention God or Christianity."[52] Finally, Thomas Jefferson, on the one hand, certainly mentioned our Creator in the Declaration of Independence, though he talked of "nature's God," which is not a conventional Christian manner of speaking. On the other hand, Jefferson also referred to the Book of Revelation, considered so important by most conservative evangelicals, as "the ravings of a maniac, no more worthy nor capable of explanation than the incoherencies of our own nightly dreams."[53]

A representative instance of dueling quotations appears in the Ten Commandments case of *McCreary County v. ACLU of Kentucky*, where

[50] http://www.yale.edu/lawweb/avalon/diplomacy/barbary/bar1796t.htm (retrieved 9-2-08).

[51] The Papers of George Washingon, http://gwpapers.virginia.edu/documents/farewell/transcript.html, 20 (retrieved 9-2-08, emphasis in original).

[52] Kramnick and Moore, *Godless Constitution*, 27–28. Arguing in the contrapositive, Kramnick and Moore maintain that because the proposed Constitution was subject to criticism in some quarters because it made no explicit reference to God or Christianity, it must not have established an essentially Christian nation. If the latter had indeed been the intention and effect of the proposed Constitution, the existence of such criticism would make no sense.

[53] Thomas Jefferson, letter to General Alexander Smyth, January 17, 1825, cited at

Justice Antonin Scalia dissents from Justice David Souter's opinion for the Court. Scalia writes, "President Washington opened his Presidency with a prayer . . . and reminded his fellow citizens at the conclusion of it that 'reason and experience both forbid us to expect that National morality can prevail in exclusion of religious principle.' "[54] Scalia cites John Adams' statement, "Our Constitution was made only for a moral and religious people. It is wholly inadequate to the government of any other," notes that Jefferson "concluded his second inaugural address by inviting his audience to pray," and quotes Madison's statement in his first inaugural address that he "placed his confidence 'in the guardianship and guidance of that Almighty Being whose power regulates the destiny of nations, whose blessings have been so conspicuously dispensed to this rising Republic, and to whom we are bound to address our devout gratitude for the past, as well as our fervent supplications and best hopes for the future.' "[55]

Souter, on the other hand, argues in his majority opinion that

> the dissent's argument for the original understanding is flawed from the outset by its failure to consider the full range of evidence showing what the Framers believed. The dissent is certainly correct in putting forward evidence that some of the Framers thought some endorsement of religion was compatible with the establishment ban. . . . But the fact is that we do have more to go on, for there is also evidence supporting the proposition that the Framers intended the Establishment Clause to require governmental neutrality in matters of religion, including neutrality in statements acknowledging religion.

---

http://www.city-data.com/forum/religion-philosophy/188445-th-jeffersons-opinion-bibles-book-revelation.html (retrieved 9-16-08).

[54] *McCreary County, Kentucky, et al. v. American Civil Liberties Union of Kentucky, et al.*, 545 U.S. 844 (2005), at 887–88, Scalia, dissenting (internal references omitted).

[55] *McCreary County* (internal references omitted). Professor Thomas B. Colby argues that in *McCreary* "Justice Scalia is selectively drawing upon the historical record to give the appearance of a historical consensus that did not exist. He holds out as unambiguous evidence of a universally understood original meaning actions that, in fact, many of the Framers themselves strongly condemned as unconstitutional. For instance, James Madison—who originally proposed the Establishment Clause—fought the First Congress's decision to hire a legislative chaplain, and condemned it as 'a palpable violation of . . . Constitutional principles.' Similarly, Thomas Jefferson refused to issue Thanksgiving prayers because he understood them to violate the Establishment Clause's prohibition against governmental 'recommendation' of religion. Madison also refused during his early years in office to issue calls for Thanksgiving prayer. Later, during the politically contentious War of 1812, he did issue such calls, but he subsequently confessed that his doing so had violated the Constitution." "A Constitutional Hierarchy of Religions? Justice Scalia, the Ten Commandments, and the Future of the Establishment Clause," *Northwestern University Law Review* 100 (2006): 1097, at 1127–28, footnotes omitted.

He, too, cites Jefferson and Madison, but on the opposite side of the issue. Jefferson, writes Souter, "refused to issue Thanksgiving Proclamations because he believed that they violated the Constitution," and Madison, he says, "criticized Virginia's general assessment tax not just because it required people to donate 'three pence' to religion, but because 'it is itself a signal of persecution. It degrades from the equal rank of Citizens all those whose opinions in Religion do not bend to those of the Legislative authority.'"[56]

Rule 11 of constitutional interpretation, according to H. Jefferson Powell some years ago in "Rules for Originalists," states, "Consensus or even broad agreement among the founders is a historical assertion to be justified, not assumed," and Rule 13 states, "History sometimes reveals a range of 'original understandings.'"[57] Indeed, recent scholarship contends that those in the founding generation did not agree even among themselves what they were supporting. According to Vincent Phillip Muñoz, the Court "has never gotten the Founders right":

> Most of the justices who have turned to history—and many of the scholars and litigators who have done the research on which those interpretations are based—have assumed that the Founders shared a uniform understanding of the right to religious liberty and that this understanding should be used to adjudicate the First Amendment's religion clauses. But the leading Founders disagreed about the proper separation of church and state. We cannot simply ask, "What would the Founders do?" and then follow their example. Whatever the merits of history-based jurisprudence, the Founders' disagreement means that there is no single church-state position that can claim the exclusive authority of America's founding history and that no one Founder's position can be assumed to reflect the original meanings of the religion clauses.[58]

[56] *McCreary County*, at 877–78, Souter (internal references omitted).

[57] H. Jefferson Powell, "Rules for Originalists," *Virginia Law Review* 73 (1987): 659, at 684, 690. His rule 1, it is worth emphasizing, is that "History itself will not prove anything nonhistorical." Powell, "Rules for Originalists," at 662.

[58] Vincent Phillip Muñoz, *God and the Founders: Madison, Washington, and Jefferson* (New York: Cambridge University Press, 2009), 206–7. See also an earlier article by Muñoz, "The Original Meaning of the Establishment Clause and the Impossibility of Its Incorporation," *University of Pennsylvania Journal of Constitutional Law* 8 (2006): 585: "The fundamental fact that almost all scholars and jurists overlook is that the Founders did not share a uniform understanding of the proper relationship between church and state" (at 604). I will address in chapter 6 the argument advanced by Muñoz, Justice Clarence Thomas, and others that "[b]ecause the original meaning only recognizes a jurisdictional boundary that protects state authority, [the Establishment Clause] cannot logically be incorporated to apply against state governments" (Muñoz, "Original Meaning," at 631).

Additionally, there is no certain way of knowing even how truly representative people like Madison, Washington, and Jefferson, among others, were of the founding

"Too often," Muñoz adds, "a single quotation or an example from one Founder is used to imply that the entire founding generation stood for a particular understanding of religious liberty."[59] The end result is that what passes for historical analysis both more and less sophisticated is merely a matter of dueling quotations.[60] According to Muñoz, "In most church-state cases, however, if one Founder supports one side, a different Founder supports the opposing side. Because the leading Founders disagreed, simply having a Founder on one's side is an inadequate legal position."[61] Similarly, Steven Smith contended in an earlier work that the historical analysis originalism attempts to provide cannot tell us what substantive principle of religious freedom the Founders embodied in the religion clauses, because there was none.[62] For Smith, so to speak, the original meaning was an empty set.

---

generation and public understanding in general. Contemporarily, we hear a great deal, perhaps inordinately so, about current issues from people like Bill O'Reilly, Rush Limbaugh, Glenn Beck, Keith Olbermann, and others, but two hundred years in the future the question would still arise as to how representative such commentators were of the public understanding of those issues. Those who talk the loudest are not necessarily representative of public opinion.

[59] Muñoz, *God and the Founders*, 207.

[60] For a nice recent survey of the back-and-forth of historical arguments, see Donald L. Drakeman, *Church, State, and Original Intent* (New York: Cambridge University Press, 2010), Introduction, 1–20. "We have access," he writes, "to a wealth of eighteenth-century newspapers and pamphlets, collections of the papers of various framers, and so on. We know with a fairly high degree of confidence what most people were saying about the establishment clause at the time it was adopted and ratified: nothing" (327). Exploring how the historical approach came to dominate contemporary discussions of church-state relations, he argues that we can say of the original meaning of the religion clauses, at best, that there was to be no national religion.

[61] Muñoz, *God and the Founders*, 207. Muñoz argues that we should turn to the founders not simply to follow them blindly but rather to learn from the profundity of their natural-rights arguments about religious liberty. "Whether we are to follow the Founders (as originalists assume we should) or to dismiss them (as progressives assume we should), we have to understand the Founders and judge the merits of their ideas" (5–6). Drakeman, *Church, State*, similarly argues, "The point is that the framers will be invoked not as speaking for a widely shared understanding of the founding generation as to what the establishment clause originally meant, but as thoughtful people whose opinions are worth considering" (344; footnote omitted).

[62] "If we ask, therefore, what principle or theory of religious liberty the framers and ratifiers of the religion clauses adopted, the most accurate answer is 'None.' They consciously chose not to answer the religion question, and they were able for the most part to avoid it (or at least thought they were) because of the way in which they answered the jurisdiction question—that is, by assigning the religion question to the states." Steven D. Smith, *Foreordained Failure: The Quest for a Constitutional Principle of Religious Freedom* (New York: Oxford University Press, 1995), 21. I will address this argument in the course of my analysis here.

Beyond inconsistencies in the historical record like these and others, there is a greater difficulty for those seeking to determine the meaning of the religion clauses by asking what the Founders intended. In the words of Justice Stevens in *Van Orden v. Perry*, "[M]any of the Framers understood the word 'religion' in the Establishment Clause to encompass only the various sects of Christianity."[63] According to Justice Joseph Story in 1833, "Now, there will probably be found few persons in this, or any other Christian country, who would deliberately contend, that it was unreasonable, or unjust to foster and encourage the Christian religion generally, as a matter of sound policy, as well as of revealed truth."[64] More to the point, Story argued this: "The real object of the amendment was, not to countenance, much less to advance Mahometanism, or Judaism, or infidelity, by prostrating Christianity; but to exclude all rivalry among Christian sects, and to prevent any national ecclesiastical establishment, which should give to an hierarchy the exclusive patronage of the national government."[65]

In other words, many writers in the founding period contended that the religion clauses were not designed to offer protection to non-Christian religions, and probably not to Roman Catholicism either. To be sure, Story also wrote, "Probably at the time of the adoption of the constitution, and of the amendment to it, now under consideration, the general, if not the universal, sentiment in America was, that Christianity ought to receive encouragement from the state, so far as was not incompatible with the private rights of conscience, and the freedom of religious worship." Yet in the very next sentence he added, "An attempt to level all religions, and to make it a matter of state policy to hold all in utter indifference, would have created universal disapprobation, if not universal indignation."[66] Free exercise of religion is to be valued, but certainly all religions were not to be treated equally. What all this means is that, on the historical approach, we are caught between the horns of a dilemma. Either the religion clauses do not offer any protections to religions that are not denominations of Protestant Christianity, which surely no one in contemporary American wants to argue,[67] or else we contemporary Americans have changed the

[63] *Van Orden v. Perry*, 545 U.S. 677 (2005), at 726 (Stevens, dissenting).

[64] Joseph Story, *Commentaries on the Constitution* 3:§§1865–73, at §1867 (http://press-pubs.uchicago.edu/founders/documents/amendI_religions69.html, retrieved 9-16-08).

[65] Story, *Commentaries*, at §1871.

[66] Story, *Commentaries*, at §1868.

[67] Yet Judge Roy Moore, the famous "Ten Commandments judge" from Alabama, stated, "By leaving religion undefined, the Court has opened the door to the erroneous assumption that, under the Establishment Clause, religion could include Buddhism, Hinduism, Taoism, and whatever might occupy in man's life a place parallel to that filled by God, or even Secular Humanism, which might be defined as man's belief in

meaning of the religion clauses, which goes against the very purpose of inquiring into the intent of the founders.

My suggestion, by contrast, is to escape both horns of the dilemma by considering a parallel interpretive issue with the Declaration of Independence. While some people prior to the Civil War considered the principle that "All men are created equal" to be completely at odds with institution of slavery, there were many who saw no inconsistency between that principle and slavery. Aside from the most retrograde of cases, I cannot imagine anyone today who does not think that the Declaration's equality principle is richer and broader than many people might have understood at that earlier time. Similarly, while some people two hundred years ago might have thought that the religion clauses allowed government to endorse or otherwise privilege Christianity, my suggestion is that the religion clauses—and especially the Establishment Clause—must be understood, when considered from the standpoint of constitutional theory rather than constitutional history, to embody a principle richer and broader than what those in the founding generation might have thought they were supporting. The meaning of the clauses does not change; rather, our understanding of that meaning changes and, we hope, for the better.[68]

Finally, much of the argument that the United States is or should be a religious community of some sort rests on two claims about morality. One claim, very familiar to readers of the ratification debates between

---

his own supremacy and sufficiency." Roy S. Moore, "Religion in the Public Square," *Cumberland Law Review* 29 (1998): 347, at 356–57 (footnote omitted).

[68] See my distinction between meaning and understanding in Goldford, *American Constitution*, 70–89. This point appears more recently in the confirmation hearings for Justice Samuel Alito:

> ALITO: Well, Senator, I would never say that it is an easy process. There are some easy cases, but there are lot [*sic*] of very difficult cases. And once you have identified the principle, the job of applying it to particular cases is often not easy at all. But what the judge has to do is make sure that the judge is being true to the principal [*sic*] that is expressed in the Constitution and not to the judge's principle, not to some idea that the judge has. And sometimes this results in groundbreaking decisions; sometimes that is because new issues come up. Sometimes it is because the principle that is embodied in a constitutional provision has long been neglected. That was certainly true with respect to the equal protection clause. There was a long period between Plessy v. Ferguson and Brown v. Board of Education when the true meaning of the equal protection clause was not recognized in the decisions of the Supreme Court.
>
> ALITO: And when Brown was finally decided, that was not an instance of the court changing the meaning of the equal protection clause; it was an instance of a court writing [*sic*] an incorrect interpretation that had prevailed for a long period of time.

Senate Confirmation Hearings for Joseph A. Alito. Day 2. *The New York Times*, January 10, 2006; no italics in original (http://www.nytimes.com/2006/01/10/politics/politicsspecial1/text-day2.html?pagewanted=all, retrieved 7-12-09).

Federalists and Anti-Federalists, is that republican self-government requires a particular kind of virtuous citizenry and thus a shared commitment to a common morality.[69] The other, perhaps less familiar claim is that any legal system is indisputably and inescapably the expression of a particular moral vision.[70] What ties both claims together is the assumption that to speak of morality is necessarily to speak of religion. In his dissent in *McCreary*, Justice Scalia stated, "Those who wrote the Constitution believed that morality was essential to the well-being of society and that encouragement of religion was the best way to foster morality."[71] On this view, to speak of law is necessarily to speak of morality, to speak of morality is necessarily to speak of religion, and thus, transitively, to speak of law is necessarily to speak of religion. On the contrary view, however, to speak of law may necessarily be to speak of morality, but to speak of morality is *not* necessarily to speak of religion—religion may be one way to foster morality, but it is not the only way. On either alternative, the issue, and thus the broader question of what the religion clauses mean for the nature of the American political order, is a matter of political and constitutional theory rather than political and constitutional history. Indeed, it is precisely the political and constitutional history that poses the question for political and constitutional theory, for it is by means of the latter that we attempt to render coherent the conflicts in the former.

[69] Muñoz, for example, writes that during the Founding period, "Some states, like Virginia, abolished official state establishments and ended direct government funding of religious clergy. What I shall call the 'Virginia Understanding' effectively privatized religion. In other states, particularly in New England, religion as such remained an object of public funding and state concern. The 'Massachusetts Way,' as I will call it, sought to use public funding and public endorsement of religion as a means to nurture and to encourage good citizenship." Muñoz, "Original Meaning," at 605. He then writes, "At the heart of the 'Massachusetts Way' lies a simple syllogism: republican government requires a virtuous citizenry; the cultivation of virtue depends on religion; therefore, supporters of republican government ought to support religion" (at 606).

[70] Though the issue is well beyond the scope of this book, I would suggest that one does not have to be a natural-law theorist to make such a claim. Even a legal positivist could say that a legal system expresses a particular moral vision, that of the sovereign authority, though not one grounded in nature, as the natural-law theorist would maintain.

[71] Justice Antonin Scalia, *McCreary County*, at 887 (dissenting opinion).

Chapter 2

Religious Minorities, Religious Freedom, and Religion

Even when not exacerbated by controversial constitutional decisions, the interrelationship of law, politics, and religion in the United States is always interesting and often contentious, particularly so in the 2008 Republican presidential nomination process. During the early stage of that process, former Massachusetts Governor Mitt Romney pursued an electoral strategy almost guaranteed to raise questions about the political importance of religion. Judged from the perspective of a long-time observer of the politics of the Iowa caucuses, the Romney strategy apparently was to assume that Senator John McCain would be, in contrast to his 2000 race, the establishment candidate for the Republican nomination, which would leave room for Romney to run to McCain's right. In the Iowa caucuses, which McCain chose not to contest in any serious manner, Romney thus targeted evangelical Christian conservatives, a constituency that in past caucuses and primaries made up 40 percent or more of the Republican base.[1]

As the campaign turned out, however, this strategy was fundamentally flawed. By attempting to win the support of religious, predominantly evangelical conservatives, the Romney campaign encountered a paradox: on the one hand, this Republican constituency considered religious values and beliefs to be of the highest importance in public as well as private life, but, on the other hand, much if not most of this very same constituency was suspicious of Romney's own Mormon religion.[2] Indeed, this dilemma

[1] In the 2008 Iowa Republican caucuses, in fact, entrance polls would indicate that approximately 60 percent of participants self-identified as evangelical or Christian conservatives. http://www.cnn.com/ELECTION/2008/primaries/results/epolls/index.html#IAREP (retrieved 8-3-10).

[2] In the words of one Southern Baptist, "I couldn't vote for him. His cross is not my cross." Private conversation with the author. That issue continued in the 2012

is what left a political opening among Iowa's evangelical Republicans for the candidacy of former Arkansas Governor—and Baptist minister—Mike Huckabee, who went on to beat Romney in the 2008 caucuses. It was in order to mitigate if not dissolve this paradox a month before the Iowa caucuses that Romney, despite some disagreement among his staff about its advisability, presented a speech on the relation between politics and religion.[3]

Although basically confused when taken as a whole, the speech in its various parts raises important issues in the interrelationship of law, politics, and religion in America. Specifically, the Romney speech often conflates two distinct concepts: religion and religious freedom. The proposition I wish to advance in this chapter is that the religion clauses of the First Amendment protect not *religion* but *religious freedom*. Moreover, once we grasp that fundamental distinction we will be able to understand how the protection of religious freedom is not equivalent to hostility to religion.

The general confusion in Romney's speech is that in appealing to conservative Christians possibly suspicious of the Mormon religion, it emphasizes both the importance of religion in American life and a separation of church and state that, put bluntly, prevents a Mormon president from acting on Mormonism as president. On the one hand, therefore, Romney sounds like many liberals in his insistence on the separation of church and state and, interestingly, on a commonality of values that appears almost as the overlapping consensus of John Rawls. "Let me assure you," Romney stated, "that no authorities of my church, or of any

---

presidential-election cycle. Reporter Sasha Issenberg wrote in the summer of 2010, "Mitt Romney and his strategists expected his Mormon faith to fade as an issue for fundamentalist Christians during his first presidential campaign. This time around, should he choose to run again, they have doubts." Referring to 2012 possibilities, Issenberg said, "[E]ven as the national Republican establishment warms to Romney as never before, the former candidate and his closest aides now believe a group of voters will always be off-limits because of his religion." See "Faith Still Sticky Issue as Romney Mulls Run: Mormonism Remains Hard Sell for Evangelicals," *Boston Globe*, July 3, 2010 (http://www.boston.com/news/nation/washington/articles/2010/07/03/faith_still_sticky_issue_as_romney_mulls_run/, retrieved 7-9-10). According to a Pew survey conducted in late May 2011, while 68 percent of the public and 58 percent of white evangelicals said a presidential candidate's Mormon religion would not matter to them, 25 percent of the public and 34 percent of white evangelicals said they would be less likely to support such a candidate. "Republican Candidates Stir Little Enthusiasm," The Pew Research Center for the People and the Press, June 2, 2011 (http://people-press.org/2011/06/02/section-2-candidate-traits-and-experience/#mormon, retrieved 6-13-11).

[3] Governor Mitt Romney, "Faith in America," speech at the George H. W. Bush Presidential Library and Museum, Texas A&M University, College Station, Tex., December 6, 2007. I cite passages from the text published at http://www.nytimes.com/2007/12/06/us/politics/06text-romney.html (retrieved 3-20-08).

other church for that matter, will ever exert influence on presidential decisions. Their authority is theirs, within the province of church affairs, and it ends where the affairs of the nation begin." Romney here not only separated church and state,[4] but also in effect made a clear distinction between the religious and the secular realms. Government, he argued, has to do with the secular realm, stating, "As governor . . . I did not confuse the particular teachings of my church with the obligations of the office and of the Constitution—and of course, I would not do so as President. I will put no doctrine of any church above the plain duties of the office and the sovereign authority of the law."

What Romney did emphasize as distinct from religious doctrine and church authority is the idea of different faiths with common values. "It is important to recognize," he stated, "that while differences in theology exist between the churches in America, we share a common creed of moral convictions. And where the affairs of our nation are concerned, it's usually a sound rule to focus on the latter—on the great moral principles that urge us all on a common course." This idea is similar to Rawls' notion of an overlapping consensus among various comprehensive doctrines set out most prominently in his book titled *Political Liberalism*.[5] Nevertheless, despite this nod in the direction of a liberal position on the question of the separation of church and state, Romney on the other hand moved immediately in his speech to the standard conservative complaint:

> But in recent years, the notion of the separation of church and state has been taken by some well beyond its original meaning. They seek to remove from the public domain any acknowledgment of God. Religion is seen as merely a private affair with no place in public life. It is as if they are intent on establishing a new religion in America—the religion of secularism. They are wrong.

Here, of course, after signaling to Christian conservatives through his affirmation of the separation of church and state that they need not fear his Mormonism, Romney endorsed their argument that religion is a necessary component of public life. "The founders proscribed the establishment of a state religion, but they did not countenance the elimination of religion from the public square. We are a nation 'Under God' and in God, we do indeed trust." The theoretical problem, of course, is the question of how to reconcile the two prongs of this argument.

[4] Later in the speech he adds, "We separate church and state in this country, and for good reason. No religion should dictate to the state nor should the state interfere with the free practice of religion."

[5] John Rawls, *Political Liberalism*, expanded ed. (New York: Columbia University Press, 2005).

Romney's concern here, of course, was political rather than theoretical. In the Huckabee campaign's second television ad in Iowa,[6] the first text on the screen was "Christian leader," and the first spoken word was "faith," leaving no doubt as to their target constituency. That was the context for a further confusion in the Romney speech. On the one hand, he decried the idea of a religious test for office: "There are some who would have a presidential candidate describe and explain his church's distinctive doctrines. To do so would enable the very religious test the founders prohibited in the Constitution." Yet on the other hand, Romney evidently felt compelled to address a theological question—"There is one fundamental question about which I often am asked. What do I believe about Jesus Christ? I believe that Jesus Christ is the Son of God and the Savior of mankind"—which implies the existence and legitimacy of at least a de facto religious test for office.

The central confusion in Romney's speech, however, came when he attempted to make what in effect is a fundamental theoretical argument. Here is the key passage:

> [The nation's founders] discovered the essential connection between the survival of a free land and the protection of religious freedom. In John Adams' words: "We have no government armed with power capable of contending with human passions unbridled by morality and religion. . . . Our constitution was made for a moral and religious people." Freedom requires religion just as religion requires freedom. Freedom opens the windows of the soul so that man can discover his most profound beliefs and commune with God. Freedom and religion endure together, or perish alone.

Romney's theoretical claims here are manifold. First, he asserts what he calls "the essential connection between the survival of a free land and the protection of religious freedom." While we can imagine a society in which individuals enjoy religious freedom but do not have political freedom, it is not problematic to suggest that in its broadest significance the concept of a "free land" would seem necessarily to include the freedom of religion.

However, in the second place, we can see in the passage how Romney moves immediately from the idea of religious freedom to the idea of religion itself. Taken at face value, the text of the Adams quotation affirms the importance of religion rather than religious freedom. Adams' argument, which appears in modern form in much religious-conservative and neoconservative discussion, is that no society can be stable, and, in particular, no self-governing republic is possible, without a moral and

[6] The first was a mostly humorous attempt to introduce him to Iowa Republicans, particularly with the co-appearance of actor Chuck Norris.

religious foundation.[7] Yet, with apologies to Adams' own views, this argument could be taken to justify the position that everyone in a society should be made to subscribe to some religion, or to an official religion, or at least to undergo some sort of religious upbringing, for the sake of social stability and self-government—a coerced form of religion that would be the denial of religious freedom. Thus, despite Romney's efforts, an argument for the political and social importance of religion does not follow from an affirmation of "the essential connection between the survival of a free land and the protection of religious freedom."

Third, and most fundamental, while we might make an analytical claim that "Freedom requires religious freedom just as religious freedom requires freedom," the claim that "Freedom requires religion just as religion requires freedom" is an empirical matter that can be true or false. And as a matter of fact, it seems to be false. Correlating the countries mentioned specifically in the summary version of a Gallup International survey of religiosity with data compiled by Freedom House,[8] we arrive at these results:

Country	*Religiosity (%)*	*Freedom House Rating*
Ghana	96	PR 1, CL 2, F
Nigeria	94	PR 4, CL 4, PF
Philippines	90	PR 3, CL 3, PF
India	87	PR 2, CL 3, F
Greece	86	PR 1, CL 2, F
Macedonia	85	PR 3, CL 3, PF
Poland	85	PR 1, CL 1, F
Romania	85	PR 2, CL 2, F
Turkey	83	PR 3, CL 3, PF

[7] As Romney stated at one point in his speech, "Our greatness would not long endure without judges who respect the foundation of faith upon which our constitution rests." Dissenting in *McCreary County, Kentucky, et al. v. American Civil Liberties Union of Kentucky, et al.*, 545 U.S. 844 (2005), Justice Scalia writes at 887, "Those who wrote the Constitution believed that morality was essential to the well-being of society and that encouragement of religion was the best way to foster morality."

[8] Gallup International, "Voice of the People 2005: Religiosity Around the World" (http://extranet.gallup-international.com/uploads/internet/Religiosity%20around%20the%20world%20VoP%2005%20press%20release.pdf, retrieved 3-21-08), and Freedom House 2005 (http://www.freedomhouse.org/template.cfm?page=15&year=2005, retrieved 3-21-08).

Country	*Religiosity (%)*	*Freedom House Rating*
Ethiopia	66	PR 5, CL 5, PF
Guatemala	64	PR 4, CL 4, PF
Canada	58	PR 1, CL 1, F
Uruguay	54	PR 1, CL 1, F
Czech Republic	49	PR 1, CL 1, F
Japan	41	PR 1, CL 2, F
Norway	36	PR 1, CL 1, F
Thailand	35	PR 3, CL 3, PF
Israel	33	PR 1, CL 2, F

Note: Religiosity = percentage of citizens considering themselves religious. PR = political rights and CL = civil liberties (top score = 1). F = free; PF = partly free; NF = not free.

Furthermore, according to Gallup's general comments, in most African countries around nine out of ten, and in most Latin American and Middle Eastern countries, countries not rated highly by Freedom House, eight out of ten, people consider themselves religious, while in Western Europe, containing countries more likely to be rated highly, six out of ten people consider themselves religious. The lowest religiosity countries on the list tend to have the more consistent ratings of fully free, while the highest religiosity countries tend to be more mixed in what Freedom House calls their freedom status.

Without putting too much weight on these data, they come close to suggesting not a direct but almost an inverse relation between religiosity and freedom. At the least, the data show that religion can exist without freedom, and freedom can exist without religion: Romney's claim that "Freedom requires religion just as religion requires freedom" is false. Religion would appear to be neither a necessary nor a sufficient condition of freedom, nor would freedom appear to be either a necessary or a sufficient condition of religion. We can make the case that freedom entails or requires religious freedom, but it is a different, and questionable, claim to argue that freedom entails or requires religion.

Mitt Romney, of course, is a businessman and politician, not a political or constitutional theorist, and it is not my intention to hold him unfairly to an inappropriate standard. Nevertheless, his conflation of religion and religious freedom in this important speech reflects the difficulty people have in understanding the nature of the religion clauses in the First Amendment in general and the nature of the Establishment Clause in particular. In the difficult and contentious course of controversies involving law, politics, and religion, most arguments about the meaning and application of the Establishment Clause are conducted in terms of views such as separationism, accommodationism, strict neutrality, benevolent neutrality, equal regard, and the like.[9] One's support or rejection of any of these views, however, necessarily presupposes an answer to a more fundamental question: is the purpose of the religion clauses the protection and special position of religion in the American constitutional scheme, or is the purpose of the religion clauses the protection and special position of religious freedom in the American constitutional scheme?

Religion is distinct from religious freedom. When we speak of religion, I suggest, we speak of religious institutions, religious beliefs, and religious practices. When we speak of religious freedom, we speak of individuals and their right to choose their own religious identities and religious positions regarding those institutions, beliefs, and practices. If the purpose of the religion clauses is to protect religion, then the question is, whose religion? Recall the well-known argument of Justice Joseph Story in his *Commentaries* about the First Amendment, cited earlier:

> The real object of the amendment was, not to countenance, much less to advance Mahometanism, or Judaism, or infidelity, by prostrating Christianity; but to exclude all rivalry among Christian sects, and to prevent any national ecclesiastical establishment, which should give to an hierarchy the exclusive patronage of the national government.[10]

On this view, the religion clauses are to protect the diversity of Christian denominations, and non-Christian faiths not at all. Indeed, Story argued, "[T]here will probably be found few persons in this, or any other Christian country, who would deliberately contend, that it was unreasonable, or unjust to foster and encourage the Christian religion generally, as a matter of sound policy, as well as of revealed truth." Presumably no one in the religious mainstream of contemporary America, however, would accept this position that favors Christianity and excludes non-Christian religions.[11]

[9] See chap. 3 *infra*.

[10] Joseph Story, "Commentaries on the Constitution 3:§1871," in *The Founders' Constitution* (http://press-pubs.uchicago.edu/founders/documents/amendI_religions69.html, retrieved 3-23-08).

[11] Note, however, the position of the American Constitution Party: "This great nation was founded, not by religionists, but by Christians; not on religions but on the Gospel of Jesus Christ. For this very reason peoples of other faiths have been and are afforded asylum, prosperity, and freedom of worship here." http://www.constitutionparty.com/documents/2004CPPlatform.pdf (retrieved 4-6-07). Similarly, according to the American Heritage Party, "the Bible is the highest and final authority to which

What, then, might we mean when we say that the religion clauses "protect" religion? Consider again, at some length, the thoughts of Justice Story:

> The real difficulty lies in ascertaining the limits, to which government may rightfully go in fostering and encouraging religion. Three cases may easily be supposed. One, where a government affords aid to a particular religion, leaving all persons free to adopt any other; another, where it creates an ecclesiastical establishment for the propagation of the doctrines of a particular sect of that religion, leaving a like freedom to all others; and a third, where it creates such an establishment, and excludes all persons, not belonging to it, either wholly, or in part, from any participation in the public honours, trusts, emoluments, privileges, and immunities of the state. For instance, a government may simply declare, that the Christian religion shall be the religion of the state, and shall be aided, and encouraged in all the varieties of sects belonging to it; or it may declare, that the Catholic or Protestant religion shall be the religion of the state, leaving every man to the free enjoyment of his own religious opinions; or it may establish the doctrines of a particular sect, as of Episcopalians, as the religion of the state, with a like freedom; or it may establish the doctrines of a particular sect, as exclusively the religion of the state, tolerating others to a limited extent, or excluding all, not belonging to it, from all public honours, trusts, emoluments, privileges, and immunities.[12]

Government, Story argues here, might aid a particular religion, while tolerating others; might establish a particular religion, again while tolerating others; or might establish a particular religion and exclude those not members of it from politics and government. Any of these measures, apparently, would count as a direction in which "government may rightfully go in fostering and encouraging religion."[13] These versions of religious establishment certainly would constitute "protecting" religion. They are analogous to government's protecting an industry from competition through granting a monopoly (establishment), preventing the entry of new firms into the market either through high barriers to entry or through legal measures, or providing subsidies.

Few people today would consider any of these measures to be consistent with the meaning of the Establishment Clause. A brief look at several

---

all other authorities and ideas must ultimately yield." In particular, the rule of law "is rooted in an authority higher than man; ultimately in God himself. The rule of law in a Christian order requires that all government policy must be consistent with God's law and the Christian-based common law." http://www.americanheritageparty.org/princ.htm (retrieved 4-6-07).

[12] Joseph Story, "Commentaries on the Constitution 3:§1866," in *The Founders' Constitution.*

[13] I raise the unremarked fourth possibility here—the idea that it is not the function of government to foster and encourage religion—below.

forms of full-blown religious establishment provides perspective on the ways one might protect religion. Here, first, are various provisions from early American state constitutions:[14]

> Delaware, Article 22 (1776): "Every person who shall be chosen a member of either house, or appointed to any office or place of trust . . . shall . . . also make and subscribe the following declaration, to whit: 'I, _____, do profess faith in God the Father, and in Jesus Christ His only Son, and in the Holy Ghost, one God, blessed for evermore; and I do acknowledge the holy scriptures of the Old and New Testament to be given by divine inspiration.'"
>
> Maryland, Article XXXII (1776): "All persons, professing the Christian religion, are equally entitled to protection their religious liberty . . . the Legislature may, in their discretion, lay a general tax and equal tax, for the support of the Christian religion."
>
> Massachusetts, First Part, Article II (1780): "The governor shall be chosen annually; and no person shall be eligible to this office, unless . . . he shall declare himself to be of the Christian religion."
>
> Massachusetts, Chapter VI, Article I (1780): "[All persons elected to State office or to the Legislature must] make and subscribe the following declaration, viz. 'I, _____, do declare, that I believe the Christian religion, and have firm persuasion of its truth.'"
>
> North Carolina, Article XXXII (1776): "That no person, who shall deny the being of God or the truth of the Protestant religion, or the divine authority either of the Old or New Testaments, . . . shall be capable of holding any office or place of trust or profit in the civil department within this State."
>
> South Carolina, Article XXXVIII (1778): "That all persons and religious societies who acknowledge that there is one God, and a future state of rewards and punishments, and that God is publicly to be worshipped, shall be freely tolerated. The Christian Protestant religion shall be deemed . . . to be the established religion of this State."
>
> Tennessee, Article VIII, Section 2 (1796): "[N]o person who denies the being of God, or a future state of rewards and punishments, shall hold any office in the civil department of this State."
>
> Vermont, Frame of Government, Section 9 (1777): "And each member [of the legislature] . . . shall make and subscribe the following declaration, viz.: 'I do believe in one god, the Creator and Governor of the universe, the rewarder of the good and punisher of the wicked. And I do acknowledge

[14] All of these are drawn from "Religious Clauses in State Constitutions" (http://www.constitution.org/primarysources/state.html, retrieved 3-22-08).

> the scriptures of the old and new testament to be given by divine inspiration, and own and profess the protestant religion.'"

And second, here are several passages from the current Iranian Constitution:[15]

> Article 2. The Islamic Republic is a system based on belief in:
>
> 1. the One God (as stated in the phrase "There is no god except Allah"), His exclusive sovereignty and the right to legislate, and the necessity of submission to His commands;
> 2. Divine revelation and its fundamental role in setting forth the laws;
> 3. the return to God in the Hereafter, and the constructive role of this belief in the course of man's ascent towards God;
> 4. the justice of God in creation and legislation;
> 5. continuous leadership (imamah) and perpetual guidance, and its fundamental role in ensuring the uninterrupted process of the revolution of Islam;
> 6. the exalted dignity and value of man, and his freedom coupled with responsibility before God.
>
> Article 4. All civil, penal financial, economic, administrative, cultural, military, political, and other laws and regulations must be based on Islamic criteria. This principle applies absolutely and generally to all articles of the Constitution as well as to all other laws and regulations, and the fuqaha' of the Guardian Council are judges in this matter.
>
> Article 12: The official religion of Iran is Islam and the Twelver Ja'fari school [in usual al-Din and fiqh], and this principle will remain eternally immutable.
>
> Article 13: Zoroastrian, Jewish, and Christian Iranians are the only recognized religious minorities, who, within the limits of the law, are free to perform their religious rites and ceremonies, and to act according to their own canon in matters of personal affairs and religious education.

We see in these examples from the early American states classic cases of establishment of religion and in the example of contemporary Iran a classic case of theocracy, in which church and state are united, fully integrated, rather than separated. Nothing we find in contemporary America approaches these versions of protecting religion. At the very least, the meaning of the religion clauses is that neither affirmation of a particular

[15] Drawn from http://www.iranonline.com/iran/iran-info/Government/constitution-1.html (accessed 3-13-08).

religious creed or faith tradition (Establishment Clause) nor rejection of a particular religious creed or faith tradition (Free Exercise Clause) can be a precondition of full participation in public life.

Nevertheless, despite the fact that in the United States we do not or no longer protect religion in the foregoing manner, consider the position of Justice Anthony Kennedy in *Allegheny County v. Greater Pittsburgh ACLU*: "Government policies of accommodation, acknowledgment, and support for religion are an accepted part of our political and cultural heritage."[16] "Rather than requiring government to avoid any action that acknowledges or aids religion," he continues in the same place, "the Establishment Clause permits government some latitude in recognizing and accommodating the central role religion plays in our society." What, however, do "accommodation," "acknowledgment," "support," and "recognition" mean? Dictionaries do not solve political conflict, to be sure—with apologies to Thomas Hobbes, political conflicts are not fundamentally about the meaning of words—but they can be suggestive when, as Kenndy is doing here, a writer is using ordinary language rather than doing technical philosophical analysis. Based upon the *Oxford English Dictionary*, "accommodate" does not appear to present much of a problem. In its most relevant *OED* definitions, it means "to adjust, reconcile (things or persons that differ), and hence, to compose, settle (their difference); to bring to harmony or agreement," or "to minister convenience to; to aid, speed, facilitate."[17] To bring to harmony and to aid or facilitate are most relevant here and certainly relate to the idea that the Free Exercise Clause requires government to lift governmentally imposed burdens on the free exercise of religion under certain conditions.

The idea of acknowledgment is more problematic. According to the most relevant *OED* definitions, "acknowledge" means "to own the knowledge of; to confess; to recognize or admit as true," or "to own as genuine, or of legal force or validity; to own, avow, or assent, in legal form, to (an act, document, etc.) so as to give it validity."[18] Acknowledgment of a religion in the sense of admitting its beliefs to be real or true, or recognizing the truth of its beliefs, or recognizing the authority, validity, or claims of its beliefs, would constitute the establishment of a set of religious beliefs in contravention of the Establishment Clause prohibition of such action. House Resolution 847, passed by a vote of 372–9 (10 members voting "present" and 40 not voting) on December 11, 2007, comes perilously close to this line:

[16] *Allegheny County v. Greater Pittsburgh ACLU*, 492 U.S. 573 (1989), at 657.

[17] "Accommodate," defs. 5 and 10. *The Oxford English Dictionary*, 2nd ed., prepared by J. A. Simpson and E. S. C. Weiner (Oxford: Clarendon, 1989).

[18] "Acknowledge," defs. 1 and 3, *OED*.

Whereas Christmas, a holiday of great significance to Americans and many other cultures and nationalities, is celebrated annually by Christians throughout the United States and the world;

Whereas there are approximately 225,000,000 Christians in the United States, making Christianity the religion of over three-fourths of the American population;

Whereas there are approximately 2,000,000,000 Christians throughout the world, making Christianity the largest religion in the world and the religion of about one-third of the world population;

Whereas Christians and Christianity have contributed greatly to the development of western civilization;

Whereas the United States, being founded as a constitutional republic in the traditions of western civilization, finds much in its history that points observers back to its Judeo-Christian roots;

Whereas on December 25 of each calendar year, American Christians observe Christmas, the holiday celebrating the birth of their savior, Jesus Christ;

Whereas for Christians, Christmas is celebrated as a recognition of God's redemption, mercy, and Grace; and

Whereas many Christians and non-Christians throughout the United States and the rest of the world, celebrate Christmas as a time to serve others: Now, therefore, be it

Resolved, That the House of Representatives—

(1) recognizes the Christian faith as one of the great religions of the world;

(2) expresses continued support for Christians in the United States and worldwide;

(3) acknowledges the international religious and historical importance of Christmas and the Christian faith;

(4) acknowledges and supports the role played by Christians and Christianity in the founding of the United States and in the formation of the western civilization;

(5) rejects bigotry and persecution directed against Christians, both in the United States and worldwide; and

(6) expresses its deepest respect to American Christians and Christians throughout the world.[19]

[19] HRES 847 EH (http://thomas.loc.gov/cgi-bin/query/z?c110:H.RES.847.EH:, retrieved 3-23-08). The original resolution prior to amendment included this text: "Whereas Christians identify themselves as those who believe in the salvation from sin offered to them through the sacrifice of their savior, Jesus Christ, the Son of God,

It is one thing to acknowledge the existence or fact of a religious tradition; it is quite another to attempt to have government acknowledge the truth or validity of that tradition.

"Recognition," already implicated in the concept of acknowledgment, has a large range of meanings. According to the *OED*, "recognition is "the action of acknowledging as true, valid, or entitled to consideration; formal acknowledgement as conveying approval or sanction of something; hence, notice or attention accorded to a thing or person." To "recognize" is "to acknowledge by special notice, approval, or sanction; to treat as valid, as having existence or as entitled to consideration; to take notice of (a thing or person) in some way."[20] Apart from showing appreciation of religion, "recognizing" religion in these senses amounts to making a normative judgment, as in the case of affirming it to be true or valid, or, as in the case of diplomatic recognition, accepting the legitimacy of a government another country as the rightful government of that country. Finally, "support" is perhaps the most problematic of the terms Justice Kennedy used in *Allegheny*. The most relevant meanings of "support" are "to strengthen the position of (a person or community) by one's assistance, countenance, or adherence; to uphold the rights, claims, authority, or status of; to stand by, back up," "to uphold or maintain the validity of (a thing); also to give support to (a course of action)," and "to furnish authority for or corroboration of (a statement, etc.); to bear out, substantiate."[21] The various synonyms—support, uphold, advocate, back, champion—mean "to favor actively one that meets opposition."

In this sense, then, Justice Kennedy's statement noted above—"Government policies of accommodation, acknowledgment, and support for religion are an accepted part of our political and cultural heritage"—appears to understand the role of government to include not just taking notice of religion (institutions, beliefs, practices) as one of many elements of American society, but also acting as a protector of and advocate for religion. On this view, therefore, the purpose of the religion clauses in the First Amendment is to protect religion. They may not allow government to prohibit criticism of religion, to prohibit blasphemy, to mandate or to prohibit certain types of religious belief and commitment, but allowing government to acknowledge, recognize, and support religion still puts the weight of government approval behind religion, thereby expressing the normative judgment that religion is a "good thing."

---

and who, out of gratitude for the gift of salvation, commit themselves to living their lives in accordance with the teachings of the Holy Bible."

[20] "Recognition," def. 4a, and "recognize," def. 4a, *OED*.

[21] "Support," defs. 2a, 2b, and 3c, *OED*.

If it is the purpose of the Constitution to protect religion, therefore, any attempt on the part of government to be neutral in regard to religion will suggest hostility to religion. As Justice Kennedy, following many justices in prior cases, states later in *Allegheny*,

> Rather than requiring government to avoid any action that acknowledges or aids religion, the Establishment Clause permits government some latitude in recognizing and accommodating the central role religion plays in our society. . . . Any approach less sensitive to our heritage would border on latent hostility toward religion, as it would require government in all its multifaceted roles to acknowledge only the secular, to the exclusion and so to the detriment of the religious.[22]

The concept of neutrality, however, despite disagreement over its meaning,[23] makes sense not with regard to the protection of religion, but to the protection of religious freedom. For example, in *The Last Freedom: Religion from the Public School to the Public Square*, Joseph Viteritti discusses *Mozert v. Hawkins City Board of Education*, the 1987 case involving religious objections to public school readings.[24] Viteritti writes, "The parents did not want their children assigned readings that contradicted their religious views, or even materials suggesting that one form of religious teaching was as good as another. They sought an alternative to the required text."[25] Furthermore, "For these fundamentalist parents, not all religions were the same. Nor was secularism a form of governmental neutrality. As they saw it, secularism was a particular worldview. This is not altogether unreasonable interpretation of the secularist perspective."[26]

Aside from his unjustified conflation of "secular" with "secular humanism,"[27] Viteritti's point depends on how we frame the issue. Consider these three options:

(1) the public school inculcates your own religious values;

(2) the public school strives for neutrality—however difficult that task is and imperfectly it can be accomplished—regarding any religious values; or

[22] *Allegheny*, at 657. Similarly, at 622 Justice O'Connor stated, "The Court has avoided drawing lines which entirely sweep away all government recognition and acknowledgment of the role of religion in the lives of our citizens for to do so would exhibit not neutrality but hostility to religion."

[23] See chaps. 3 and 4 *infra*.

[24] *Mozert v. Hawkins City Board of Education*, 827 F.2d 1058 (1987).

[25] Joseph P. Viteritti, *The Last Freedom: Religion from the Public School to the Public Square* (Princeton, N.J.: Princeton University Press, 2007), 56.

[26] Viteritti, *Last Freedom*, 60.

[27] See chap. 6 *infra*.

(3) the public school inculcates values contrary or even hostile to your own religious values.

It is one thing to accept (2) because we cannot allow (1), that is, to say that because we cannot allow the public school to teach your own religious values, we ask that the school strive for neutrality regarding any religious values. It is something entirely different, however, to argue that (2) is essentially (3) and thus we must revert to (1)—that is, that neutrality itself is a religious value contrary or even hostile to our own, and consequently we must have the school teach our own religious values. That move is simply unacceptable in a pluralist society, and those who make that argument are necessarily out of luck. Any opposition to the universalistic claims of a religious group in the name of pluralism is going to constitute a rejection of those universalistic claims. No matter what we do, if we have a universalistic religion—i.e., one that claims its truths are valid for everyone everywhere, any religious views to the contrary notwithstanding—any opposition to those claims to keep open a space for other religions is going to be taken by the former as an attack on—hostility to—its universalistic claims. In that sense, protection of religious freedom is distinct from protection of religion. It is, in fact, the protection of religious freedom *against religion itself*.[28] Consequently, because the principal danger to *your* religious freedom is frequently *someone else's* religion, an attempt to preserve and protect your religious freedom can appear—perhaps unavoidably—to that someone else to be an instance of hostility to his or her religion.

It is helpful to recall a key, if usually unremarked, statement by Justice Blackmun in *Allegheny County*: "A secular state, it must be remembered, is not the same as an atheistic or antireligious state. A secular state establishes neither atheism nor religion as its official creed."[29] The reason people on and off the Court worry that the religion clauses, and particularly the Establishment Clause, might be interpreted and applied in a way that evinces hostility toward religion is that it is often religion itself that is the main threat to religious freedom. Using Blackmun's terms, both atheism and religion are arguably religious positions, and the idea of the secular state refers to the principle that the government's role as mandated

[28] Thus, regarding Viteritti's remarks on secularism, we have to ask, if one were to argue that conventional Establishment Clause jurisprudence actually establishes "secular humanism," is this an argument on the basis of religious liberty (government is advantaging a religion), or an argument against "secular humanism" because it is the wrong religion? In other words, is it an argument against the idea of advantage, or against the wrong religions receiving the advantage? See also what Story calls case 1 and case 2 in the passage cited in the text accompanying note 12 *supra*.

[29] *Allegheny*, at 610.

by the Establishment Clause is not to take a position on religious matters, pro or con, at all. In order to protect religious freedom, the Constitution prohibits the government from either mandating religion or prohibiting religion. Yes, religious conflict in America can take place between the more religious and the less religious, but, as I suggested in chapter 1, it perhaps takes place more often between one "more religious" and another "more religious." Consider the plea of the police chaplain in the Santeria case of the Lukumi:

> The chaplain of the Hialeah Police Department told the city council that Santeria was a sin, "foolishness," "an abomination to the Lord," and the worship of "demons." He advised the city council: "We need to be helping people and sharing with them the truth that is found in Jesus Christ." He concluded: "I would exhort you . . . not to permit this Church to exist.[30]

This was a matter not of a religious group being persecuted by secularists, but of one religious group attacked by another religious group.[31]

We could say, therefore, that the existence of the religion clauses indicates that religion is different, singled out for special benefits (the guarantee of free exercise) and burdens (limitations and restrictions imposed by the prohibition on laws respecting establishment). On the other hand, it makes more sense to say that it is not religion that is singled out by the religion clauses, but religious freedom, precisely because religion is of such importance to people. The biggest threat to religious freedom can be religion itself, the sectarianism of religion that can lead believers to worry that some people may believe in and belong to the "wrong" religion. Perhaps the paradox of the religion clauses is that the best way to protect religion is not to protect religion, but to let it fend for itself. One could support religious freedom because one is hostile to religion, certainly, but one could support religious freedom also because one favors religion and sees religious freedom as contributing to the vitality of religion. Thus, if a broad conception of neutrality ascribed to the Establishment Clause appears to be unfavorable or even hostile to religion, the response must be that while neutrality is not hostile to religion, it sometimes may appear so because its purpose is to protect not religion per se but religious freedom.

[30] *Church of Lukumi Babalu Aye v. City of Hialeah*, 508 U.S. 520 (1993), at 541–42.

[31] Indeed, from a critical but more scholarly perspective, Richard T. Hughes, in *Christian America and the Kingdom of God* (Urbana and Chicago: University of Illinois Press, 2009) makes an essentially religious—indeed, Christian—argument against the idea of a Christian America. His principal thesis, he writes, is this: "the notion of Christian America and the notion of the kingdom of God are polar opposites whose values could not be further apart. This means that the idea of Christian America is in every key respect an oxymoron—essentially a contradiction in terms—when measured by the most sacred document of the Christian tradition: the Bible itself" (3–4).

Protecting religious freedom means protecting your right to believe in and belong to a religion or belief system different from my own, whereas protecting religion does not necessarily mean protecting your right to believe differently.

The fundamental reason why this distinction between religion and religious freedom is important, and important to recognize, such that religious freedom trumps religion in the American political order, is that, in the last analysis, everyone is actually or potentially a member of some religious minority or another. Because of that fact, everyone has a substantial interest in the protection of his or her religious freedom from possible majority intrusion.[32] While casual thinking in American political culture quite rightly points to the country's commitment to both majority rule and individual rights,[33] serious consideration of the nature of the American constitutional order reveals that those two principles are in fact in tension with each other. The major problem is that even with its democratic legitimacy, majority rule means that in a situation where we require a social or collective policy decision, such a decision will be binding on everyone regardless of individual values, beliefs, and preferences. When the majority rules, to put it bluntly, individuals must defer to the majority's wishes, under threat of penalty for noncompliance. By contrast, when we say that an individual has a right in a particular matter, we are saying that the individual may make his or her own decision in that matter and that the majority must defer to the individual even if the majority's values, beliefs, and preferences are to the contrary.

The tension between majority rule and individual rights, consequently, is that to affirm the majority's claim is to reject the (opposing) individual's claim, and to affirm the individual's claim is the reject the (opposing) majority's claim. If the concept of democracy refers, strictly speaking, to the question of who rules—the people, which, in practical terms and based upon the idea of equal voice, means the majority—without regard to the question of over what matters, then, as we saw in chapter 1, the concept of liberal democracy refers to the idea that the majority rules, but not over everything. To tell the majority that they may not rule

[32] As Prof. Allen D. Hertzke of the University of Oklahoma states in regard to the Free Exercise Clause, "The ruling [in *Employment Division v. Smith*, 494 U.S. 872 (1990)] galvanized virtually the entire American religious landscape, in part because every faith can envision itself as a vulnerable minority in some situation." See "The Supreme Court and Religious Liberty," in *Weekly Standard* 16, no. 5 (October 18, 2010): 22–28, 25. As chap. 6 *infra*, will attempt to argue, this perspective applies equally to questions in Establishment Clause jurisprudence.

[33] Indeed, popular culture usually refers to majority rule and minority rights, but here I assume the proposition that it is individuals rather than "minorities" who have rights.

over issue X even though they are the majority, however, is usually not going to make the majority happy. The tension between majority rule and individual rights reflects the difficult constitutional purpose of preventing the tyranny of the majority over the minority without creating a tyranny of the minority over the majority.

That tension between majority rule and individual rights lies at the heart of conflict over the public status and role of religion in the United States. So much of the constitutional politics of religion in contemporary American has to do with the argument made by conservative evangelicals and conservative Catholics that religion-clause jurisprudence has moved from the protection of the religious rights of the minority to the actual subordination of the religious rights of the Christian majority to those of the minority. The Family Research Council, for example, states on its website, "We believe in religious liberty for people of all faiths and of no faith, but we deny that minority religions are entitled to greater protection than members of the country's majority Christian faith."[34] Likewise, in his argument with Justice Stevens in *McCreary County v. ACLU of Kentucky*, Justice Scalia writes,

> [I]n the context of public acknowledgments of God there are legitimate *competing* interests: On the one hand, the interest of that minority in not feeling "excluded"; but on the other, the interest of the overwhelming majority of religious believers in being able to give God thanks and supplication *as a people*, and with respect to our national endeavors. Our national tradition has resolved that conflict in favor of the majority.[35]

And, as Scalia himself notes, the Court held in *Marsh v. Chambers* that "[t]o invoke Divine guidance on a public body entrusted with making the laws is not, in these circumstances, an 'establishment' of religion or a step toward establishment; it is simply a tolerable acknowledgment of beliefs widely held among the people of this country."[36] As these examples suggest, we do confront in the area of religion a highly charged tension between the rights of the majority versus the rights of the minority: apparently, either the majority rules over the minority, or the minority rules over the majority.

[34] Family Research Council (http://www.frc.org/religion-culture#public, retrieved 8-17-09).

[35] *McCreary County, Kentucky, et al. v. American Civil Liberties Union of Kentucky, et al.*, 545 U.S. 844 (2005), dissenting opinion. Scalia also took a majoritarian approach to free-exercise issues in *Employment Division v. Smith*, 494 U.S. 872 (1990), writing at 890, "Values that are protected against government interference through enshrinement in the Bill of Rights are not thereby banished from the political process." This holding engendered widespread concern about free-exercise rights across the religious spectrum.

[36] *Marsh v. Chambers*, 463 U.S. 783 (1983), 792 (Burger, C.J.).

Let us proceed according to the principle of charity and assume that a claim like the Family Research Council's contention that minority religions are not entitled to greater constitutional protection than members of the country's majority Christian religion is a call not for subordinating the former to the latter but rather for restoring a balance that the Family Research Council and other like-minded advocates believe has disappeared over the past half-century.[37] Madison's argument in Federalist 10 about factions, sketched here in chapter 1, bears close examination in this regard, for its overarching concern was precisely this question of how to preserve the rights of the majority without trampling those of the minority and, at the same time, how to preserve the rights of the minority without trampling those of the majority. The argument I wish to sketch in the remainder of this chapter is that returning to Federalist 10 is particularly helpful in the difficult matter of protecting both the minority against majority tyranny and the majority against minority tyranny. Specifically, if we recognize that in fact we are all members of actual or potential religious minorities, we can reframe the debate over religion-clause jurisprudence by rethinking it in terms of Madison's argument about factions and thereby provide a better understanding of the meaning and operation of those clauses. In particular, the logic of the Establishment Clause becomes clearer. If we understand, first, that we are all members of actual or potential religious minorities and, second, that the Constitution protects not religion but religious freedom—a significant difference, as we have seen—then the Establishment Clause can and must be understood as a protection of our religious freedom and not, as many religious conservatives have come to believe, a restriction of our religious freedom or hostility toward religion.

[37] At present we also hear claims of "anti-Christian bigotry." For a broad argument covering evangelicals and Catholics alike, see Stanley Kurtz, "Scary Stuff," *National Review Online*, April 28, 2005 (http://www.nationalreview.com/kurtz/kurtz200504280758.asp, retrieved 8-22-09). Andrea Lafferty of the Traditional Values Coalition, an evangelical-based advocacy group, asks, "Who Says Anti-Christian Bigotry Is Not on the Rise?" April 21, 2009 (http://www.andrealafferty.org/2009/04/who-says-anti-christian-bigotry-is-not.html, retrieved 8-22-09). The Family Research Council states, "FRC will continue to speak out when bigotry against people of faith, especially Christians (who are the most frequent target), is expressed in the media and in the political sphere" (http://www.frc.org/religion-culture#public, retrieved 8-17-09). William Donahue of the Catholic League, a Catholic advocacy group, argues that "today's brand of anti-Catholicism is more virulent and more pervasive than ever before in American history. While it is true that Catholics as individuals have made progress in securing their rights, the degree of hostility exhibited against the Catholic Church is appalling. Quite simply, Catholic bashing has become a staple of American society" (http://www.catholicleague.org/about.php, retrieved 8-17-09). However, the question of "anti-Christian bigotry," even if true, is a social issue in principle distinct from, even if it can manifest itself in, a political and legal issue.

Is there in fact a religious majority in the United States? At first glance, this seems to be a ridiculously uninformed or even simple-minded question. Even the most casual observers would readily say that most Americans are Christian. My argument, however, is that there is a significant difference between what I would call a nominal religious majority and a substantive religious majority in the United States. Most Americans, as we will see, are Christian in a generic sense; this is what I call a nominal religious majority. Nevertheless, individuals themselves are not religious in a generic sense; they are religious in terms of the substantive, concrete particularities of a specific religious tradition, and in this sense there is no substantive religious majority in the United States. In biology, numerous individual species may constitute a genus, but that fact does not eliminate or override the fundamental differences between them. So, too, Republican men and Democratic men are all men, and the New York Yankees and the Boston Red Sox are all men, but their lived reality is not their generic maleness but their specific partisan or baseball identities.

The 2008 U.S. Religious Landscape Survey from the Pew Forum on Religion & Public Life provides us with the rich set of data necessary to make this argument.[38] Nominally, it is indeed the case that there is a Christian majority in the United States:

Religion	*Adult Self-Identifiers (%)*
Christian	78.4
Other religions	4.7
Unaffiliated	16.1
Don't know/refused	0.8
Total	**100.0**

[38] "2008 U.S. Religious Landscape Survey" (http://religions.pewforum.org, retrieved 9-13-08), published by the Pew Forum on Religion & Public Life. Unless noted otherwise, all data are drawn from this source. A similar survey, though not as detailed in ways helpful here, is the Trinity College (Hartford, Conn.) American Religious Identification Survey 2008 (http://www.americanreligionsurvey-aris.org/, retrieved 8-22-09). Another interesting trove of survey data appears in Rachel Laser, Nikki Yamashiro, Jim Kessler, Robert P. Jones, and Daniel Cox, "Beyond the God Gap: A New Roadmap for Reaching Religious Americans on Public Policy Issues," published by The Culture Program, Third Way, and Public Religion Research (http://www.publicreligion.org/objects/uploads/fck/file/Third%20Way-PRR%20Report%20-%20Beyond%20the%20God%20Gap.pdf, retrieved 8-2-10).

Nevertheless, the fact that 78.4 percent of American adults self-identify as Christian does not mean, as we certainly know, that they are all "Christian" in the same way or even in compatible ways. The Pew data reveal, first, this general diversity:

Christian Denomination	*Adult Self-Identifiers (%)*[39]
Protestant	51.3
Catholic	23.9
Mormon	1.7
Jehovah's Witnesses	0.7
Orthodox	0.6
Other Christian	0.3
Total	**78.3**

Thus, approximately half of all American adults are Protestant and one-fourth of all American adults are Catholic. They nominally constitute a three-fourths majority but, as history tells us, with significant and even fundamental differences among them.[40]

Surely, however, there is a meaningful, if narrow (51.3 percent), Protestant majority in the country, and until recently there certainly has been a de facto Protestant hegemony throughout American history. As Joseph Bottum writes in *First Things*, "In truth, all the talk, from the eighteenth century on, of the United States as a religious nation was really just a make-nice way of saying it was a Christian nation—and even to call it a Christian nation was usually just a soft and ecumenical attempt to gloss over the obvious fact that the United States was, at its root, a *Protestant* nation."[41] Nevertheless, no single Protestant tradition or denomination is

[39] This column is the percentage of all adults who self-identify in these denominations; it is not the percentage of all self-identified Christians who self-identify in these denominations.

[40] See, however, the argument by James Davison Hunter that a shift has occurred in the nature of religious cleavage in the United States. Whereas the fundamental religious cleavage used to be Catholics vs. Protestants vs. Jews, by the 1990s that cleavage had become liberal Catholics, liberal Protestants, and liberal Jews vs. conservative Catholics, conservative Protestants, and conservative Jews. *Culture Wars: The Struggle To Control The Family, Art, Education, Law, And Politics In America* (New York: Basic Books, 1992).

[41] Joseph Bottum, "The Death of Protestant America: A Political Theory of the Protestant Mainline," *First Things*, August–September 2008 (http://www.firstthings.com/article/2008/08/001-the-death-of-protestant-america-a-political-theory-of-the

itself a religious majority in the country. The Religious Landscape Survey shows that there are, rather, hundreds of denominations clustered loosely into three basic Protestant traditions:

Protestant Tradition	*Adult Self-Identifiers (%)*
Evangelical churches	26.3
Mainline churches	18.1
Historically black churches	6.9
Total	**51.3**

If the differences among Protestant traditions are real, then the apparent 51.3 percent Protestant majority dissolves into a group of competing traditions and denominations, no one of which comes close to constituting a national religious majority. Indeed, these traditions themselves subdivide and fragment into a remarkable range of different and at times antagonistic denominations. The Religious Landscape Survey divides the evangelical tradition in way seen in the chart on the following page.

The only evangelical denomination in double figures is the Baptists, with 10.8 percent of all adults, and of the others only the Pentecostals and the nondenominationalists total as much as 3.4 percent of all adults each.

Even these top three evangelical groups subdivide and fragment. Consider just the Baptists and the Pentecostals. The Baptists in the evangelical tradition (and the Religious Landscape Survey elsewhere notes Baptists in the mainline tradition) include the Southern Baptist Convention (6.7 percent of all adults); independent Baptists in the evangelical tradition (2.5 percent); the Baptist Missionary Association, Free Will Baptist, General Association of Regular Baptists, and other Baptist denominations in the evangelical tradition, all less than 0.3 percent each; and Baptists in the evangelical tradition, not further specified (0.9 percent). Pentecostals in the evangelical tradition include Assemblies of God (1.4 percent); Church of God Cleveland Tennessee (0.4 percent); Four Square Gospel, Pentecostal Church of God, Pentecostal Holiness Church, nondenominational independent Pentecostal, Church of God of the Apostolic Faith, apostolic Pentecostal in the evangelical tradition, other Pentecostal denomination in the evangelical tradition, all less than

-protestant-mainline-19, retrieved 8-15-08). According to the Religious Landscape Survey, "[T]he United States is on the verge of becoming a minority Protestant country; the number of Americans who report that they are members of Protestant denominations now stands at barely 51%" (http://religions.pewforum.org/reports, retrieved 8-22-09).

Evangelical Denomination	*Adult Self-Identifiers (%)*
Baptist in the evangelical tradition	10.8
Methodist in the evangelical tradition	< 0.3
Nondenominational in the evangelical tradition	3.4
Lutheran in the evangelical tradition	1.8
Presbyterian in the evangelical tradition	0.8
Pentecostal in the evangelical tradition	3.4
Anglican/Episcopal in the evangelical tradition	< 0.3
Restorationist in the evangelical tradition	1.7
Congregationalist in the evangelical tradition	< 0.3
Holiness in the evangelical tradition	1.0
Reformed in the evangelical tradition	< 0.3
Adventist in the evangelical tradition	0.5
Anabaptist in the evangelical tradition	< 0.3
Pietist in the evangelical tradition	< 0.3
Other evangelical/fundamentalist	0.3
Protestant nonspecific in the evangelical tradition	1.9

0.3 percent each; and Pentecostal in the evangelical tradition, not further specified (0.7 percent). Yes, these religious denominations are all "Christian," but their differences matter and can be intense. For example, Pentecostals were unhappy that Baptist minister Jerry Falwell was appointed to oversee Jim and Tammy Faye Bakker's scandal-ridden PTL television ministry in 1987. "Mr. Bakker said his fellow Pentecostal Christians are upset that PTL is now in the hands of Falwell and other fundamentalists. Pentecostalism stresses a personal experience of God, an emphasis often frowned upon by fundamentalists."[42]

[42] "Evangelist Says He Was Misled in Giving Up PTL," *The New York Times*, May 27, 1987 (http://www.nytimes.com/1987/05/27/us/evangelist-says-he-was-misled-in-giving-up-ptl.html?scp=3&sq=fundamentalists%20vs.%20pentecostals%20ptl%20scandal&st=cse, retrieved 8-22-09).

Beyond the 26.3 percent of American adults who place themselves in the evangelical Protestant tradition, 18.1 percent place themselves in the mainline Protestant tradition and 6.9 percent place themselves in the historically black Protestant tradition. The Religious Landscape Survey shows that these traditions too contain substantial diversity:

Mainline Denomination	*Adult Self-Identifiers (%)*
Baptist in the mainline tradition	1.9
Methodist in the mainline tradition	5.4
Nondenominational in the mainline tradition	0.9
Lutheran in the mainline tradition	2.8
Presbyterian in the mainline tradition	1.9
Anglican/Episcopal in the mainline tradition	1.4
Restorationist in the mainline tradition	0.4
Congregationalist in the mainline tradition	0.7
Reformed in the mainline tradition	< 0.3
Anabaptist in the mainline tradition	< 0.3
Friends in the mainline tradition	< 0.3
Other/protestant nonspecific in the mainline tradition	2.5
Historically Black Churches	*Adult Self-Identifiers (%)*
Baptist in the historically black tradition	4.4
Methodist in the historically black tradition	0.6
Nondenominational in the historically black tradition	< 0.3
Pentecostal in the historically black tradition	0.9
Holiness in the historically black tradition	< 0.3
Protestant nonspecific in the historically black tradition	0.5

The mainline Methodists (5.4 percent) and Lutherans (2.8 percent) are the only two denominations in that tradition claiming more than 2 percent of American adults, and black Baptists (4.4 percent) are the only denomination among historically black churches that claim more than 1 percent of American adults. American Christianity, then, while nominally the majority religion in terms of adult self-identification, is fragmented to the point that the two largest individual denominations are Catholics (23.9 percent of all adults) and Southern Baptists (6.7 percent of all adults), amounting together to less than a third of all Americans.[43]

Despite the fact of denominational fragmentation, perhaps Christians constitute a majority religion in terms of beliefs. Here too we encounter significant diversity among Christian traditions and denominations. Consider one doctrinal question posed by the Religious Landscape Survey: "Do you believe in God or a Universal Spirit, and, if so, with what degree of certainty?" Members of evangelical churches and historically black churches, Mormons, and Jehovah's Witnesses believe with absolute certainty at a rate of 90 to 93 percent, whereas only around 71 to 73 percent of members of mainline churches, Catholics, and the Orthodox so believe.[44] As to the importance of religion in one's life, 79 to 86 percent of members of evangelical churches and historically black churches, Mormons, and Jehovah's Witnesses say it is very important, whereas 52 to 60 percent of those from mainline churches, Catholics, the Orthodox, and other Christians say the same.

Three more doctrinal issues provide interesting evidence of Christian diversity. First, the Religious Landscape Survey asked whether "There is only ONE true way to interpret the teachings of my religion" or "There is MORE than one true way to interpret the teachings of my religion." Self-identified Christian adults answered as follows ("neither/both equally" and "don't know/refused" omitted):

[43] The Religious Landscape Survey indicates that besides Protestant and Catholic Christianity, what we normally consider to be truly minority religions are themselves fragmented and diverse as well. The Church of Jesus Christ of Latter-day Saints comprises most of those who self-identify as Mormons, but there are Mormon groups as well. American Jews can be Reform, Conservative, or Orthodox, while American Muslims can be Sunni or Shia, among others. The small Orthodox population here is predominantly either Greek Orthodox or Russian Orthodox, while Buddhists and Hindus have their own internal differentiations. Even the largest group after Protestants (51.3 percent) and Catholics (23.9 percent), the unaffiliated (16.1 percent), includes those who are atheist, agnostic, or "nothing in particular."

[44] By contrast, though we are concerned here with the nominal Christian majority, 82 percent of American Muslims and only 41 percent of American Jews believe in God with absolute certainty.

Tradition	*Only One Way (%)*	*More Than One Way (%)*
Evangelical churches	41	53
Historically black churches	39	57
Mormons	54	43
Jehovah's Witnesses	77	18
Mainline churches	14	82
Catholics	19	77
Orthodox	28	68
Other Christians	13	82

The first four traditions are much more likely to oppose interpretive pluralism than the last four, though it is interesting and perhaps surprising to note that the majority of members of even evangelical and historically black churches support interpretive pluralism. Second, the Religious Landscape Survey asked whether one believes that the Bible is the word of God and "literally true word for word," the word of God but not "literally true word for word," or a book written by men and not the word of God:

Tradition	*Word of God, Literally True (%)*	*Word of God, Not Literally True (%)*	*Written by Men (%)*
Evangelical churches	59	29	07
Historically black churches	62	22	09
Mormons	35	57	04
Jehovah's Witnesses	48	45	01
Mainline churches	22	38	28
Catholics	23	39	27
Orthodox	26	33	29
Other Christians	05	30	44

Once again, a major division lies between the same first four Christian traditions and the last four. Finally, in response to the question "Is your religion the one true faith leading to eternal life, or do many religions lead to eternal life?" roughly one-third each of the members of evangelical and historically black churches believe that their religion is the one true faith, as do 57 percent of Mormons and 80 percent of Jehovah's Witnesses. On the other hand, roughly 85 percent of mainline Protestants, along with 79 percent of Catholics and even 58 percent of members of evangelical and historically black churches, believe that many faiths can lead to eternal life.

The point, then, is that within the demographic Christian majority in the United States, there are differences, and these differences *matter* to the contending traditions and denominations. When Justice Scalia refers, as we saw earlier in his *McCreary* dissent, to "the interest of the overwhelming majority of religious believers in being able to give God thanks and supplication *as a people*, and with respect to our national endeavors," the foregoing data require us to ask, skeptically, whether such a national religious community actually exists. Americans are not constituted as a religious people, for the question always arises, whose religion? For example, as commentator Michael Kinsley has said on various occasions, a gaffe "is when a politician tells the truth—or more precisely, when he or she accidentally reveals something truthful about what is going on in his or her head."[45] In that light, consider two nonpolitician incidents two decades apart. First, speaking at a 1980 religious convention that was also addressed by Ronald Reagan, Bailey Smith, a former president of the Southern Baptist Convention, declared, "God Almighty does not hear the prayer of a Jew."[46] This is a position that the Reverend Jerry Falwell at first supported but later opposed.[47] Second, there developed a controversy about the legitimacy of interfaith and ecumenical services around the country honoring the memory of the victims of the 9/11 attacks in 2001. According to the Rev. Karl K. Schmidt, pastor of Bethany Lutheran Church in Alexandria, Virginia, "An interfaith event is inappropriate . . . if it 'gives the impression that various religions are equally valid and equally true.'"[48] Richard Cizik, a former official with the National

[45] Michael Kinsley, "Gaffes to the Rescue," *Time*, February 8, 2007 (http://www.time.com/time/magazine/article/0,9171,1587283,00.html, retrieved 8-23-09).

[46] South Of Heaven blog. http://southofheaven.typepad.com/south_of_heaven/2008/05/god-does-not-he.html (retrieved 6-12-08).

[47] Marjorie Hyer, "Evangelist Reverses Position on God's Hearing Jews," *Washington Post*, October 11, 1980 (http://www.washingtonpost.com/wp-dyn/content/article/2007/05/15/AR2007051501197_pf.html, retrieved 6-12-08).

[48] *Washington Post*, November 24, 2001 (http://www.washingtonpost.com/ac2/wp-dyn?pagename=article&node=&contentId=A7821-2001Nov23, retrieved 9-6-11).

Association of Evangelicals, stated, "There's a movement afoot toward a kind of universalism that evangelicals do not accept, that we all pray to the same God and have different paths and the result is the same. . . . We want it understood that Christians, Buddhists and Muslims are not praying to the same god. Allah is not Jehovah."[49] One might argue that these two incidents are outliers, but *pace* Kinsley, they do reveal what was actually going on in someone's head. Speakers like these do not believe there is a truly national religious community; based upon these statements, they would appear to define a national religious community through the lens and with the premises of their own particular religious commitments.

Beyond inter- and intrafaith doctrinal differences, religions, and Christianity itself, differ as to fundamental texts that they might be presumed to share. Catholics and Protestants might both be "Christian," but, in the words of the United States Conference of Catholic Bishops,

> Catholic and Protestant Bibles both include 27 books in the New Testament. Protestant Bibles have only 39 books in the Old Testament, however, while Catholic Bibles have 46. The seven books included in Catholic Bibles are Tobit, Judith, 1 and 2 Maccabees, Wisdom, Sirach, and Baruch. Catholic Bibles also include sections in the Books of Esther and Daniel which are not found in Protestant Bibles.[50]

According to the National Bible Association, "Catholic and Protestant versions of the Bible are different because Catholics and Protestants have different doctrine and dogma which result in differences in word choice, translation style and explanatory notes."[51] Indeed, in the *McCreary* case cited earlier no less an authority than Justice Scalia admitted, though did not care, that there are linguistically and, more important, theologically distinct and sometimes conflicting Jewish, Catholic, Lutheran, and Protestant translations of the Decalogue.[52]

[49] *Washington Post*, November 24, 2001.

[50] United States Conference of Catholic Bishops. http://www.usccb.org/nab/faq.shtml (retrieved 9-13-08).

[51] National Bible Association. http://www.nationalbible.org/read-the-bible/difference/ (retrieved 9-13-08).

[52] "Because there are interpretational differences between faiths and within faiths concerning the meaning and perhaps even the text of the Commandments, *Justice Stevens* maintains that any display of the text of the Ten Commandments is impermissible because it 'invariably places the [government] at the center of a serious sectarian dispute.' *Van Orden, ante*, at 13 (dissenting opinion). I think not. The sectarian dispute regarding text, if serious, is not widely known. I doubt that most religious adherents are even aware that there are competing versions with doctrinal consequences (I certainly was not). In any event, the context of the display here could not conceivably cause the viewer to believe that the government was taking sides in a doctrinal controversy." Footnote 12, Scalia dissent, *McCreary County*, at 909, emphasis in original.

Perhaps, then, we should speak more broadly of the Judeo-Christian tradition as the substance of an American religious majority. This, too, is problematic, for the Jewish tradition and the Christian tradition do not really share a common text. First, following the *McCreary* point in the last paragraph, there are significant differences between the Hebrew Bible and the various Christian versions of the Old Testament: the foundational texts are different, the total number of biblical books is different, the arrangement of the categories of books is different, the titles of some of the books are different, and the categorization of some books is different.[53] Second, strictly speaking, there is for Jews no such text as the Old Testament, for the reason that the term implies what Jews do not believe—that the Torah or Hebrew bible has been superseded by a new testament.

Third, the very term "Judeo-Christian" implies that the trajectory of Judaism necessarily leads to Christianity (Jews, Ann Coulter has stated, need to be perfected by becoming Christians[54]). The campaign to privilege a Judeo-Christian tradition, according to religion scholar Martin Marty,

> succeeds old and failed ones that would have passed a Christian amendment to the Constitution officially designating America a Christian nation. This new campaign stands a better chance of success than did the older, more restrictive-sounding ones, though not a few Jews and other Americans think that "Judeo-Christian" is often a code word for those promoting a Christian America.[55]

Thus, according to Frederick Mark Gedicks and Roger Hendrix:

> In fact, Judeo-Christianity is far more congenial to the beliefs of Christians than it is to those of Jews. Because conventional Christian theology generally characterizes Judaism as a proto-Christianity that was "completed" or "fulfilled" with Jesus and the resurrection, Christians can incorporate Judaism into their faith in a way that Jews cannot incorporate Christianity into theirs. To the extent that the "Judeo-Christian" tradition symbolizes essential Christian beliefs, its symbolism obviously and necessarily excludes Jews. Notwithstanding its name, "Judeo-Christianity" is essentially a Christian

[53] Felix Just, S.J., "Jewish and Christian Bibles: A Comparative Chart" (http://catholic-resources.org/Bible/Heb-Xn-Bibles.htm, retrieved 9-13-08).

[54] "Columnist Ann Coulter Shocks Cable TV Show, Declaring 'Jews Need to Be Perfected by Becoming Christians.'" *Fox News*, October 11, 2007. http://www.foxnews.com/story/0,2933,301216,00.html (retrieved 9-13-08).

[55] Martin E. Marty, "A Judeo-Christian Looks at the Judeo-Christian Tradition," *Christian Century* (October 5, 1986): 858–60 (http://www.religion-online.org/showarticle.asp?title=188, retrieved 9-4-08). Marty draws upon Arthur A. Cohen, *The Myth of the Judeo-Christian Tradition* (New York: Harper & Row, 1970), who suggests that the term was "essentially an invention of American politics."

> tradition whose symbols and observances include a symbolic meaning that Jews do not accept.[56]

Finally, many of those who lean most heavily on the concept of a Judeo-Christian tradition clumsily betray their agenda. The website of the Traditional Values Coalition, noted *supra*, is revealing in this regard. Its first sentence, about "a moral code and behavior based upon the Old and New Testaments,"[57] suggests some degree of commonality between Jews and Christians, though the Religious Landscape Survey shows substantial differences on social and political questions.[58] The second sentence, though, is a theological statement and as such is particularistic and exclusionary.

The argument here, then, is that even when we leave aside non-Christian religions and unaffiliated people, 78.4 percent of American adults may be Christian in some generic sense—but no one is generically Christian as an individual. Whatever our particular religious affiliations and beliefs, we are all religious minorities. As Christopher Eisgruber and Lawrence Sager have written, "America's religious heterogeneity means that any religious group will be a minority in parts of the country."[59] While there is a Christian majority in the country in a generic sense, what I have called a nominal national majority, no specific religious denomination within *any* faith tradition, defined and constituted in terms of its own substantively concrete religious beliefs and practices, composes a national religious majority. *Every* religious adherent belongs to a minority group. At the individual level, people are not religious in a generic sense, whether that is monotheist or "Judeo-Christian." For Christians, they are not generically Christian—they are Catholic or Protestant, and in the latter case they are Baptist or Methodist or Lutheran and so on, not generically Protestant. Jews are not generically Jewish—they are Orthodox, Conservative, or Reform—and Muslims are not generically Muslim—they are Sunni or Shia or possibly something else as well.

Yet if there is no substantive national religious majority, perhaps there are indeed substantive regional, state, or local religious majorities. The Religious Landscape Survey data do not speak to local situations,

[56] Frederick Mark Gedicks and Roger Hendrix, "Uncivil Religion: Judeo-Christianity and the Ten Commandments," *West Virginia Law Review* 110 (2007): 275, at 296–97 (footnotes omitted).

[57] Traditional Values Coalition, "Traditional Values Defined: What Are Traditional Values?" (http://www.traditionalvalues.org/defined.php, retrieved 8-17-09, original emphasis omitted).

[58] See http://religions.pewforum.org/comparisons#.

[59] Christopher L. Eisgruber and Lawrence G. Sager, "The Supreme Court's Hands-Off Approach to Religious Doctrine: Does It Matter What Religion Is?" *Notre Dame Law Review* 84 (2009): 807, at 813.

but they do provide interesting evidence at the regional and state levels. Regionally, the survey unsurprisingly says,

> The Midwest most closely resembles the religious makeup of the overall population. The South, by a wide margin, has the heaviest concentration of members of evangelical Protestant churches. The Northeast has the greatest concentration of Catholics, and the West has the largest proportion of unaffiliated people, including the largest proportion of atheists and agnostics.[60]

On a state-by-state level, there are in fact, according to the survey, only three states in which there is anything approaching a religious majority. Arkansas (53 percent), Oklahoma (53 percent), and Tennessee (51 percent) are majority evangelical Protestant—and yet we have already explored the significant diversity in that general classification. There is a majority tradition in these states, in other words, but no denominational majority. In the following twenty states, listed in declining order, we find an evangelical Protestant plurality (refer to the chart on the left):

State	%
Alabama	49
Kentucky	49
Mississippi	47
South Carolina	45
North Carolina	41
Georgia	38
Missouri	37
West Virginia	36
Indiana	34
Texas	34
Louisiana	31
Virginia	31
Oregon	30
Kansas	29
Hawaii	26
Montana/Wyoming	26
Michigan	26
Ohio	26
Washington	25

State	%
Connecticut and Rhode Island	43
Massachusetts	43
New Jersey	42
New York	39
Illinois	32
California	31
Nebraska	31
Maine	29
New Hampshire/Vermont	29
Pennsylvania	29
Wisconsin	29
Delaware	27
Nevada	27
Florida	26
New Mexico	26
Arizona	25
Iowa	25
Maryland/DC	18

[60] 2008 Religious Landscape Survey highlights (http://religions.pewforum.org/reports, retrieved 8-17-09).

The Religious Landscape Survey shows no majority mainline Protestant states, listing only Minnesota (32 percent) and North and South Dakota (35 percent) as plurality mainline Protestant states. There are no majority Catholic states either, with twenty plus the District of Columbia listed as plurality Catholic (here refer to the chart on the right above).

Finally, there is one majority Mormon state, Utah (58 percent), one plurality Mormon state, Idaho (23 percent), and, interestingly, two plurality unaffiliated states, Alaska (27 percent) and Colorado (25 percent). Thus, only four states have a religious majority: Arkansas, Oklahoma, and Tennessee, where the majority is nevertheless a tradition—evangelical Protestant—rather than a specific denomination, and Utah, where the majority is both a tradition and a denomination.

The fact that there is no substantive national religious majority, then, affirms the continuing relevance of Madison's sociological solution to the potential problem of majority tyranny. Recall his definition of a faction: "By a faction I understand a number of citizens, whether amounting to a majority or a minority of the whole, who are united and actuated by some common impulse of passion, or of interest, adverse to the rights of other citizens, or to the permanent and aggregate interests of the community."[61] What is fundamental to the balance between the rights of the majority and the rights of the minority, however, is Madison's claim here that a majority can be a faction no less than a minority can. That is, a majority, and not just a minority, can be "united and actuated by some common impulse of passion, or of interest, adverse to the rights of other citizens, or to the permanent and aggregate interests of the community." It can be constituted by and act in accordance with interests harmful to those of a minority, clearly enough, but also to the common good. As Madison states, "When a majority is included in a faction, the form of popular government, on the other hand, enables it to sacrifice to its ruling passion or interest both the public good and the rights of other citizens."[62] In that sense, a majority is not self-legitimating; its views are not automatically right just because it is a majority. The majority position may represent the common good, but, then again, it may not.

With regard to religion, then, Madison's argument suggests that a Christian majority may well act adversely "to the rights of other citizens, or to the permanent and aggregate interests of the community." His solution to the danger of such a majority faction is the familiar contention that

[61] Federalist 10, in Alexander Hamilton, James Madison, and John Jay, *The Federalist Papers*, ed. Clinton Rossiter, with a new introduction and notes by Charles R. Kesler (New York: New American Library, 1961 and 1999), 46.

[62] Federalist 10, 48.

there is no natural national majority. The descriptors "natural national" sound a bit odd, but they are fundamental. Madison writes, "A religious sect may degenerate into a political faction in a part of the Confederacy; but the variety of sects dispersed over the entire face of it must secure the national councils against any danger from that source."[63] Any national religious majority would never be natural, as the Religious Landscape Survey data show, in the sense of there being one common religion national in scope; instead, any national religious majority would be an artificial majority, in the sense that it would consist of a coalition of numerous religious minorities aligned temporarily around one or two dominant issues. This was, famously, one of Madison's arguments for the extended republic:

> [T]he greater number of citizens and extent of territory which may be brought within the compass of republican than of democratic government . . . renders factious combinations less to be dreaded in the former than in the latter. The smaller the society, the fewer probably will be the distinct parties and interests composing it; the fewer the distinct parties and interests, the more frequently will a majority be found of the same party; and the smaller the number of individuals composing a majority, and the smaller the compass within which they are placed, the more easily will they concert and execute their plans of oppression. Extend the sphere, and you take in a greater variety of parties and interests; you make it less probable that a majority of the whole will have a common motive to invade the rights of other citizens; or if such a common motive exists, it will be more difficult for all who feel it to discover their own strength, and to act in unison with each other.[64]

Increase the territorial size of the republic, therefore, and a natural majority of national scope and cohesion becomes less likely.

Yet even assuming this sociological claim was and continues to be true, Madison clearly allows for the possibility or even probability of a natural state or local majority. "The smaller the society, the fewer probably will be the distinct parties and interests composing it; the fewer the distinct parties and interests, the more frequently will a majority be found of the same party," he writes. Particularly in regard to religion, what protects a religious minority against the interests and actions of a state or local religious majority? The federalism solution to the problem of living under the religious choices of a majority not of one's own religion would allow local majorities to provide governmental support to religion—in

[63] Federalist 10, 52.
[64] Federalist 10, 51.

effect, the majority religion—while allowing those of other faiths to continue to live peacefully under that policy. If one were to object to this arrangement, the federalism solution is for the objectors to move somewhere else where their religious beliefs would be in the majority. Thus, for example, *Santa Fe Independent School District v. Doe* raises the question as to the constitutionality of the practice of having an elective student council chaplain offer a prayer over the school's public-address system before each game of the Texas high school's football season. The original plaintiffs were a Mormon family and a Catholic family whom the district court identified as Doe in order to protect them against harassment and intimidation due to their challenge of religious practices sponsored by the Baptist majority.

> In their complaint the Does alleged that the District had engaged in several proselytizing practices, such as promoting attendance at a Baptist revival meeting, encouraging membership in religious clubs, chastising children who held minority religious beliefs, and distributing Gideon Bibles on school premises. They also alleged that the District allowed students to read Christian invocations and benedictions from the stage at graduation ceremonies, and to deliver overtly Christian prayers over the public address system at home football games.[65]

The federalism response to this minority challenge of a majority practice would be simple: Move.

Even assuming this is possible, however—whatever Catholic or particular Protestant or even Mormon state or local majorities there might be, Jews, Muslims, Hindus, Jehovah's Witnesses, and so on are highly unlikely for the foreseeable future to find a state or locality where they constituted a religious majority themselves[66]—it would have the effect of creating an American version of *cuius regio, eius religio* (whose realm, his religion).[67] "Under this principle," John Witte writes of the Peace of Augsburg (1555), "princes, dukes, or city councils were authorized to establish by civil law the appropriate forms of religious doctrine, liturgy, charity, and education for their polities—with religious dissenters granted the

[65] *Santa Fe Independent School District v. Doe*, 530 U.S. 290 (2000), at 295 (footnote omitted).

[66] Hence the discussion of the need for special judicial protection of "discrete and insular minorities" in the famous footnote 4 of *United States v. Carolene Products Co.*, 304 U.S. 144 (1938).

[67] *The Concise Oxford Dictionary of World Religions*, 1997 (http://www.encyclopedia.com/doc/1O101-Cuiusregio.html, retrieved 8-19-09).

[68] John Witte Jr., *Religion and the American Constitutional Experiment*, 2nd ed. (Boulder, Colo.: Westview, 2005), 10–11.

right to worship privately in their homes or to emigrate peaceably from the polity."[68] In the American context, it would not be princes, dukes, or city councils setting—establishing—the religious order, but state or local majorities acting through their appropriate legislative bodies. The result of the federalism approach would be a potential religious balkanization of the country resulting from the choice by religious minorities in one state to move to another where they would constitute a religious majority. Turning the nation into a collection of officially Catholic states, officially Baptist states, officially Lutheran states, officially Mormon states, and so forth, would dissolve the *unum* into the *pluribus*.

In view of the extensive and ineradicable diversity of religious commitments, beliefs, and practices in the United States, therefore, the very existence of the religion clauses is thus evidence of the principle that religious matters are reserved to the individual and protected against majority intrusion. Constitutionally, we do not say, "If you are a religious minority and object to the practices of the religious majority or even plurality, go find your own religious majority somewhere else if you want to enact and enforce your own religion-related policy X or Y." This constitutional premise is what grounds the opposition to Scalia's contention in *Smith* that "leaving accommodation to the political process will place at a relative disadvantage those religious practices that are not widely engaged in" but is an "unavoidable consequence of democratic government."[69]

Therefore, when the Family Research Council states, as noted earlier, "We believe in religious liberty for people of all faiths and of no faith, but we deny that minority religions are entitled to greater protection than members of the country's majority Christian faith,"[70] the tacit claim is that the rights of minority religious adherents should not be allowed to block governmental support for the beliefs and practices of a religious majority. In other words, on this view the rights of the minority have been preferred to those of the majority. Nevertheless, we do well to remember Madison's concern in Federalist 10 to provide protection for the minority in a republican form of government where in most cases the majority rules. Federalist 10 is not hostile to the majority rule—that is, in contemporary terminology, the default condition of the republican form of government; instead, it seeks to carve out a space in the sea of majority rule for islands of minority rights.

In the light of Federalist 10, consequently, two central premises lead to the conclusion I seek in this chapter. First, I have advanced and, I

[69] Employment Division, *Oregon Department of Human Resources v. Smith*, 494 U.S. 872 (1990), at 890.

[70] Family Research Council (http://www.frc.org/religion-culture#public, retrieved 8-17-09).

believe, justified at length the premise that that there is no natural substantive national religious majority in the Untied States, nor even, with the exception of Utah, a natural substantive state religious majority. We Americans are all members of actual or potential religious minorities in our religious affiliations. Second, I rely on the premise that the purpose of the religion clauses is to protect not religion but religious freedom, which is something very different from religion per se. As Justice Stewart noted in *Abington*, "That the central value embodied in the First Amendment—and, more particularly, in the guarantee of 'liberty' contained in the Fourteenth—is the safeguarding of an individual's right to free exercise of his religion has been consistently recognized."[71]

Given these two premises, my argument is that then when a member of a religious minority invokes the Establishment Clause to protect himself or herself against government support for or the imposition of the beliefs and practices of some putative religious majority to which he or she does not belong, or the Free Exercise Clause to protect himself or herself against government disfavor or hostility toward his or her own religious beliefs and practices, that appeal to the Constitution does not amount to either hostility toward or a restriction of the majority's rights, or a favoring of the minority over the majority. It is, rather, a condition of reciprocal respect for everyone's religious freedom. If we consider ourselves as members of a religious majority, then the clauses appear to be restrictions or limitations on our power as a religious majority and our subordination to "the Other"—a religious minority. If, instead, we understand that we are all actually or potentially members of religious minorities, and that everyone has an equal right to religious freedom, then the religion clauses operate as a protection of our religious freedom as individuals against the eventuality that we ourselves at some point will be on the outside of some majority coalition. This is a version of the social-contract bargain that I will refrain from infringing upon your religious freedom on the condition that you will refrain from infringing upon my religious freedom. We do not like the fact that at times when we claim to have a majority of our own that the religion clauses restrict our exercise of that majority power, blocking us from acting on our agenda, but that is the very purpose of the religion clauses. It is not preferring the rights of the minority over the majority but preferring the rights of everyone since everyone is at some point a member of a minority confronting a majority in a republican polity. A majority that can impose my religious beliefs and values on you, I must always bear in mind, can impose your religious beliefs and values on me.

[71] *Abington School District v. Schempp*, 374 U.S. 203 (1963), at 312.

The whole American constitutional system is designed to safeguard the viability of long-term interests and principles against the strength and intensity of short-term passions and inclinations that would otherwise obscure and overrule the former. "When occasions present themselves, in which the interests of the people are at variance with their inclinations," Hamilton writes in Federalist 71, "it is the duty of the persons whom they have appointed to be the guardians of those interests, to withstand the temporary delusion, in order to give them time and opportunity for more cool and sedate reflection."[72] Although Hamilton writes here in the context of the executive branch, his admonition applies to the judicial branch as well. When the courts prevent the representatives of a temporary, contemporary majority from enacting and enforcing certain policies, we do not ordinarily refer to that as a case of their being hostile to that majority or favoring a minority. We say, rather, that the courts are safeguarding the long-term interests of the people as expressed in the Constitution against the short-term inclinations of a contemporary majority. Those who argue that this is a matter of preferring the interests of the minority to those of the majority seem to forget that, according to Federalist 10, a majority could well be a faction itself, "united and actuated by some common impulse of passion, or of interest, *adverse to the rights of other citizens, or to the permanent and aggregate interests of the community*" (emphasis added). In such a situation, the majority counterposes its interests not just to those of the minority, thus eliciting the contemporary allegations of imbalance or preference for the latter, but, more fundamentally, to the "permanent and aggregate interests of the community." If this is the case, then there is no issue of a tension among putative equals, majority interests, and minority interests; the issue is one between the majority and the broader common good to which it is constitutionally subordinate.

[72] Federalist 71, 400.

Chapter 3

Conventional vs. Radical Establishment Clause Jurisprudence

Whatever the religion clauses of the U.S. Constitution represent and however they function in particular cases and controversies, from the standpoint of American political and constitutional theory they have to do with the relation between an individual's religious orientation and his or her status as an American citizen. Regarding government, the religion clauses stand for the proposition, as we saw Justice Robert Jackson put it in chapter 1, that "[i]f there is any fixed star in our constitutional constellation, it is that no official, high or petty, can prescribe what shall be orthodox in politics, nationalism, religion, or other matters of opinion or force citizens to confess by word or act their faith therein."[1] Regarding the individual, the religion clauses stand for the proposition that the affirmation of a particular religion, religious belief, or religious practice cannot be a condition of full participation in the rights and responsibilities of American citizenship (Establishment Clause), and the rejection of a particular religion, religious belief, or religious practice cannot be a condition of full participation in the rights and responsibilities of American citizenship (Free Exercise Clause). However, the devil, as they say, is in the details. It is easy enough to say that any law or government action that establishes religion or prohibits the free exercise thereof is unconstitutional, but the question is, what counts as the establishment of religion or an infringement of its free exercise?

Even at this level of generality and abstraction, however, the religion clauses entail that the Constitution rules out any possibility of what I call a hard theocracy. To take an extreme example, consider the principles of the American Heritage Party and the American Constitution Party, the two minor, essentially theocratic American political parties to which we

[1] *West Virginia v. Barnette*, 319 U.S. 624 (1943), at 642.

referred in chapter 2. According to the American Heritage Party, "[T]he Bible is the highest and final authority to which all other authorities and ideas must ultimately yield."[2] In particular, the rule of law "is rooted in an authority higher than man; ultimately in God himself. The rule of law in a Christian order requires that all government policy must be consistent with God's law and the Christian-based common law."[3] Any political-legal system, the American Heritage Party argues, is necessarily a theocracy: "*All power and authority is ordained of God* for His glory and for the government and welfare of His creation. All law and government is therefore religious, being founded upon basic presuppositions about God, man & law. Every government legislates the morality of its underlying religion, whether of belief or of unbelief toward God."[4] A hard theocracy, then, would be a political order in which the fundamental law is itself or at least immediately a religious text, religious revelation, or religious institution, such that the legitimacy and legality of law and social practices are to be assessed in terms of their conformity to a fundamental law of a religious nature. According to *The Catholic Encyclopedia*, a theocracy is

> [a] form of civil government in which God himself is recognized as the head. The laws of the commonwealth are the commandments of God, and they are promulgated and expounded by the accredited representatives of the invisible Deity, real or supposed—generally a priesthood. Thus in a theocracy civic duties and functions form a part of religion, implying the absorption of the State by the Church or at least the supremacy of the latter over the State.[5]

Article 1 of the Saudi Arabian Constitution states, for example, "The Kingdom of Saudi Arabia is a sovereign Arab Islamic state with Islam as its religion; God's Book and the Sunnah of His Prophet, God's prayers and peace be upon him, are its constitution, Arabic is its language and Riyadh is its capital," while Article 23 states, "The state protects Islam; it implements its Shari'ah; it orders people to do right and shun evil; it fulfills the duty regarding God's call."[6] Understood in these terms, then, the American Heritage Party conceives of the American polity as a hard theocracy.

What, however, about a polity in which the government is permitted, even while guaranteeing everyone the right to the free exercise of his or

[2] On September 18, 2010, the American Heritage Party formally changed its name to the Christian Liberty Party. See http://www.christianlibertyparty.org/ (retrieved 9-06-11).

[3] Christian Liberty Party (http://www.christianlibertyparty.org).

[4] Christian Liberty Party (http://www.christianlibertyparty.org, emphasis in original).

[5] "Theocracy," in *The Catholic Encyclopedia* (http://www.newadvent.org/cathen/14568a.htm, retrieved 4-17-10).

[6] The Constitution of Saudi Arabia (http://www.servat.unibe.ch/icl/sa00000_.html, retrieved 4-17-10).

her religion, to endorse or privilege a particular religion or set of religious beliefs and values? In contrast to a hard theocracy, what I call a "soft theocracy" would be a political order that, on the one hand, did not ground ordinary law in a fundamental law consisting of the religious truths or values to be found in a particular religious text, vision, or revelation, but did posit a link between one's civic identity as a citizen and a particular religious identity. If we said, for example, that to be truly an American one had to be a Christian (of some sort), such that one who is not a Christian is not truly an American, then that would be an instance of what I am calling a soft theocracy. The Jeremiah Project, for example, claims that the American founders "believed that although no one Christian denomination should dominate the nation, the principles of the Bible and Christianity should underlie our government and American education as well."[7] Similarly, the American Constitution Party, which has run presidential candidates in recent elections,[8] states that its goal "is to restore American jurisprudence to its Biblical foundations and to limit the federal government to its Constitutional boundaries. . . . The U.S. Constitution established a Republic rooted in Biblical law, administered by representatives who are Constitutionally elected by the citizens."[9] This idea that the American political system is in some manner rooted in Biblical law, advanced by advocates of the claim that the United States is a Christian nation, is what I mean by soft theocracy. The Constitution is our fundamental law, not some distinctly religious text, but the Constitution is to be interpreted and understood as based upon, rooted in, or expressive of Biblical principles. Thus, when, as we have seen, Justice Scalia argues in *McCreary* that government may favor monotheistic over non-monotheistic religions, his position amounts to saying that the American polity is a soft theocracy. In other words, a soft theocracy would plausibly be a political order that did not ground ordinary law in a fundamental law that itself was a particular religious text, vision, or revelation, but instead conceived interpretation of its fundamental law as necessarily informed by some religious text, vision, or revelation. Thus, to assert that the Constitution must be understood as embodying certain religious beliefs and values even though it is not itself understood to be a religious text itself would be to maintain that our political order is a soft theocracy.

[7] Jeremiah Project (http://www.jeremiahproject.com/culture/heritage.html, retrieved 4-16-10).

[8] Howard Phillips in 2000, who also ran in 1992 and 1996 when the Constitution Party was formerly called the U.S. Taxpayers Party; Michael Peroutka in 2004; and Charles Baldwin in 2008. Source: Dave Leip, "Atlas of U.S. Presidential Elections" (http://uselectionatlas.org/RESULTS/, retrieved 4-17-10).

[9] Preamble, Constitution Party Platform (http://www.constitutionparty.com/party_platform.php, retrieved 4-16-10).

In that light, we can distinguish between what we might call conventional Establishment Clause jurisprudence and the radicalization of conventional Establishment Clause jurisprudence. The usual question in conventional Establishment Clause jurisprudence is this: should government—i.e., a political and legal order, or a political-legal system—endorse religion in general, a particular religion, or a set of religious beliefs, values, and practices, or should government remain neutral and not endorse religion in general, a particular religion, or a set of religious beliefs, values, and practices? We could ask also whether government should enforce a particular religion or set of religious beliefs, values, and practices, but everyone who accepts the conventional version of the Establishment Clause question rejects, often on Free Exercise grounds, any policy of enforcement even if he or she accepts the act of endorsement. What is important to recognize here is that conventional Establishment Clause jurisprudence is centered on a conflict between two doctrinal positions that share a common premise. Separationism employs a concept known as strict neutrality, the position that government should be neutral not only between religion A and religion B but also between religion and nonreligion. The Court sets forth the classic statement of the separationist position in *Everson v. Board of Education*:

> The "establishment of religion" clause of the First Amendment means at least this: Neither a state nor the Federal Government can set up a church. Neither can pass laws which aid one religion, aid all religions, or prefer one religion over another. Neither can force nor influence a person to go to or to remain away from church against his will or force him to profess a belief or disbelief in any religion. No person can be punished for entertaining or professing religious beliefs or disbeliefs, for church attendance or non-attendance. No tax in any amount, large or small, can be levied to support any religious activities or institutions, whatever they may be called, or whatever form they may adopt to teach or practice religion. Neither a state nor the Federal Government can, openly or secretly, participate in the affairs of any religious organizations or groups and vice versa. In the words of Jefferson, the clause against establishment of religion by law was intended to erect "a wall of separation between church and State."[10]

Put more succinctly, separationists, according to Clyde Wilcox, believe "that the First Amendment establishment clause mandates that government not become entangled in religion in any way and remain neutral between religion and secularism."[11] On this reading, government must be

[10] *Everson v. Board of Education*, 330 U.S. 1 (1947), at 15–16.

[11] Clyde Wilcox, *Onward Christian Soldiers? The Religious Right in American Politics*, 4th ed. (Boulder, Colo.: Westview, 2010), 165.

neutral between one religion and another, *and* must be neutral between religion and nonreligion.

Accommodationism, or what is sometimes called nonpreferentialism, by contrast, employs a concept known as benevolent neutrality, the position that government should be neutral solely between religion A and religion B, but not between religion and nonreligion; government may prefer or support religion without doing the same for nonreligion. Perhaps the classic statement of the accommodationist position is to be found in Justice Douglas' opinion for the Court in *Zorach v. Clauson*:

> We are a religious people whose institutions presuppose a Supreme Being. We guarantee the freedom to worship as one chooses. We make room for as wide a variety of beliefs and creeds as the spiritual needs of man deem necessary. We sponsor an attitude on the part of government that shows no partiality to any one group and that lets each flourish according to the zeal of its adherents and the appeal of its dogma. When the state encourages religious instruction or cooperates with religious authorities by adjusting the schedule of public events to sectarian needs, it follows the best of our traditions. For it then respects the religious nature of our people and accommodates the public service to their spiritual needs. To hold that it may not would be to find in the Constitution a requirement that the government show a callous indifference to religious groups. That would be preferring those who believe in no religion over those who do believe.[12]

As Wilcox aptly notes, the focus of the accommodationist position is simply a prohibition of the establishment of any particular religion as our national religion:

> **Accommodationists** believe that the Constitution merely prohibits the establishment of a national religion. They point out that many colonies had established churches at the time of the founding and indeed for many years afterward. They argue that the First Amendment merely prohibits the government from tilting to one religious group over another but does not mean that the government may not prefer religion generally to nonreligion.[13]

On the accommodationist position, then, government must be neutral between one religion and another, neither benefiting nor burdening one religion over another, but, as opposed to the separationist position, it may prefer or privilege religion over nonreligion. The premise common to both positions is the proposition that some form of neutrality is possible, desirable, and mandated by the Establishment Clause.

[12] *Zorach v. Clauson*, 343 U.S. 306 (1952), at 313–14.
[13] Wilcox, *Onward Christian Soldiers?* 13, emphasis in original.

The radical Establishment Clause question, by contrast, is this: Is such a choice between endorsing and not endorsing religion in general, a particular religion, or particular religious beliefs and values indeed possible? In other words, can government—again, a political and legal order, or a political-legal system—*not* not endorse, even if it does not enforce, a religious orthodoxy? Can a political-legal system be truly neutral regarding religion, religious beliefs and values, and religious practices, or does any political-legal system always, necessarily, inescapably constitute the establishment of religious beliefs and values? Conventional Establishment Clause jurisprudence accepts as valid the concept of neutrality and argues merely over the nature and extent of that neutrality; in that sense neutrality is the common premise of both separationism and accommodationism. Radical Establishment Clause jurisprudence rejects that premise; it rejects the very possibility of neutrality, and with it the argument that such neutrality is desirable and mandated by the Establishment Clause. The radicalization of Establishment Clause jurisprudence is based upon a rejection of the very distinction between the religious and the secular—i.e., between religion and "nonreligion"—a rejection the consequence of which is the claim that the American political order, like any political order, is at bottom at least a soft or, more likely, a hard theocracy.

This is the fundamental theoretical issue that has come to the fore with the rise of religious conservatism in late-twentieth-century American politics, a phenomenon centered on what is also known as Christian conservatism and popularly known as the Christian Right, though the issue is not limited to that rise. According to Wilcox,

> The Christian Right is a social movement that attempts to mobilize evangelical Protestants and other orthodox Christians into conservative political action. Many Christian Right leaders object to the term "Christian Right," which they believe depicts a narrow movement. Some prefer the term "religious Right," which would encompass all "people of faith" including conservative Jews and possibly even Muslims. Yet despite the visible presence of orthodox Jews at Christian Coalition conventions, the movement remains a Christian one concentrated primarily among white evangelical Christians.[14]

This phenomenon, Wilcox accurately reports, reflects a broad, contemporary debate over the role of religion in American politics. "At stake," he writes, "are two competing visions for American democracy: One holds that the United States is a Christian nation specially blessed by God; the other maintains that it is a secular state with a high wall of separation between church and state."[15] While Free Exercise jurisprudence generally

[14] Wilcox, *Onward Christian Soldiers?* 5.

[15] Wilcox, *Onward Christian Soldiers?* 11–12.

conceptualizes freedom-of-religion questions as a matter of whether or not private individuals may be left to practice their religious beliefs as they see fit, it is principally in Establishment Clause jurisprudence that we encounter the debate over the public status of religion. The Christian Right's critique of Establishment Clause jurisprudence in that debate has two prongs, one of which is fairly conventional while the other, vis-à-vis that jurisprudence, is more fundamental and radical in the sense just described. The first prong of that critique is the proposition that the Establishment Clause presupposes and allows us to be an essentially Christian nation, and simply, though importantly, mandates equal treatment of Christian, if not all, denominations. This is the idea that governmental neutrality is neutrality among religions, not neutrality between religion and nonreligion. As such, this position is not inconsistent with the possibility of neutrality and a distinction between the religious and the secular.

The second prong, however, is the more fundamental and radical argument made by some, though not all, associated with the Christian Right.[16] It is the claim that the very attempt to be neutral between

[16] In *The Democratic Virtues of the Christian Right* (Princeton: Princeton University Press, 2009), Jon A. Shields argues that "the vast majority of Christian Right leaders have long labored to inculcate deliberative norms in their rank-and-file activists—especially the practice of civility and respect; the cultivation of real dialogue by listening and asking questions; the rejection of appeals to theology; and the practice of careful moral reasoning" (2). In particular, Shields cautions against the danger of assuming that the more extreme activists associated with the Christian Right speak for everyone in that movement:

> Mistaking such marginal fundamentalists [Shields is speaking of Randall Terry and Jerry Falwell] as representative of the Christian Right as a whole prevents us from undertaking a thoughtful assessment of the right or understanding the complex relationship between Christianity and deliberation. Because we have regarded fringe fundamentalists as paradigmatic representatives of the Christian Right, we have assumed falsely that orthodox believers more broadly are a grave threat to a democratic culture that depends on civil and reasonable citizens. The reality is far more complicated: some orthodox faiths shore up deliberative ideals, while others compromise them. (4)

Similarly, Timothy Beal argues in a very informative article surveying recent scholarly literature that "recent studies by more-or-less outsiders show there is no such thing as evangelicalism. The term represents a broad range of significantly different theologies, practices, and religious movements within Christianity, and there are often tensions among and within them." "Among the Evangelicals: Inside a Fractured Movement," *The Chronicle of Higher Education*, December 12, 2010 (http://chronicle.com/article/Among-the-Evangelicals/125647/, retrieved 6-17-11).

Nevertheless, while the Christian Right theorists this chapter explores in detail are not in a theological mainstream, their radicalization of Establishment Clause jurisprudence articulates well the Christian America position and, more broadly and importantly, the argument that any political order is necessarily also a religious order. Their writings will thus function in this chapter as a theoretical foil that raises important questions about the meaning of the religion clauses in the American political order.

religion and nonreligion is itself a religious position and thus violates Establishment Clause prohibitions. It is, more specifically, the claim that purported neutrality between the religious and the secular is itself a secular position, that secularism is what the Christian Right calls secular humanism, that secular humanism is itself a religion, that government endorsement and advancement of secular humanism thus contravene the Establishment Clause, and that, consequently, neutrality itself violates the Establishment Clause. This second proposition is a fundamental and radical critique of conventional Establishment Clause jurisprudence, then, because it challenges the two main premises of that jurisprudence, namely, the intelligibility of the distinction between religion and nonreligion and the intelligibility of the concept of neutrality. The burden of this chapter is to dissect and challenge that radical challenge itself by arguing that because accepting the radicalization of Establishment Clause jurisprudence undermines the intelligibility of the religion clauses, affirming the intelligibility of the religion clauses requires rejecting the radicalization of Establishment Clause jurisprudence. That is, there are two central premises at the core of the religion clauses in general and Establishment Clause jurisprudence in particular: (1) the intelligibility of the distinction between the religious and the secular and (2) the intelligibility of the concept of governmental neutrality. The presence of the religion clauses in the First Amendment make sense only upon the premise that we can distinguish clearly between religion and nonreligion and upon the premise that government can be truly neutral among different religions and between religion and nonreligion.

What, exactly, does the term "secular" mean, definitionally as opposed to philosophically? According to the *Oxford English Dictionary*, secular means "of or pertaining to the world"; or "belonging to the world and its affairs as distinguished from the church and religion; civil, lay, temporal. Chiefly used as a negative term, with the meaning non-ecclesiastical, non-religious, or non-sacred"; or "of or belonging to the present or visible world as distinguished from the eternal or spiritual world; temporal, worldly."[17] In *Black's Legal Dictionary* we find a similar definition: "Not spiritual; not ecclesiastical; relating to affairs of the present (temporal) world."[18] Common to both definitions is the idea that the secular refers to or involves the temporal rather than spiritual dimension of human reality, and implicit here are both an ontological claim and an epistemological claim. As a matter of ontology, the concept of the secular suggests the idea of two distinct realms or spheres, the secular and the

[17] "Secular," defs. I, 2a, and 3a, *OED*.

[18] *Black's Legal Dictionary*, 6th ed. (St. Paul, Minn.: West Publishing, 1990), 1353.

religious, which in turn implies both a notion of separate principles that govern these realms and a notion of a relation between these realms. Perhaps the most famous idea of this sort is to be found in St. Augustine's *City of God*, where he distinguishes between the City of God and the City of Man.[19] As a matter of epistemology, second, the concept of the secular suggests the not uncontroversial idea of a neutral, value-free perspective from which particular religious perspectives are merely private, relative worldviews. This is tantamount to the claim that, by way of analogy, I can play baseball, I can play basketball, I can play football, I can play chess, but most of the time I am not playing any game at all. Just as I start from the latter standpoint, the "real" world, and then choose to play, for awhile, a particular game with its own rules and discourse, I take as my baseline the secular and then choose to hold a particular set of religious beliefs. Michael Perry sets out with his customary thoroughness the idea of a secular belief in contrast to a religious belief:

> By a "religious" argument, I mean an argument that relies on (among other things) a religious belief: an argument that presupposes the truth of a religious belief and includes that belief as one of its essential premises. . . . A belief can be "nonreligious," then, in one of two senses. The belief that God does not exist is nonreligious in the sense of "atheistic." A belief that is about something other than God's existence or nonexistence, nature, activity, or will is nonreligious in the sense of "secular."[20]

The concept of the secular, then, presumes that something is capable of *not* pertaining to religion. Thus, in one sense, a secular *polity* would be created by an Establishment Clause whose meaning is that affirmation of or allegiance to a faith tradition can*not* be a condition of citizenship and full participation in American public life. In another sense, "secular society" refers to the notion that social institutions are the expression of values that are either nonreligious or neutral vis-à-vis religion.[21]

[19] Augustine, *The City of God against the Pagans* (New York: Cambridge University Press, 1998).

[20] Michael J. Perry, *Religion in Politics: Constitutional and Moral Perspectives* (New York: Oxford University Press, 1997), 31.

[21] It is necessary to refrain from the implication drawn by some groups that "secular society" means "value free." There was much discussion of the role of "values voters" during and after the 2004 presidential election. (See, e.g., Larry Eichel, "'Values Voters': Credit and More," *Philadelphia Inquirer,* November 7, 2004, http://philly.newspaperdirect.com/epaper/viewer.aspx.) The term has been applied to conservative Christians (see, more recently, the 2010 Values Voter Summit, http://www.valuesvotersummit.org/, retrieved 8-31-10, sponsored by FRC Action, the legislative arm of the religious-conservative Family Research Council), with the implication that anyone who does not support their particular agenda thereby lacks values.

Accepting these background considerations uncritically for the moment, let us see how the Supreme Court has employed the concepts of neutrality and the secular. The central motif running through the Court's decisions in Establishment Clause matters has been the distinction between the religious and the secular, and the concomitant concept of neutrality, both between religion and religion and between religion and nonreligion. Without undertaking an exhaustive survey of all or even most of the Court's rulings in this area, we can get a feel for this motif by looking at statements by the justices in a number of the most famous Establishment Clause decisions. The *Everson* prohibition against aid to or preference for one or all religions, cited above, tacitly raises the concept of government neutrality, the concept stated more explicitly in this passage in the *Everson* opinion:

> [The First] Amendment requires the state to be a neutral in its relations with groups of religious believers and non-believers; it does not require the state to be their adversary. State power is no more to be used so as to handicap religions, than it is to favor them.[22]

Significantly, the Court argues that neutrality is not hostility; there is, the Court suggests here, a middle position between advocacy of religion and hostility toward religion. In his dissenting opinion, Justice Jackson implicates this concept of neutrality and additionally, in the notion of the isolation of the secular from the religious, the idea of two distinct spheres:

> Our public school, if not a product of Protestantism, at least is more consistent with it than with the Catholic culture and scheme of values. It is a relatively recent development dating from about 1840. It is organized on the premise that secular education can be isolated from all religious teaching so that the school can inculcate all needed temporal knowledge and also maintain a strict and lofty neutrality as to religion. The assumption is that after the individual has been instructed in worldly wisdom he will be better fitted to choose his religion.[23]

Finally, Justice Rutledge, speaking for all four dissenters, also employs a distinction between spheres:

> The Amendment's purpose was not to strike merely at the official establishment of a single sect, creed or religion, outlawing only a formal relation such as had prevailed in England and some of the colonies. Necessarily it was to uproot all such relationships. But the object was broader than separating church and state in this narrow sense. It was to create a complete and permanent separation of the spheres of religious activity and civil

[22] *Everson*, at 18.

[23] *Everson*, at 23–24, footnote omitted.

> authority by comprehensively forbidding every form of public aid or support for religion.[24]

Despite their disagreement as to the particulars of the case, the *Everson* justices hold to the idea of a distinction between a religious sphere and a secular sphere, and to the idea of government neutrality between the two.

In *McCollum v. Board of Education*,[25] *Engel v. Vitale*,[26] and *Abington School District v. Schempp*,[27] the Court continues to rely on these two fundamental premises, even as it does not explore them. Consider this passage by Justice Frankfurter in *McCollum*:

> The non-sectarian or secular public school was the means of reconciling freedom in general with religious freedom. The sharp confinement of the public schools to secular education was a recognition of the need of a democratic society to educate its children, insofar as the State undertook to do so, in an atmosphere free from pressures in a realm in which pressures are most resisted and where conflicts are most easily and most bitterly engendered. Designed to serve as perhaps the most powerful agency for promoting cohesion among a heterogeneous democratic people, the public school must keep scrupulously free from entanglement in the strife of sects. The preservation of the community from divisive conflicts, of Government from irreconcilable pressures by religious groups, of religion from censorship and coercion however subtly exercised, requires strict confinement of the State to instruction other than religious, leaving to the individual's church and home, indoctrination in the faith of his choice.[28]

We see here the distinction between the secular and the religious, of course, but additionally we see, in the first sentence of the passage, the assumption that secular means nonsectarian—an assumption, we will see below, questioned by the radicalization of Establishment Clause jurisprudence. In *Engel*, Justice Douglas in his concurring opinion reaffirms the Court's position on the concept of neutrality:

> The First Amendment leaves the Government in a position not of hostility to religion but of neutrality. The philosophy is that the atheist or agnostic—the nonbeliever—is entitled to go his own way. The philosophy is that if government interferes in matters spiritual, it will be a divisive force. The First Amendment teaches that a government neutral in the field of religion better serves all religious interests.[29]

[24] *Everson*, at 31–32.
[25] *McCollum v. Board of Education*, 333 U.S. 203 (1948).
[26] *Engel v. Vitale*, 370 U.S. 421 (1962).
[27] *Abington School District v. Schempp*, 374 U.S. 203 (1963).
[28] *McCollum*, at 216–17.

In *Abington* the Court defends what it calls the "wholesome neutrality" which runs through its previous Establishment Clause case law, stating that while the state may not advance religion, it "may not establish a 'religion of secularism' in the sense of affirmatively opposing or showing hostility to religion, thus 'preferring those who believe in no religion over those who do believe.'"[30] Justice Goldberg, concurring, likewise writes,

> It is said, and I agree, that the attitude of government toward religion must be one of neutrality. But untutored devotion to the concept of neutrality can lead to invocation or approval of results which partake not simply of that noninterference and noninvolvement with the religious which the Constitution commands, but of a brooding and pervasive devotion to the secular and a passive, or even active, hostility to the religious. Such results are not only not compelled by the Constitution, but, it seems to me, are prohibited by it.[31]

Similarly, Justice Brennan in concurrence writes, "[T]he First Amendment commands not official hostility toward religion, but only a strict neutrality in matters of religion."[32] More broadly, according to Brennan, the Establishment Clauses prohibits "those involvements of religious with secular institutions which (a) serve the essentially religious activities of religious institutions; (b) employ the organs of government for essentially religious purposes; or (c) use essentially religious means to serve governmental ends, where secular means would suffice."[33] The state, he adds, "must be steadfastly neutral in all matters of faith, and neither favor nor inhibit religion."[34] We see in these passages from his concurring opinion both the concept of neutrality and, particularly in item (c) of this last citation, the distinction between the religious and the secular.

Similarly strong statements of governmental neutrality appear in other major cases in Establishment Clause jurisprudence. Speaking for the Court in *Epperson v. Arkansas*, Justice Fortas states,

> Government in our democracy, state and national, must be neutral in matters of religious theory, doctrine, and practice. It may not be hostile to any religion or to the advocacy of no-religion; and it may not aid, foster, or promote one religion or religious theory against another or even against the militant opposite. The First Amendment mandates governmental neutrality between religion and religion, and between religion and nonreligion.[35]

[29] *Engel*, at 443.
[30] *Abington*, at 225 (citing *Zorach v. Clauson*, 343 U.S. 306 [1952], at 314).
[31] *Abington*, at 306.
[32] *Abington*, at 295.
[33] *Abington*, at 295.
[34] *Abington*, at 299.
[35] *Epperson v. Arkansas*, 393 U.S. 97 (1968), at 103–4.

Concurring in *Walz v. Tax Commission*, Justice Harlan writes, "[T]he Government must neither legislate to accord benefits that favor religion over nonreligion, nor sponsor a particular sect, nor try to encourage participation in or abnegation of religion."[36] Dissenting in the same case, Justice Douglas argues that "one of the mandates of the First Amendment is to promote a viable, pluralistic society and to keep government neutral, not only between sects, but also between believers and nonbelievers."[37] In *Marsh v. Chambers*, Justice Brennan writes in his dissenting opinion, "It may be true that individuals cannot be 'neutral' on the question of religion. But the judgment of the Establishment Clause is that neutrality by the organs of government on questions of religion is both possible and imperative."[38]

The proper conceptualization of this focus on neutrality lies at the root of the conflict over the intelligibility and practicality of the *Lemon* test. Drawing together the strands of previous Establishment Clause cases, Chief Justice Burger states for the Court in *Lemon v. Kurtzman*,

> Every analysis in this area must begin with consideration of the cumulative criteria developed by the Court over many years. Three such tests may be gleaned from our cases. First, the statute must have a secular legislative purpose; second, its principal or primary effect must be one that neither advances nor inhibits religion . . . ; finally, the statute must not foster "an excessive government entanglement with religion."[39]

The purpose prong necessarily presumes the possibility of distinguishing between a secular and a religious legislative purpose. Teaching religion—as opposed to teaching about religion—is obviously a religious activity, whereas teaching math or physics or chemistry is evidently a secular activity. But are math and physics and chemistry secular subjects if they are taught as evidence of divine intelligence or design?[40] Similarly, if someone justifies government by reference to Augustine's doctrine of original sin and government's role to provide order in a fallen world, is

[36] *Walz v. Tax Commission*, 397 U.S. 664 (1970), at 694.

[37] *Walz*, at 716.

[38] *Marsh v. Chambers*, 463 U.S. 783 (1983), at 821 (footnote omitted).

[39] *Lemon v. Kurtzman*, 403 U.S. 602 (1971), at 612. Compare *Abington*, at 222:

> The test may be stated as follows: what are the purpose and the primary effect of the enactment? If either is the advancement or inhibition of religion then the enactment exceeds the scope of legislative power as circumscribed by the Constitution. That is to say that to withstand the strictures of the Establishment Clause there must be a secular legislative purpose and a primary effect that neither advances nor inhibits religion.

[40] E.g., if a grade-school teacher conducts a lesson in basic arithmetic by asking, "If four disciples walked with Jesus and were joined by another three, how many disciples walked with Jesus?" exactly what is the teacher teaching?

government concern with law and order a "secular purpose"? The purpose prong attempts to tread that very thin line of neutrality. Likewise the effect prong assumes that there is some space, some position, between advancing and inhibiting religion, but, as indicated by the references to hostility we have seen, the attempt to avoid advancing religion can appear to some to be inhibiting religion, and the attempt to avoid inhibiting religion can appear to some to be advancing religion.

In an attempt to deal with difficulties in the *Lemon* test, Justice O'Connor in *Lynch v. Donnelly* suggests that the "proper inquiry under the purpose prong of *Lemon* . . . is whether the government intends to convey a message of endorsement or disapproval of religion."[41] From this perspective, she writes further in *Wallace v. Jaffree*, "*Lemon*'s inquiry as to the purpose and effect of a statute requires courts to examine whether government's purpose is to endorse religion and whether the statute actually conveys a message of endorsement."[42] Although the language differs from *Lemon*, here too the assumption is that it is possible for government neither to endorse a particular religion or religious belief nor to disapprove of a particular religion or religious belief. It is, in other words, the presumption of neutrality. Government, she writes in *Allegheny County v. Greater Pittsburgh ACLU*, "is to be neutral in matters of religion, rather than showing either favoritism or disapproval towards citizens based on their personal religious choices."[43] Writing for the Court in *Allegheny*, Justice Blackmun states, "Whether the key word is 'endorsement,' 'favoritism,' or 'promotion,' the essential principle remains the same. The Establishment Clause, at the very least, prohibits government from appearing to take a position on questions of religious belief or from 'making adherence to a religion relevant in any way to a person's standing in the political community.' "[44] And, significantly, Blackmun adds this key point: "A secular state, it must be remembered, is not the same as an atheistic or antireligious state. A secular state establishes neither atheism nor religion as its official creed."[45] A secular state, he insists, establishes no orthodoxy of any sort on religious matters.

Most, if not all, of the justices whose views I have cited as to the necessity of governmental neutrality vis-à-vis religion would likely fall into the separationist camp, insisting on strict neutrality between religion and religion and between religion and nonreligion. What is striking, however, is that justices one would consider advocates of the

[41] *Lynch v. Donnelly*, 465 U.S. 668 (1984), at 691.
[42] *Wallace v. Jaffree*, 472 U.S. 38 (1985), at 69.
[43] *Allegheny County v. Greater Pittsburgh ACLU*, 492 U.S. 573 (1989), at 627.
[44] *Allegheny*, at 593–94 (citing O'Connor in *Lynch v. Donnelly*, at 687).
[45] *Allegheny*, at 610.

accommodationist position employ the concept of neutrality as well. In *Abington*, for example, while justices in the majority insist, as we have seen, that neutrality requires prohibition of religious exercises, Justice Stewart in dissent argues that "permission of [religious] exercises for those who want them is necessary if the schools are truly to be neutral in the matter of religion."[46] The dissenters in *Wallace v. Jaffree*, cited above in regard to Justice O'Connor's discussion of the endorsement test, are particularly interesting instances of a reference to neutrality from the accommodationist position. According to Chief Justice Burger,

> If the government may not accommodate religious needs when it does so in a wholly neutral and noncoercive manner, the "benevolent neutrality" that we have long considered the correct constitutional standard will quickly translate into the "callous indifference" that the Court has consistently held the Establishment Clause does not require.[47]

Dissenting also in *Wallace*, Justice Rehnquist argues that it is "indisputable" that Madison saw the First Amendment "as designed to prohibit the establishment of a national religion, and perhaps to prevent discrimination among sects. He did not see it as requiring neutrality on the part of government between religion and irreligion."[48] Moreover, he adds,

> None of the other Members of Congress who spoke during the August 15th debate expressed the slightest indication that they thought the language before them from the Select Committee, or the evil to be aimed at, would require that the Government be absolutely neutral as between religion and irreligion. The evil to be aimed at, so far as those who spoke were concerned, appears to have been the establishment of a national church, and perhaps the preference of one religious sect over another; but it was definitely not concerned about whether the Government might aid all religions evenhandedly.[49]

Based upon his account of the historical sources, then, Rehnquist concludes that neutrality between religion and nonreligion—irreligion, in his words—is not a requirement of the Establishment Clause:

> It would seem from this evidence that the Establishment Clause of the First Amendment had acquired a well-accepted meaning: it forbade establishment of a national religion, and forbade preference among religious sects or denominations. . . . The Establishment Clause did not require government neutrality between religion and irreligion nor did it prohibit the Federal

[46] *Abington*, at 313.
[47] *Wallace*, at 90.
[48] *Wallace*, at 98.
[49] *Wallace*, at 99.

> Government from providing nondiscriminatory aid to religion. There is simply no historical foundation for the proposition that the Framers intended to build the "wall of separation" that was constitutionalized in *Everson*.[50]

Whether Rehnquist's accommodationist position is truer to the Establishment Clause than the separationist position is an important question, but it is secondary to my concern here. The important point here is Rehnquist's—along with Burger's and Stewart's—assumption that neutrality is possible. Rehnquist rejects the claim the government must be neutral between religion and nonreligion, saying merely that government must be neutral between one religion and another.

In other words, it is not the case that separationists argue for neutrality and accommodationists argue against neutrality. Rather, they both presume the possibility of neutrality toward religion on the part of government, disagreeing in particular cases simply over whether a given government program or action counts as neutral. They can disagree as to whether government should be neutral between religion and nonreligion, but there appears to be no disagreement that government *can* be neutral between religion and nonreligion, and between one religion and another.[51] Thus, in an apt if lengthy passage, Michael Perry summarizes the concept of freedom of religion in American jurisprudence:

> [T]he central point of the free exercise and non-establishment norms, taken together, is that government may not make judgments about the value or disvalue—the truth value, the moral value, the social value—of religions or religious practices or religious (theological) tenets as such (i.e., as religious). Government has no such power, and government may not arrogate to itself any such power. Whereas the free exercise norm forbids government to take prohibitory action disfavoring one or more religious practices as such, the nonestablishment norm forbids government to discriminate in favor of membership in one or more churches or other religious communities or in favor of the practices or tenets of one more churches. No matter how much some persons might prefer one or more religions, government may not take any action based on the view that the preferred religion or religions are, as religion, better along one or another dimension of value than one or more other religions or than no religion at all. So, for example, government may not take any action based on the view that Christianity, or Roman Catholicism, or the Fifth Street Baptist Church, is, as a religion or a church, closer to the truth than one or more other religions or churches or than no religion at all—or, if

[50] *Wallace*, at 106.

[51] Even if Justice Scalia argues in *McCreary*, as we have seen, that government does not have to be neutral between monotheistic religions, on the one side, and polytheistic religions and atheism, on the other, he still assumes the possibility of neutrality among monotheistic religions.

> not necessarily closer to the truth, at least a more authentic reflection of the religious history and culture of the American people.[52]

The fundamental assumption of conventional Establishment Clause, along with Free Exercise Clause, jurisprudence is that it is possible for government to be agnostic, as it were, regarding religious beliefs. It is the assumption that there exists a truly neutral position between religions and between religion and nonreligion.

However, in the course of the Establishment Clauses cases, the Court, at least through the words of certain justices, quietly, probably unintentionally, provided the basis for a theoretically radical attack on those precedents. Two cases are especially noteworthy. In *Torcaso v. Watkins*, Justice Black, speaking for the Court, states that

> neither a State nor the Federal Government can constitutionally force a person "to profess a belief or disbelief in any religion." Neither can constitutionally pass laws or impose requirements which aid all religions as against non-believers, and neither can aid those religions based on a belief in the existence of God as against those religions founded on different beliefs.[53]

This is the standard language of neutrality, as we have seen earlier, but in a footnote at the very end of this passage Black, perhaps inadvertently, leaves a gift for the future: "Among religions in this country which do not teach what would generally be considered a belief in the existence of God are Buddhism, Taoism, Ethical Culture, *Secular Humanism* and others."[54] The other case of interest here is *Abington*, to which we attended earlier. I cited this statement by Justice Stewart: "[P]ermission of [religious] exercises for those who want them is necessary if the schools are truly to be neutral in the matter of religion."[55] The statement following this sentence immediately, however, is crucial: "And a refusal to permit religious exercises thus is seen, not as the realization of state neutrality, but rather as *the establishment of a religion of secularism*, or at the least, as government support of the beliefs of those who think that religious exercises should be conducted only in private."[56] While religious conservatives at minimum subscribe, as do some other religious groups, to the accommodationist critique of the separationist position, the basis for the radical theoretical attack on conventional Establishment Clause jurisprudence is the proposition, contained in both of these passages, that secularism or secular humanism is not a neutral position, but a religion itself.

[52] Perry, *Religion in Politics*, 14–15.
[53] *Torcaso v. Watkins*, 367 U.S. 488 (1961), at 495 (footnotes omitted).
[54] *Torcaso*, at 495n11, emphasis added.
[55] *Abington*, at 313.
[56] *Abington*, at 313, emphasis added.

Specifically, the fundamental and radical move on the part of some Christian Right thinkers is to reject the two central premises that ground Establishment Clause jurisprudence: (1) the intelligibility of the distinction between the religious and the secular and (2) the intelligibility of the concept of governmental neutrality. I should note that it is not just some thinkers associated with the Christian Right who challenge conventional wisdom here. Richard John Neuhaus, while critical of many aspects of the Christian Right, subscribes to much of the latter's argument in *The Naked Public Square*.[57] There he argues, "When religion in any traditional or recognizable form is excluded from the public square, it does not mean that the public square is in fact naked. . . . When recognizable religion is excluded, the vacuum will be filled by *ersatz* religion, by religion bootlegged into public space under other names."[58] Secularism, he states more fully, becomes a religion:

> The notion that this is a secular society is relatively new. It might be proposed that, while the society is incorrigibly religious, the state is secular. But such a disjunction between society and state is a formula for governmental delegitimation. In a democratic society, state and society must draw from the same moral well. In addition, because transcendence abhors a vacuum, the state that styles itself as secular will almost certainly succumb to secular*ism*. Because government cannot help but make moral judgments of an ultimate nature, it must, if it has in principle excluded identifiable religion, make those judgments by "secular" reasoning that is given the force of religion. Because this process is already advanced in the spheres of law and public education, there is a measure of justice in the complaints about "secular humanism." Secular humanism, in this case, is simply the term unhappily chosen for *ersatz* religion.[59]

"What is called neutrality toward religion," he adds, "is an invitation for a substitute religion."[60] Consequently, he concludes, "The conflict in American public life today, then, is not a conflict between morality and secularism. It is a conflict of moralities in which one moral system calls itself secular and insists that the other do likewise as the price of admission to the public arena."[61]

[57] Richard John Neuhaus, *The Naked Public Square: Religion and Democracy in America*, 2nd ed. (Grand Rapids: Eerdmans, 1986).

[58] Neuhaus, *Naked Public Square*, 80.

[59] Neuhaus, *Naked Public Square*, 82. Despite Neuhaus' contention here that we cannot have an "incorrigibly" religious society but a secular government, my overarching argument in this book is that however difficult that pairing may be, it is just what the religion clauses mandate and indeed what those clauses require if they are to make sense.

[60] Neuhaus, *Naked Public Square*, 102.

[61] Neuhaus, *Naked Public Square*, 125–26. Nevertheless, when Neuhaus writes that "state and society must draw from the same moral well," he makes a tacit jump from

It is this rejection of the concept of neutrality and the distinct status of the secular that is typical of the radical version of the Christian Right critique. We can grasp the outlines of that critique by looking at three representative examples of the writings in this area. In *A Time for Anger: The Myth of Neutrality*,[62] Franky Schaeffer maintains that secular humanism "is a philosophy which holds that God is nonexistent or irrelevant to human affairs, and that man must choose or invent his own ethics; secular humanism makes man the measure of all things."[63] His book is a call to arms to resist and overthrow secular humanism:

> Using politics and what's left of the law, we must stall the advance of secularism and then, in the name of liberty, regain the ground we have lost. Our insane society must be put right once again. The innocent must be protected, the sanctity of each life upheld. If it takes one or fifty years, compassionate Judeo-Christian truth *must be reestablished*.[64]

Noteworthy here, of course, is the tacit claim that "Judeo-Christian" truth—not something, in point of fact, with which Jews would associate themselves—was once our established truth and now must be reestablished. The background assumption of this claim by Schaeffer is his denial of the possibility of neutrality:

> In the guise of advocating "neutrality," secular humanists have replaced our nation's set of operating principles which derive from the Judeo-Christian tradition with another set of principles: these commit the United States to a materialistic view of truth, and have effectively established secular humanism as the only national religion.[65]

"moral" to "religious" that is itself contentious. People of diverse religious orientations can share a common commitment to the moral and political principles of the Declaration of Independence, unless one claims that those principles express an essentially and uniquely religious vision. Yet if that is the case, the claim that the Declaration has universal applicability dissolves.

Additionally, Neuhaus writes that "government cannot help but make moral judgments of an ultimate nature," but what would such judgments be? In the American political order, they cannot be judgments as to theological issues like the nature and fate of the soul. A governmental decision to impose the death penalty qualifies as a "moral judgment of an ultimate nature," but surely that does not require a theological underpinning.

[62] Franky Schaeffer, *A Time for Anger: The Myth of Neutrality* (Westchester, Ill.: Crossway Books, 1982). Lest we dismiss Schaeffer as a marginal figure, we do well to note that 2012 presidential candidate Michele Bachmann was influenced by him. See Michelle Goldberg, "Bachmann's Unrivaled Extremism," *The Daily Beast*, June 14, 2011 (http://www.thedailybeast.com/articles/2011/06/14/michele-bachmanns-unrivaled-extremism-gay-rights-to-religion.html, retrieved 6-16-11).

[63] Schaeffer, *Time for Anger*, 24.

[64] Schaeffer, *Time for Anger*, 77, emphasis in original.

[65] Schaeffer, *Time for Anger*, 59–60.

Morality, for Schaeffer, is never, simply, morality; it is always someone's morality: "All law is, in fact, some form of legislated morality. The question is whose morality will dominate."[66] Most strikingly, along with this rejection of neutrality Schaeffer rejects the distinction between the religious and the secular:

> Every human being has a religion: he holds certain values, and these values imply a rationale; in this it makes no difference whether someone has accepted the values of an organized religion or has chosen his own. Everyone believes in something, even if that "something" is his repudiation of all organized religions. Although man is capable of dispassionate inquiry, there is, finally, no such thing as a nonreligious view of truth: to value one thing as opposed to another is to make a declaration of faith. All life is religious, and all life is secular. There is no real division between the two.[67]

For Schaeffer, then, religion is not merely a private belief system. We all live within an essentially, and essentially public, religious world, and the only question is whose religion it is going to be. We cannot not be religious.

In a popular work titled *The Second American Revolution*[68] and, with John Conlan, a law review article titled "The Establishment of the Religion of Secular Humanism and Its First Amendment Implications,"[69] John Whitehead develops in more detail the ideas advanced by Schaeffer. The former work defines humanism similarly as

> the fundamental idea that men and women can begin from themselves without reference to the Bible and, by reasoning outward, derive the standards to judge all matters. For such people, there is no absolute or fixed standard of behavior. They are quite literally autonomous (from the Greek *autos*, self, and *nomos*, law), a law unto themselves.[70]

Whitehead, we notice here, quietly makes the usual Christian Right claim that without reference to the Bible there can be no absolute or fixed standards of conduct, a logical jump that involves hidden premises he leaves unexplored. His view of the history of the relationship between American government and religion is that it is a story of an original establishment followed by an increasing disestablishment of Christianity. The First Amendment, he states, "provides freedom *for* the Christian religion, not

[66] Schaeffer, *Time for Anger*, 25.

[67] Schaeffer, *Time for Anger*, 23–24.

[68] John W. Whitehead, *The Second American Revolution* (Elgin, Ill.: David C. Cook, 1982).

[69] John W. Whitehead and John Conlan, "The Establishment of the Religion of Secular Humanism and Its First Amendment Implications," *Texas Tech Law Review* 10 (1978): 1.

[70] Whitehead, *Second American Revolution,* 38.

from the Christian religion,"[71] for "the principal religion to be protected by the First Amendment was Judeo-Christian theism."[72] In the law review article, Whitehead and Conlan state more forthrightly, in view of their agenda, that "[t]he religion of the first amendment is traditional theism and, in particular, Christianity."[73] More specifically,

> A central concern of those who drafted the First Amendment was to prevent the federal government from establishing a national denominational church. This protected the state-established or state-preferred Christian denominations that existed in many of the colonies of that era. Thus the philosophical base of the First Amendment was that of *denominational pluralism*—a healthy coexistence between the various Christian denominations. Such practical denominational pluralism is not to be confused with the new concept of pluralism, which commands complete acceptance of all views, even secular humanism.[74]

It is to the development of what he calls this new concept of pluralism that Whitehead attributes the progressive disestablishment of Christianity: "From a preferred position within the religion clauses, Judeo-Christian theism has been relegated to the level of all other systems of belief—and of unbelief."[75]

The crux of this development, according to Whitehead, was a shift, fostered by the federal courts, from the content of belief to the structure and function of belief. *Davis v. Beason*,[76] for example, illustrates what Whitehead and Conlan consider the original understanding of religion:

> Religion, as defined in *Davis*, involves a belief in a "Creator," which, the Court held, imposes certain obligations upon each individual to obey the will of the "Creator," or Supreme Being. This definition of religion mirrors that understood by James Madison, and those within the historical milieu that drafted the first amendment, and is, therefore, both historically

[71] Whitehead, *Second American Revolution*, 100.

[72] Whitehead, *Second American Revolution*, 101. Again, it is typically not Jews who make this argument about "Judeo-Christian theism."

[73] Whitehead and Conlan, "Establishment of the Religion," at 3, footnote omitted.

[74] Whitehead, *Second American Revolution*, 96, emphasis in original. In their article, similarly, Whitehead and Conlan, "Establishment of the Religion," at 3, state, "The concern of Madison and the founding fathers was that one Christian denomination would prevail over the others. Thus, the first amendment was not meant to prevent the 'establishment' of Christianity as a religion, but to prevent one Christian denomination from dominating the others."

[75] Whitehead, *Second American Revolution*, 108. Similarly, 103, he writes, "[T]he Christian theistic religious practices that the Reynolds Court presupposed have now judicially been reduced to 'mere opinion' or belief. Christianity has lost its historically preferred position."

[76] *Davis v. Beason*, 133 U.S. 333 (1890).

> and constitutionally accurate. Moreover, the Court's definition corresponds with American religious heritage and was applicable to a society overwhelmingly dominated by theistic Christianity. This non-sectarian definition, applied to a Judaeo-Christian society, is clearly compatible with the first amendment religion clauses.[77]

The federal courts, however, reflecting broad social and intellectual currents in post–Civil War America, began to depart from the traditional theistic conception of religion.

> *Davis* reaffirms the heritage of ideas and commentaries concerning the nature of religion. Beginning in the 1940's, however, traditional theistic religion came under increasing attack. The federal courts began to broaden and diversify the definition of "religion," until by the end of the 1960's the judicial definition of religion was altered from sustenance of belief—belief in and obligation owed to the "Creator"—to the *impact* of the belief on the *life* of the person expressing and holding it. The judicial transformation of "religion" corresponds to the change that was taking place in a previously theistic society. Society's basis of truth was shifting from traditional theism's emphasis on God-centeredness, with the result being that the finite man of society ignores the absolutes revealed by God and instead relies upon the rationalization of his own mind.[78]

The key cases in this transition, according to Whitehead, are *United States v. Ballard* and *Torcaso v. Watkins*.[79] The former marks the move toward the replacement of traditional theism by secular humanism:

> In *Ballard* the Supreme Court made it clear that the classification of a "belief" as religion does not depend upon the tenets of the creed, but rather the *sincerity* of the belief. . . . Thus, the Supreme Court has adopted a concept of religion which is tantamount to Secular Humanism's position of the centrality of man, because the basis of both is the deification of man's reason.[80]

And *Torcaso*, in effect, completes the transition and spawns the controversial decisions of the 1960s: "By repudiating Maryland's theistic preference and, thus, leveling all religions, the Court in *Torcaso* rejected Judeo-Christian theism as the religion and foundation of the United States."[81]

Whitehead's argument amounts to the claim that if the defining characteristic of religion has changed from the content of belief to the

[77] Whitehead and Conlan, "Establishment of the Religion," at 8, footnotes omitted.

[78] Whitehead and Conlan, "Establishment of the Religion," at 10.

[79] *United States v. Ballard*, 322 U.S. 78 (1944), and *Torcaso v. Watkins*, 367 U.S. 488 (1961).

[80] Whitehead and Conlan, "Establishment of the Religion," at 11–12.

[81] Whitehead, *Second American Revolution*, 109.

structure of belief—i.e., to belief itself—then any and all beliefs are inherently religious. This claim is grounded in his rejection of the distinction between the religious and the secular: "Christ is Lord over *all* areas of life—not merely the spiritual. Indeed, it is incorrect to make a fundamental distinction between spiritual and secular. Christ is Lord of the intellectual life, the business life, the political life."[82] At the same time, though he apparently criticizes the proposition that any and all beliefs are inherently religious, Whitehead employs that proposition to attack the concept of neutrality. He does so by attempting to establish the claim that law is necessarily an expression of religious belief: "Any legal system, humanistic or Christian," he states, "necessarily has a kind of 'religious' foundation."[83] The reason, Whitehead maintains, is that "all substantial laws—as opposed to mere regulations, such as specific traffic rules—necessarily involve judgments between right and wrong. Therefore, they involve moral principles and establish what is necessarily a kind of religious concern (although it may not be that of Christianity or any other organized religion)."[84] Or, as he writes later, "Historically morals have always been a religious concern. Therefore, because law establishes and declares the meaning of justice and righteousness, law is inescapably religious."[85] Yet law is not only "inescapably religious" but also necessarily exclusionary:

> All pronouncements of right and wrong—laws—are, after all, moral concerns. Such issues have always been at their base religious, even if this religion is the belief system of materialism, humanism, and rationalism. As such, a moral order will maintain that foundation by some form of hostility, subtle or otherwise, to any other religious moral order. Real tolerance among religious systems (in the sense of one system accepting another as equally true) is, as history teaches, nonexistent. For this reason, the new "religion" of secular humanism cannot and will not be tolerant of the biblical, Judeo-Christian values still embodied in the American legal and social structure.[86]

"Any legal system, secular or otherwise," he argues, "must develop a religious foundation of law, and maintain that foundation by hostility to any other law order or it will falter."[87] Our current "culture war," therefore,

[82] Whitehead, *Second American Revolution*, 39–40, emphasis in original.

[83] Whitehead, *Second American Revolution*, 86.

[84] Whitehead, *Second American Revolution*, 87.

[85] Whitehead, *Second American Revolution*, 111. At 20 Whitehead and Conlan, "Establishment of the Religion," footnotes omitted, write, "All law, and therefore, the legal system in its totality, is based upon moral principle. Historically, morals have always been a religious concern; therefore, it can be concluded that law is religious in origin and should be interpreted and adhered to in a religious fashion."

[86] Whitehead, *Second American Revolution*, 86.

[87] Whitehead, *Second American Revolution*, 112.

is from this perspective, as Pat Buchanan told the Republican national convention in 1992, necessarily a religious war.[88] In Whitehead's words,

> Just as Christian theism was once the foundation undergirding law and government, a religious origin in contemporary law exists by province of the Supreme Court, but it has shifted from biblical revelation to humanism. The denial of God does not eliminate the fact that there is an operative god in every religious system or faith. The religious motivation and impetus for the present American law and governmental system is humanism, which has become, in effect, a state-established religion.[89]

Governmental neutrality is impossible, on this view, because an agnostic position vis-à-vis religion is itself a religious position.

It should be clear, then, that Whitehead objects to the disestablishment of Christianity. The question, however, is whether once a religion is disestablished we are left in a position of neutrality, or whether the disestablishment of one religion can be effected only by the establishment of another. The latter is the view for which Whitehead contends: "Traditional theism, particularly Christianity, has been disestablished as the State's presuppositional base in exchange for the religion of Secular Humanism."[90] The key step is the argument that secular humanism is not the rejection of religion but rather an affirmation of a nontheistic religion:

> "Secularism" is nontheistic and "humanism" is secular because it excludes the basic tenets of theism. Therefore, Secular Humanism is nontheistic. However, while Secular Humanism is nontheistic, it is *religious* because it directs itself toward religious beliefs and practices, that are in active opposition to traditional theism. Humanism is a doctrine centered solely on human interests or values. Therefore, humanism [deifies] Man collectively and individually, whereas theism worships God. Moreover, while humanism draws its values and absolutes from the finite reasoning of relativistic Man, theism has received its values and absolutes through the revelation of the infinite Deity or Creator. Both humanism and theism worship their own "god." The difference is the object of worship not the act. Therefore, Secular Humanism is a religion whose doctrine worships Man as the source of all knowledge and truth, whereas theism worships God as the source of all knowledge and truth.[91]

[88] Buchanan stated, "My friends, this election is about much more than who gets what. It is about who we are. It is about what we believe. It is about what we stand for as Americans. There is a religious war going on in our country for the soul of America. It is a cultural war, as critical to the kind of nation we will one day be as was the Cold War itself" (http://www.buchanan.org/pa-92-0817-rnc.html).

[89] Whitehead, *Second American Revolution*, 111–12, footnote omitted.

[90] Whitehead and Conlan, "Establishment of the Religion," at 23, footnote omitted.

[91] Whitehead and Conlan, "Establishment of the Religion," at 30–31, emphasis in original.

The consequence is that purported neutrality itself becomes subject to Establishment Clause prohibitions. In Whitehead and Conlan's words:

> The apparent outcome of the Supreme Court's absolute acceptance of belief-as-religion is that all religious expression, including Secular Humanism, in state programs is unconstitutional. The Court's acceptance of belief-as-religion has virtually eliminated theism from the public educational system while the religion of Secular Humanism has become entrenched in the public schools. Secular humanism, being no less a religion than theism, is equally susceptible to the establishment clause, and its expression, in any form, is clearly unconstitutional.[92]

Or, as they conclude more succinctly, "it logically follows that the State is prohibited from establishing nontheistic or secular ideologies under the same authority as it is prohibited from establishing theistic practices."[93] There is, consequently, no nonpreferential position to which we can repair. For example,

> If all moral teaching is eradicated in public education the problem of religious secularism is still present because the state would be effectively establishing a preference for those who believe in no morals over those who do. A belief in morals is undoubtedly a belief-as-religion. Moreover, if moral teaching is eliminated in the public schools, then the ideology of the religion of Secular Humanism would be the only ideology in public education offering answers to moral questions.[94]

Whitehead and Conlan's main argument, then, is that governmental neutrality is simply impossible, because any governmental system is the institutionalization of a particular set of religious beliefs. In their words,

> The Supreme Court's theory of neutrality by the State is merely a hopeful illusion. Neutrality presupposes objectivity, but value determination between right and wrong is a moral principle and establishes a religious concern. Therefore, all laws promulgated by the State are enforced morality, which is a religious concern. All law, including the legal system[,] is based upon moral principle, and, therefore, is a religious concern.[95]

Their chain of reasoning is this: law is grounded in morality, morality is grounded in religion, and consequently law is grounded in religion.

The third example of the Christian Right critique of conventional Establishment Clause assumptions is Rousas John Rushdoony, whose

[92] Whitehead and Conlan, "Establishment of the Religion," at 17–18, footnotes omitted.

[93] Whitehead and Conlan, "Establishment of the Religion," at 18, footnote omitted.

[94] Whitehead and Conlan, "Establishment of the Religion," at 19–20.

[95] Whitehead and Conlan, "Establishment of the Religion," at 22, footnote omitted.

work provides the theoretical basis for much of what we have seen Schaeffer and Whitehead and Conlan argue.[96] The title of one particular article, "The State as an Establishment of Religion,"[97] states his central proposition:

> The state is a law structure, and every law structure is inescapably a religious establishment. All law is an expression of some form of moral order, codified and made legal by acts of state. Moral order rests on a concept of ultimate order, on a theology. The source of law in any system is the god of that system, in that law-making is an attribute of sovereignty. This "god" can be man, the state, or some other entity which is made ultimate and sovereign, and is thus the working "god" of the system.[98]

Every political system, according to Rushdoony, is a religious establishment, that is, an institutionalization of religion. To be sure, there may be a bit of sleight of hand here, in the statement, "The source of law in any system is the god of that system, in that law-making is an attribute of sovereignty." On the one hand, we can understand this claim as the contentions that (1) the source of law in any political order is the ultimate authority of that order, (2) a god is the ultimate authority of any political order, and (3) therefore the source of law is the god of that political order.[99] "God" here could be simply a metaphor for the concept of an ultimate authority. On the other hand, given Rushdoony's overall argument, he most likely takes this claim to be not just metaphorically true but literally true: every political order rests on its god.

Second, but equally important, every political system, in his view, is the establishment of a *particular* religion:

[96] In *Republican Gomorrah: Inside the Movement That Shattered the Party* (New York: Nation Books, 2009), author Max Blumenthal identifies Rushdoony as the theoretical and theological godfather of the Christian Right. See the text at 17–22. See also Frederick Clarkson's extensive discussion of Christian Reconstructionism at Political Research Associates (http://www.publiceye.org/magazine/v08n1/chrisrec.html, retrieved 8-6-10).

[97] Rousas John Rushdoony, "The State as an Establishment of Religion," chap. 3 of *Freedom and Education: Pierce v. Society of Sisters Reconsidered*, ed. Donald P. Kommers and Michael J. Wahoske (South Bend, Ind.: Center for Civil Rights, University of Notre Dame Law School, 1978), 37–46.

[98] Rushdoony, "The State," 37, emphasis in original. In his main work, *The Institutes of Biblical Law* (Phillipsburg, N.J.: Presbyterian and Reformed Publishing, 1973), he writes at 4: "Law is in every culture religious in origin. Because law governs man and society, because it establishes and declares the meaning of justice and righteousness, law is inescapably religious, in that it establishes in practical fashion the ultimate concerns of a culture. Accordingly, a fundamental and necessary premise in any and every study of law must be, first, a recognition of this religious nature of law."

[99] The apparent sleight of hand has this form: X is the ultimate authority in the political order, God is the ultimate authority, therefore X is God.

> Each religion has had its characteristic law structure, so that Buddhist law and Islamic law are reflections of the basic faiths of their respective cultures. These law structures are incompatible one with another, so that the idea of freedom of religion as commonly accepted is a myth: such a radical freedom is an impossibility, and religious toleration is possible only within very narrow and restrictive limits.[100]

Complete religious freedom, he maintains, is simply impossible:

> *Reynolds* [*v. United States*, 98 U.S. 145 (1878)] did presuppose that the existing law structure was Christian in character. The Court did recognize the impossibility of religious freedom. There is scarcely a criminal practice, i.e., criminal in terms of the Biblical tradition and as maintained in Judaic and Christian traditions, which is not somewhere legitimate in some tribe, society, or culture. Human sacrifice, bestiality, homosexuality, cannibalism, ritual prostitution, and much else have been aspects of religious practice at some time or another. The Court was right: no state or civil government can exist if a full-scale religious freedom be permitted.[101]

No political system—no state—therefore, can be truly neutral or value free:

> The structure of a state represents, implicitly or explicitly, a particular religion. Implicit in the Court's decision [in *Reynolds*] was the equation of Christian moral standards with Civilization. It is impossible for a state to cease being a religious establishment. To do so would require that the state abolish itself and all its law-making power and declare a permanent state of anarchy.
>
> The state, however, is still with us, although under a pretended or illusory neutrality and objectivity. The state cannot be neutral. Its laws reflect not neutrality but a passionate partisanship.[102]

Nonestablishment is simply impossible, according to Rushdoony; there is never not an established religion. In the *Institutes* he writes,

> [N]o disestablishment of religion as such is possible in any society. A church can be disestablished, and a particular religion can be supplanted by another, but the change is simply to another religion. Since the foundations of law

[100] Rushdoony, "The State," 38.

[101] Rushdoony, "The State," 39.

[102] Rushdoony, "The State," 39. Moreover, he argues, "there can be no tolerance in a law-system for another religion. Toleration is a device used to introduce a new law-system as a prelude to a new intolerance. . . . Every law-system must maintain its existence by hostility to every other law-system and to alien religious foundations, or else it commits suicide." Rushdoony, *Institutes*, 5–6.

> are inescapably religious, no society exists without a religious foundation or without a law-system which codifies the morality of its religion.[103]

The reason for this is that human beings are essentially, inescapably, religious creatures: "Because men are not gods, and reason is not god, all human thinking and rationality rests on certain pretheoretical presuppositions concerning the nature of reason, reality, life, and history which are in essence religious."[104] The question, then, is not *whether* there should be an establishment of religion; rather, the question is always which religion will be the established religion. Rushdoony's argument is that some religion will always be the dominant or hegemonic religion, for there can be no political order in which there is not a hegemonic religion. The only meaningful question is which religion will be hegemonic, and in the American political order it will be either Christianity or humanism.

Like Schaeffer and Whitehead and Conlan, Rushdoony argues that in the United States traditionally established Christianity has been giving way to the establishment of the new religion of humanism:

> What we are witnessing at present, amid much tension and conflict, is a shift in the American legal establishment, a shift from Christianity to humanism. Humanism is a religion no less than Christianity. Paul Tillich's definition of religion as ultimate concern does the most justice to all religions and clearly defines religions, both theistic and non-theistic. Theistic here has reference to belief in a personal God. Non-theistic religions make some entity, such as the state, or a creature, such as man, or men in general (as with humanism), the working god of their system. The denial of God does not eliminate the fact that there is an operative god in every religious system or faith. The religious motivation, impetus, and fervor behind our present law structure, our state establishment of religion, is humanism.[105]

Reflecting the hot-button concerns of the Christian Right, Rushdoony draws from this argument the consequence that "the state schools are also religious schools whose curriculum embodies and incarnates the religion of humanism. The state schools are an establishment of religion. Education is inevitably religious."[106] Ending up in the same place as Schaeffer and Whitehead and Conlan, then, he tells us that we are faced with a battle, a religious conflict: "Either the established religion of the state, humanism, will in the years ahead move steadily to alter and in effect destroy Christianity in church and school, or else it will give way to the

[103] Rushdoony, *Institutes*, 5.
[104] Rushdoony, "The State," 44.
[105] Rushdoony, "The State," 40.
[106] Rushdoony, "The State," 43.

re-establishment of Christianity as the religious foundation of the law structure of the state."[107]

If we can say fairly, as I believe we can, that these writers are representative of the radical Christian Right's critique of conventional Establishment Clause jurisprudence,[108] then it is clear that that critique, beyond its support for the mainstream accommodationist position, advances the more fundamental and radical claim that the very attempt to be neutral between religion and nonreligion is itself a religious position and thus violates Establishment Clause prohibitions. This claim, I have suggested, challenges the two main premises of that jurisprudence, namely, the intelligibility of the distinction between religion and nonreligion,

[107] Rushdoony, "The State," 45. There is an interesting irony in Rushdoony's critique of conventional Establishment Clause jurisprudence: the theoretical radicalism of that conservative or right-wing critique may stem from the essentially Thrasymachean premise that the critique shares with what would ordinarily be considered the left-wing position of Marxism. That premise, encapsulated in Thrasymachus' statement in Plato's *Republic* that justice is the interest or advantage of the stronger, is the proposition that purportedly neutral and universal values and norms are at bottom the biased and particular interests of some dominant group such as a sex or a race or a class. Consider this statement by Rushdoony:

> Although the state is an establishment of religion, it does not acknowledge that it is one, and this creates a major social problem. For the central religious institution to assume that its religion is simply an objective and neutral position creates a devastating social distortion. This is compounded when the state's schools naively back this doctrine to their pupils. Since close to half the population is Roman Catholic, fundamentalist, Lutheran, and Calvinist, it means that by implication their position is factional and partial whereas the state's position is neutral and impartial. Rushdoony, "The State," 44.

Rushdoony's claim that what is presented as neutral and impartial actually masks particular interests and partisanship makes him a strange bedfellow with the Marxist concept of ideology, which holds that the ruling ideas of the age are the ideas of the ruling class. Whereas the ruling class for Marx was always defined in economic or material terms, for Rushdoony it would always be defined in religious terms.

[108] Julie Ingersoll has argued "that a small group within fundamentalism known as Christian Reconstructionists played an important but unexplored part of the rise of the Christian Right and that, though unacknowledged, the influence of this group continues today. The published works of the Reconstructionists influenced the leaders of the Christian Right. . . . The ideas of Reconstructionists helped to frame the worldview of the Christian Right, and helped weave together the issues that have dominated the Christian Right's political agenda while grounding those issues in a specific understanding of the family." "Mobilizing Evangelicals: Christian Reconstructionism and the Roots of the Religious Right," in *Evangelicals and Democracy in America*, Vol. 2: *Religion and Politics*, ed. Steven Brint and Jean Reith Schroedel (New York: Russell Sage, 2009), chap. 6, 179–208, 179. She continues, "Briefly, Christian Reconstructionism is a label for a small group of conservative Christians who want to reconstruct society to conform to biblical law: they wish, that is, to build a theocracy. Many consider Rousas John Rushdoony the father of this movement."

or the religious and the secular; and the intelligibility of the concept of governmental neutrality. The logic of the radical version of the Christian Right position seems to be this: (1) any political system—any government and legal system—by its very nature is the institutionalization of certain values and beliefs; (2) values and beliefs are necessarily and inescapably religious in nature; thus (3) any political system by its very nature is the institutionalization of religion. One question that arises immediately is the connection between religion and belief presupposed by the Christian Right: religion is certainly a form of belief, but is belief necessarily religious? There is at least the hint of inconsistency in the fact that Whitehead and Conlan, for example, appear to criticize what they consider the Supreme Court's transmutation of religion into belief, yet use the claim that Secular Humanism is a belief to argue that it is a religion.[109] If the transmutation of religion into belief is what led to the disestablishment of (Protestant) Christianity and is to be regretted and, if possible, reversed, then it would seem that a distinction between religion and belief would allow space for belief that is not religious, and thus a political system as the institutionalization of nonreligious belief. The Christian Right argument, in order words, might well be parasitic on a premise it decries.

A second question presents itself: how does the Christian Right claim, as we have seen it in Schaeffer, Whitehead and Conlan, and Rushdoony, that government cannot be neutral vis-à-vis religion square with the idea they and other mainstream accommodationists advance of governmental neutrality among (Christian) religions? If governmental neutrality is indeed possible between one religion and another, then there would seem to be at least a prima facie case to be made that such neutrality is possible between religion and nonreligion—thus weakening if not undermining a core element of the Christian Right critique. On the other hand, if governmental neutrality is in fact not possible, as our representative writers have insisted, then that would seem to prove too much: not only would government have to be seen to be the institutionalization of Christianity, but also, and necessarily, government would have to be seen to be the institutionalization of a particular denomination of Christianity. The slippery slope here is that not only would we have to say that American government is Christian as distinct from non-Christian, but Protestant as

[109] There is hint here of the fallacy of the undistributed middle: "A fallacy of the form 'All A are B. All C are B. Therefore, all A are C.' Consider: All elms are trees. All oaks are trees. Therefore, all elms are oaks" (http://www.philosophicalsociety.com/Logical%20Fallacies.htm#affirm-consequent, retrieved 8-1-10). In this case, the reasoning seems to be: religion is a belief system; X is a belief system; therefore, X is religion.

distinct from Catholic or Greek Orthodox, and one Protestant faith tradition as opposed to all the others.

Still, what about the argument that all values are essentially religious in nature? That argument is what constitutes the radical character of the Christian Right's approach to religion-clause issues. If Rushdoony is correct in his argument, then the question arises, what remains of substance to the Establishment Clause, not to mention the Free Exercise Clause? The claim that the state is an establishment of religion makes the phrase "Congress shall make no law respecting an establishment of religion" either meaningless or at least an impossible mandate. The religion clauses, by singling out religion, necessarily suggest that there are things that are *not* religion (that is what it means to single out something); they make sense only on that assumption, without which the clauses would be unnecessary, incoherent in purpose, or redundant. In conventional Establishment Clause jurisprudence we do not ordinarily take the phrase "Congress shall make no law respecting an establishment of religion" to mean "Congress shall make no law respecting an establishment of a political theory" or "Congress shall make no law respecting an establishment of a moral theory." Religion is simply different, if not unique. Therefore, the claim that government's position of neutrality regarding religious commitments is itself a religious commitment becomes the claim that religion is "in" everything, or that everything is at bottom religious, and thus undermines the intelligibility of the religion clauses by making the Establishment Clause a self-refuting mandate.

The radicalization of Establishment Clause jurisprudence, then, is inconsistent with the religion clauses themselves. To accept the radical formulation of the essential Establishment Clause question—Can a political-legal order be truly neutral regarding religion, religious beliefs and values, and religious practices, or does any political-legal order always, necessarily, inescapably constitute the establishment of religious beliefs and values?—makes the religion clauses meaningless. To be sure, those who wrote and ratified the First Amendment could have been wrong in their assumptions, but the presence of the Establishment Clause in that amendment suggests that they themselves did not take it to be meaningless or an impossible mandate. As much as those who radicalize Establishment Clause jurisprudence might claim to be interpreting the clause properly and accurately, their quarrel is not with other interpretations of the clause but in fact with the very existence of that clause. Consequently, if we wish to continue to regard the religion clauses as meaningful, we must reject the radicalization of Establishment Clause jurisprudence.

Chapter 4

Orthodoxy and Neutrality

In radicalizing conventional Establishment Clause jurisprudence, the Christian Right certainly pursues a distinct religio-political agenda of a return to what they consider traditional family values accompanied and reinforced by an increased public role for religion.[1] At the same time, there is, however, a less distinctly political, more academic version of the argument that any political order necessarily and inevitably embodies some set of religious beliefs and values. In this version, a political order may not be a hard theocracy, but it will always be, in the terms I have suggested here, at least a soft theocracy. That is, any concept of religious freedom will always be itself a religious rather than "neutral" conception. The prime examples of this position are to be found in the work of two law professors, Stephen Feldman and Steven Smith, that appeared, coincidentally in the mid-1990s. The purpose of this chapter is to offer an exploration and analysis of their work, both interesting in their own

[1] See, e.g., the mission statement of the Family Research Council: "Family Research Council (FRC) champions marriage and family as the foundation of civilization, the seedbed of virtue, and the wellspring of society. FRC shapes public debate and formulates public policy that values human life and upholds the institutions of marriage and the family. Believing that God is the author of life, liberty, and the family, FRC promotes the Judeo-Christian worldview as the basis for a just, free, and stable society" (http://www.frc.org/mission-statement, retrieved 9-2-10). However, it is important to note that many Christian conservatives advocate simply an accommodationist reading of the Establishment Clause rather than the more radical approach of Rushdoony and others. For the latter, see the Chalcedon Center, at http://chalcedon.edu/. Still politics, famously, makes strange bedfellows, and religious politics makes even stranger bedfellows. Consider, for example, the confluence of interest between the late Rev. Jerry Falwell and the feminist group Women Against Pornography (see "Sexes: Women's War on Porn," *Time*, August 27, 1979 [http://www.time.com/time/magazine/article/0,9171,920580,00.html, retrieved 9-1-10]).

right but especially the latter's, that will help to set the stage for what I will argue is the principle behind the religion clauses in general and the Establishment Clause in particular.

In *Please Don't Wish Me a Merry Christmas*, Stephen Feldman "approach[es] the question of power in society from a postmodern perspective."[2] The dominant story of separation of church and state, he writes, maintains that "the separation of church and state stands as a constitutional principle that promotes democracy and equally protects the religious freedom of all Americans, especially religious outgroups, including Jews."[3] Like our Christian Right authors, however, Feldman argues against the presumption of neutrality: "Contrary to the dominant story, the separation of church and state stands, to a great extent, as a political and religious development that manifests and reinforces Christian domination in American society."[4] Far from serving the needs of all religious groups equally, he states, "the constitutional principle of the separation of church and state [is] a highly complex social phenomenon that flows primarily from and helps reproduce the Christian domination of American society and culture."[5] Feldman focuses specifically on the principle's effect on Jews:

> All in all, the religion clauses of the first amendment looked radically different when viewed from the position of a religious outgroup, such as the Jews, instead of from the viewpoint of the Protestant majority. From the Protestant perspective, on the one hand, the free exercise clause protected the individual faculty—conscience—needed for a meaningful religious (Christian) experience, and the establishment clause protected against the traditional nemesis (in England) of Protestant freedom of conscience—the national established churches. From the Jewish standpoint, on the other hand, the religion clauses failed either to protect the central component of orthodox Judaism or to confront the traditional hazards to Jewish life. The orthodox Jew must follow the mitzvot (which translates as commandments, laws, or good deeds) of the Torah because, with the ethical, social, and ritual injunctions of the mitzvot, God (supposedly) has specified a comprehensive way and content for human fulfillment in this world. But freedom of conscience is primarily an orientation toward other-worldly Christian salvation; hence freedom of conscience, as protected by the free exercise clause, is a Protestant concept that is largely unrelated to a Jewish understanding of a religious life.[6]

[2] Stephen M. Feldman, *Please Don't Wish Me a Merry Christmas* (New York: New York University Press, 1997), 5.

[3] Feldman, *Please Don't Wish*, 4.

[4] Feldman, *Please Don't Wish*, 5.

[5] Feldman, *Please Don't Wish*, 9.

[6] Feldman, *Please Don't Wish*, 169, footnote omitted.

The First Amendment, then, as Feldman sees it, simply reinforces the de facto establishment of Protestant Christianity. The belief-practice distinction so central to religion-clause jurisprudence, according to which government may regulate practice but never belief,[7] is for Feldman an essentially Christian distinction. Our very concept of religious freedom, in his view, is an essentially Christian concept. Indeed, whereas the Christian Right argues that the phrase "separation of church and state" does not appear in the Constitution, based upon their belief that separation of church and state would undermine the essentially Christian character of the American political-legal order, Feldman argues that the separation of church and state actually produces and maintains the essentially Christian character of the American political-legal order. As he summarizes his view,

> [T]he free exercise and establishment clauses were intended primarily to reaffirm federal protection of the religious and political well-being of Protestants and their City Upon a Hill (the United States). Any benefit that flowed to non-Protestant religions was merely incidental to the protection of Protestantism; religious toleration of outgroups was, for the most part, a by-product of the predominant thrust of the religion clauses. As Joseph Story, a constitutional scholar and Supreme Court justice, observed early in the nineteenth century, the first amendment was not intended to countenance or advance no-Christian religions such as Judaism.[8]

The irony of the Christian Right critique, then, is that authors such as Schaeffer, Whitehead and Conlan, and Rushdoony on the right agree with Feldman on the left that the United States is an essentially Christian nation with an essentially Christian constitutional and political system. The principal differences between the two camps are two: one is that where Schaeffer, Whitehead and Conlan, and Rushdoony praise this "fact," Feldman laments it, and the second is that where Schaeffer, Whitehead and Conlan, and Rushdoony see modern Supreme Court decisions as disestablishing America's Protestant hegemony, Feldman sees those same decisions as maintaining and reinforcing that hegemony.

Where Feldman sees religion-clause jurisprudence as governed by a Christian hegemony that renders it coherent, Steven Smith writes against the background of the dissatisfaction with the fragmentation of religious-clause doctrine. In the light of such free-exercise decisions as

[7] Laws are made for the government of actions, and while they cannot interfere with mere religious belief and opinions, they may with practices. *Reynolds v. United States*, 98 U.S. 145 (1878), at 166.

[8] Feldman, *Please Don't Wish*, 167, footnotes omitted.

Employment Division v. Smith[9] and such establishment-clause decisions as *Lee v. Weisman*,[10] many commentators have complained that contemporary religion-clause jurisprudence is at best tangled and confusing, and at worst incoherent. As Justice Antonin Scalia has argued, "Our Religion Clause jurisprudence has become bedeviled (so to speak) by reliance on formulaic abstractions that are not derived from, but positively conflict with, our long-accepted constitutional traditions."[11] Smith puts forth an interesting and provocative argument questioning the entire enterprise of constructing a coherent and principled theory of the religion clauses. In *Foreordained Failure* he writes, "The entire body of modern constitutional discourse on the subject of religious freedom, I came to believe, was founded on empty premises and false assumptions," in that "virtually the whole of modern religion clause discourse is misconceived in its very foundations."[12] Smith argues that neither an originalist nor what he calls a theoretical approach will yield an acceptable general principle of religious freedom. I wish to examine critically this conceptualization of the problem in contemporary religion-clause jurisprudence. Specifically, at the risk of sounding too cute by half, I want to say that Smith makes a theoretical argument against theory and in favor of prudentialism, whereas I want to make a prudentialist argument against prudentialism and in favor of theory.

The basic premise that Smith challenges is the very notion that there is a single general or overarching principle of religious freedom. He writes, "Judges and constitutional scholars have been asking, in one form or another, something like the following question: 'What is the meaning and scope of the principle of religious freedom embodied in the Constitution?' "[13] This, argues Smith, is the wrong question. The reason judges and scholars have failed to answer this question successfully, he maintains, is not that they have somehow given erroneous answers to a proper question, but rather that they have presumed that such a question has a univocal answer:

[9] Employment Division, *Oregon Department of Human Resources v. Smith*, 494 U.S. 872 (1990).

[10] *Lee v. Weisman*, 505 U.S. 577 (1992).

[11] *Lee v. Weisman*, at 644 (dissenting). Referring in *Edwards v. Aguillard*, 482 U.S. 578 (1987), at 639 to what he calls "our embarrassing Establishment Clause jurisprudence," Scalia says of the "purpose" prong of the *Lemon* test, "Our cases interpreting and applying the purpose test have made such a maze of the Establishment Clause that even the most conscientious governmental officials can only guess what motives will be held unconstitutional." *Edwards*, at 636.

[12] Steven D. Smith, *Foreordained Failure: The Quest for a Constitutional Principle of Religious Freedom* (New York: Oxford University Press, 1995), vi.

[13] Smith, *Foreordained Failure*, 6.

> It may be that the source of our present frustrations in the area of religious freedom is not that judges and scholars have given careless answers, but rather than they have asked wrong questions. If so, then no amount of rethinking, however meticulous or energetic, is likely to improve the situation as long as we insist on pressing the same bad questions.[14]

In other words, according to Smith, we have been unable successfully to uncover a single, overarching principle of religious freedom not because we have engaged in the task incompetently, but rather because we have been looking for what is not there. That is, "One consequence of the question [as to the meaning a scope of the principle of religious freedom embodied in the Constitution] is that by quietly suggesting that religious freedom is something that can be reduced to or presented in the form of a 'principle,' the question may tempt us to think of religious freedom as if it were some singular ideal or state of affairs."[15] The plurality of opinions as to the meaning of religious freedom, Smith argues, does not indicate error, as would a plurality of opinions as to the sum of 2 and 2 in a base-10 system, but rather reflects the fact that there is indeed no single, overarching meaning of the concept. This is how we deal with the incongruity of views of religious freedom:

> We might simply relinquish the singular conception of religious freedom and admit that there are potentially many versions of religious freedom. To put it differently, we might acknowledge that there is no single of self-subsisting "principle" of religious freedom; there is only a host of individuals with a host of different opinions and notions about how much and what kind of scope government ought to give to the exercise of religious beliefs and practices.[16]

From this perspective, then, we give up any notion of a Platonist "essence" of religious freedom, leaving us with the ongoing debate we already have. Thus, Smith argues,

> In short, the pluralistic approach allows us to say much of what we already say about religious freedom but denies any self-subsisting status to "the principle" of religious freedom. There is, consequently, no unitary principle of religious freedom; rather there are numerous versions of religious freedom, which may be more or less attractive and defensible.[17]

[14] Smith, *Foreordained Failure*, 5.
[15] Smith, *Foreordained Failure*, 6.
[16] Smith, *Foreordained Failure*, 11.
[17] Smith, *Foreordained Failure*, 12.

There are, then, no right or wrong conceptions of religious freedom. Rather, there are, depending upon the circumstances, simply more or less persuasive conceptions of religious freedom.

This is the point at which Smith arrives. The argument by which he gets there, in brief, is that the two standard interpretive approaches by which we normally seek to answer the question as to meaning of the principle of religious freedom embodied in the Constitution do not and cannot provide that answer. We normally assume, Smith maintains, that a principle of religious freedom can be grounded either in historical fact or in abstract theory. The former approach is, of course, originalism: "The 'originalist' approach holds that the Constitution's version of religious freedom is the one that its framers and ratifiers intended to adopt."[18] The problem with originalism, according to Smith, is not that we face any empirical or historiographical difficulties in determining what it was that the framers and ratifiers thought they were doing. Rather,

> I maintain that we *can* ascertain the probably original meaning of those clauses, and when we do we also discover, paradoxically, that the religion clauses have nothing of substance to say on questions of religious freedom. The original meaning supplies us neither with concrete answers to particular legal questions nor with any general principle, norm, value, or theory that might serve as a basis for working out such answers.[19]

The reason the religion clauses have nothing of substance to say about the meaning of religious freedom, Smith argues, is that they "were purely jurisdictional in nature; they did not adopt any substantive right or principle of religious freedom."[20] Putting the matter simply, Smith writes, "The religion clauses, as understood by those who drafted, proposed, and ratified them, were an exercise in federalism."[21]

Smith sets out this jurisdictional argument by drawing a helpfully clear distinction between two types of questions we can ask about the meaning of religious freedom. The first is the substantive question:

> One kind of question may be thought of as first-order or substantive: This was the question of the proper relation between government and religion. Should government establish one religion as the official state religion? Should the state subsidize a religion? Should it support all religions, or at least all Protestant religions, on equal terms? Should religious heresy or blasphemy be punished? Should conventional religious practices—Sabbath observance, for example—be enforced by law?[22]

[18] Smith, *Foreordained Failure*, 14.
[19] Smith, *Foreordained Failure*, 16, emphasis in original.
[20] Smith, *Foreordained Failure*, 16.
[21] Smith, *Foreordained Failure*, 18.
[22] Smith, *Foreordained Failure*, 19.

This is ordinarily what we are concerned to discuss when we address the problem of religious freedom. The second type of question, however, is jurisdictional: "A second-order question was one of governmental organization, or of the allocation of jurisdiction. Which level of government, state or national, should be responsible for addressing the first-order question?"[23] The relevant historical context for these questions, Smith maintains, was an emerging dispute during the Founding period between two positions on the relation between religion and government. "The first position," he writes, "and the one supported by received wisdom and tradition, can be described in two claims or propositions. First, religion is essential to a stable social and political order. Second, governmental support is needed to maintain this essential religious foundation."[24] In contrast to this traditional position, others held what Smith calls a voluntarist position:

> This view accepted the first but not the second of the claims associated with the traditional position; it agreed that a religious foundation was vital to the political and social order, but it insisted that governmental support was not essential, and indeed might well be harmful, to the cause of religion.[25]

Smith's argument is that the conflicting sides here essentially decided not to decide their dispute; they

> chose in effect to avoid answering the first-order question by leaving it to the states. The religion clauses kept the national government out of religion not because governmental support for religion was generally regarded as improper—*that* was precisely the issue on which the traditional and voluntarist positions divided—but rather because the religion question was within the jurisdiction of the states.[26]

The implication of this jurisdictional point for the originalist approach to the meaning of the religion clauses is, from Smith's perspective, profound. It empties them of substantive content:

> If we ask, therefore, what principle or theory of religious liberty the framers and ratifiers of the religion clauses adopted, the most accurate answer is "None." They consciously chose not to answer the religion question, and they were able for the most part to avoid it (or at least thought they were) because of the way in which they answered the jurisdiction question—that is, by assigning the religious question to the states. This observation suggests that it is futile to try to extrapolate or reconstruct a principle or theory

[23] Smith, *Foreordained Failure*, 19.
[24] Smith, *Foreordained Failure*, 19.
[25] Smith, *Foreordained Failure*, 20.
[26] Smith, *Foreordained Failure*, 21, emphasis in original.

> of religious liberty from the original meaning of the religion clauses. Those clauses quite simply were not based on any such principle or theory.[27]

The originalist approach to the question as to meaning of the principle of religious freedom embodied in the Constitution, Smith concludes, provides no substantive answer. It tells us only that the framers and ratifiers "punted" the problem to the states.

The second interpretive approach to the meaning of the principle of religious freedom embodied in the Constitution is ordinarily conceptualized as nonoriginalism, although Smith never refers to it that way:

> The theoretical approach, by contrast, does not assume that the Constitution's version of religious freedom was fixed by human intentions at the time of the First Amendment's enactment. Instead, this approach seeks to articulate the best, or the most plausible, or the most theoretically attractive version of religious freedom.[28]

Here is where we find Smith's interesting and provocative argument about the enterprise of constructing a coherent and principled theory of the religion clauses, for, in a nutshell, he maintains that "no adequate theory or principle of religious freedom is possible."[29] The reason for this conclusion is his argument that since a principle of religious freedom depends upon the possibility of theoretical neutrality and such theoretical neutrality is impossible, so too is a principle of religious freedom. The problem, he believes, is that any theory necessarily loads the dice:

> Any effort to articulate a theory of religious freedom . . . founders on a basic theoretical conundrum. The function of a theory of religious freedom is to mediate among a variety of competing religious and secular positions and interests, or to explain how government ought to deal with these competing positions and interests. To perform that function, however, the theory will tacitly but inevitably privilege, or prefer in advance, one of those positions while rejecting or discounting others. But a theory that privileges one of the competing positions and rejects others a priori is not truly a theory of religious freedom at all—or, at least, it is not the sort of theory that modern proponents of religious freedom have sought to develop.[30]

To explain this, Smith starts with the claim that "any account of religious freedom will necessarily depend upon—and hence will stand or fall along with—more basic background beliefs concerning matters of religion and

[27] Smith, *Foreordained Failure*, 21.
[28] Smith, *Foreordained Failure*, 14.
[29] Smith, *Foreordained Failure*, 61.
[30] Smith, *Foreordained Failure*, 63.

theology, the proper role of government, and 'human nature.'"[31] Thus, at length,

> The problem, simply put, is that theories of religious freedom seek to reconcile or to mediate among competing religious and secular positions within a society, but those competing positions disagree about the very background beliefs on which a theory of religious freedom must rest. One religion will maintain beliefs about theology, government, and human nature that may support a particular version of religious freedom. A different religion or a secular viewpoint will support different background beliefs that logically generate different views or theories of religious freedom. In adopting a theory or religious freedom that is consistent with some background beliefs but not with others, therefore, government (or the judge or the legal scholar) must adopt, or privilege, one of the competing secular or religious positions. Yet this adopting or preferring of one religious or secular position over its competitors is precisely what modern theories of religious freedom seek to avoid. Hence, theories of religious freedom can function only by implicitly betraying their own objective.[32]

Since any theory necessarily presupposes some particular view or perspective, Smith thus argues that particular view or perspective will occupy a preferred position. Hence, we cannot avoid what he calls the "preferred position" approach to theorizing.

The preferred position, then, necessarily becomes the de facto establishment that serves as the baseline for the range of possible religious freedom. In Smith's words,

> Indeed, a theory derived from the preferred position might as accurately be called a theory of "official orthodoxy" or of religious or secular "establishment." The theory in essence asserts (or assumes) that government should operate in accordance with the standards and values of some religious or secular orthodoxy and should grant dissenters the freedom to deviate from the orthodoxy only insofar as the orthodoxy itself allows.[33]

The notion of orthodoxy, however, contradicts the notion of neutrality at the root of our quest for a principle of religious freedom:

> The theorist of religious freedom, it seems, must ground her theory in premises or background beliefs compatible with one (or perhaps, insofar as they sometimes happen to converge, some) of the competing religious or secular positions whose claims a theory of religious freedom seeks to mediate. The theorist in effect adopts one among the competing positions and then grants

[31] Smith, *Foreordained Failure*, 63.
[32] Smith, *Foreordained Failure*, 68.
[33] Smith, *Foreordained Failure*, 74.

> other faiths only the freedom that the preferred position permits. Whether such a theory deserves to be called a theory of religious freedom at all seems doubtful, and it is certain that modern judges and theorists have aspired to do much more.
>
> They have aspired, more specifically, to develop a theory that is "neutral" as among competing religious and secular positions—neutral, as the Supreme Court has repeatedly put it, both among religious and between religion and nonreligion. The foregoing discussion is in fact an argument against the possibility of a "neutral" theory.[34]

The emphasis on neutrality, Smith notes, "can be understood as an effort to avoid or transcend the kind of theorizing that adopts or prefers in advance one of the competing religious or secular positions within a community and then allows other positions only as much freedom as the preferred position prescribes."[35] Nevertheless, he insists that neutrality is a chimera:

> A genuine theory of religious neutrality . . . would of necessity be a "neutral" theory in the sense that it would not begin by adopting or favoring one of the competing religious or secular positions. Unfortunately, since every theory of religious freedom depends on background beliefs that will be derived from and compatible with one or some of those positions but not others, this sort of neutral theory also appears to be unattainable.[36]

There is, consequently, no free-floating set of background beliefs, no value-free, pretheoretical commitments on which we could ground a neutral theory. Thus, Smith concludes,

> Descriptions of reality are always undertaken from a point within reality. In the same way, theories of religious freedom are always offered from the viewpoint of one of the competing positions that generate the need for such a theory; there is no neutral vantage point that can permit the theorist or judge to transcend these competing positions. Hence, insofar as a genuine and satisfactory theory of religious freedom would need to be "neutral" in this sense, rather than one that privileges one of the competing positions from the outset, a theory of religious freedom is as illusory as the ideal of neutrality it seeks to embody.[37]

His argument, finally, is that since a theory of religious freedom must be neutral, the impossibility of neutrality implies the impossibility of a

[34] Smith, *Foreordained Failure*, 74–75.
[35] Smith, *Foreordained Failure*, 77.
[36] Smith, *Foreordained Failure*, 77–78.
[37] Smith, *Foreordained Failure*, 97.

theory of religious freedom. Hence, "no adequate theory or principle of religious freedom is possible."[38]

What would Smith have us do, then, in the absence of a theory of religious freedom? While he does not advance a fully developed argument here, he does point us in two directions as worthy of our consideration. First, he suggests the possibility that, since the driving force behind the concern for a theory of religious freedom has been the need for a principle to govern the practice of judicial review, one could argue either (1) that judicial review might not have to be a principled exercise in the way we have supposed for so long or (2) that judicial review, principled or not, might not be the best way to protect religious freedom. We should, instead, entrust the protection of religious freedom to the political process:

> The curtailment of judicial review under the religion clauses would not mean, of course, that religious freedom would disappear from the public agenda. The imposing presence of a judicial overseer may have lulled us into forgetting that religious freedom is properly the concern of citizens and governmental institutions generally. To be sure, leaving religious freedom to the political process has its risks. Most obviously, unpopular religious minorities may have little power in the political process. On the other hand, it is arguable that the political process is more responsive to religious freedom concerns than the courts have been.[39]

This move, of course, points us toward Justice Scalia's opinion in *Smith*:

> It may fairly be said that leaving accommodation to the political process will place at a relative disadvantage those religious practices that are not widely engaged in; but that unavoidable consequence of democratic government must be preferred to a system in which each conscience is a law unto itself or in which judges weigh the social importance of all laws against the centrality of all religious beliefs.[40]

This amounts to a Madisonian reliance on the multiplicity of factions described in Federalist 10, such that there is no natural majority in the country but an "artificial" majority which is a coalition of minorities. However, Madison's theory, on which Scalia and, evidently, Smith rely works under two conditions that seem to be absent when it comes to religion: (1) the loser has to agree to lose, in the sense that the loser sees no vital interest at stake, yet vital interests are precisely at stake in the case of

[38] Smith, *Foreordained Failure*, 61.

[39] Smith, *Foreordained Failure*, 126.

[40] Employment Division, *Oregon Department of Human Resources v. Smith*, 494 U.S. 872 (1990) at 890.

something as personal, strong, and all-encompassing as religion; and (2) there are no discrete and insular minorities—i.e., groups who are almost never part of a majority coalition and are thus condemned to be permanently among the losers—and yet so many of our religious-freedom cases arose due to the concerns of such minorities.[41]

The second direction in which Smith points us in the absence of a theory of religious freedom is more directly of interest here. He argues, as we have seen, that a substantive conception of religious freedom is a state rather than federal matter, and then argues that there can be no theory or principle of religious freedom that a state could adopt.[42] Given the unavailability of a (macro-level) theory of religious freedom, we are left with a micro-level prudentialism. As Smith states the point, "[R]eligious freedom, like many other matters of both personal and political concern, is inherently a prudential matter that cannot plausibly be confined to or regulated by 'theory.'"[43] The relationship between government and religion, he says, is governed "by judgments based on shifting conditions and concerns, and these judgments cannot sensibly be reduced to any governing principle or domesticated under the roof of any theory."[44] Revealingly, to illustrate his conception of what he considers to be theory-free prudentialism, Smith chooses the example of deciding what movie to go see as a way of understanding that we make decisions and have reasons without having a theory. When giving reasons why you go to see one movie as opposed to another, your companion

> might suggest that your reasons express an unarticulated, perhaps subconscious "theory" of movie selection. But this characterization is dubious because there is no basis to assume that your reasons add up to or reflect any coherent pattern or method for choosing movies. Some of your reasons ("Oh, I just felt like it") seem too specific, and too whimsical, to represent any general theory. . . . Other reasons *might* be generalizable, but there is no assurance that this is the case.[45]

Such a model of decision making, Smith suggests, applies as well to the problems we encounter in answering questions about religious freedom:

[41] Most famously, the Jehovah's Witnesses in *Murdock v. Pennsylvania*, 319 U.S. 105 (1943), and *West Virginia State Board of Education v. Barnette*, 319 U.S. 624 (1943) (overruling *Minersville School District v. Gobitis*, 310 U.S. 586 [1940]).

[42] This is similar, I would suggest without further detail here, to the Court's commerce-clause position in the 1880–1930 period that economic regulation (e.g., of monopoly) is a state matter, and then its Due Process position at the time that the states could not engage in such regulation either.

[43] Smith, *Foreordained Failure*, 16.

[44] Smith, *Foreordained Failure*, 60.

[45] Smith, *Foreordained Failure*, 58, emphasis in original.

> Upon reflection, it seems that most of the decisions we make are more like movie selections than like "theory"-driven decisions. There is no clearly correct answer, and yet We make a choice. We may think and give reasons. . . . We may even invoke general guidelines or maxims that might be loosely described as "principles," but we do not assume that these guidelines fit nicely together into any complete and internally consistent framework from which we can deduce right answers. In short, our choices do not depend on anything resembling a "theory"—unless, that is, the term is stretched so far as to lose its meaning.[46]

This argument is problematic, however. We choose what movie to go see on the basis of various whims, desires, tastes, and prejudices because we do not *have* to choose on a principled basis. Smith says, "[M]any of our activities and practices are not, and perhaps could not be, governed by any theory."[47] But to say "many" is not to say "all," especially in an area like religious freedom in which courts are required to choose on a principled basis, wherever one sees the source of principle to lie. He states that "most of our personal decisions—selecting a movie, choosing a career, deciding whether to marry or have children—do not seem to lend themselves to resolution through the application of any theory. The same is true for many, perhaps most, political decisions."[48] But, again, "many" and "most" are not "all," yet Smith moves seamlessly to the claim that "religious freedom is likewise, for better or worse, a prudential matter."[49]

Now, legislatures may indeed choose prudentially, but may courts? We can check legislators' judgments by voting them out of office. How other than by principle and theory do we check judges? We have seen that Smith suggests the courts may well not be the best place to resolve our problems of religious freedom, yet he still indicates a balancing role for courts:

> Whether, how, and to what extent religious freedom should be respected might depend on a context-specific balancing of competing interests, and that balancing might not be reducible to any consistent theory or general principle—except, of course, for the "principle" of doing whatever is best under the circumstances.[50]

Yet consider the questions this position raises but leaves unaddressed. First, what interests count as competing and thus worthy of balancing?

[46] Smith, *Foreordained Failure*, 58.
[47] Smith, *Foreordained Failure*, 58.
[48] Smith, *Foreordained Failure*, 60.
[49] Smith, *Foreordained Failure*, 60.
[50] Smith, *Foreordained Failure*, 100.

Second, what counts as "best" in a given context? Third, the very notion of balancing is not uncontroversial and requires some theory or principle to establish its legitimacy. Finally, even a prudential approach would have to employ, however tacitly, a theory of what constitutes "religion" in order to identify when a religious issue arises. It would appear that theory, for all of Smith's persuasiveness, sneaks in through the back door.

Smith's concern, nevertheless, is that the theory road leads inexorably to a dead end. The immovable obstacle, once again, is the problem of neutrality. Consider this important passage:

> The notion of neutrality holds that government should be impartial toward, and should treat equally, all religious beliefs, neither privileging nor disfavoring any set of beliefs. Consequently, the demand for neutrality calls for the relationship between government and religion to be determined without privileging or adopting any of the competing religious and secular positions within the culture. But this aspiration is not merely unrealistic or difficult to attain *in practice*; upon reflection, the aspiration is scarcely intelligible. How *could* a regime or theory regulating the relations between government and religion be elaborated and defended except on the basis of beliefs and values of one or more of the competing religious and secular positions within the culture.[51]

Note that in this passage, as in others cited above, Smith tacitly asserts an equivalence between the two concepts in the phrase "competing religious and secular positions." He appears to suggest that a belief system is a belief system, and since a secular position is a belief system, it as such a belief system is epistemologically on the same footing as a religious position and hence has no special status as neutral. Yet this is to treat the secular as a version of atheism, which arguably is a kind of "antireligion," but his suggestion implies that agnosticism, perhaps more the essence of secularism than is atheism, is not a separate and distinct position. He runs together the claim that the state should be agnostic about religious values and the claim that the state should be atheistic about religious values, implying the proposition that the state cannot not take a position on the truth of religious beliefs. Smith chooses not to address the work of John Rawls, which is his prerogative, but Rawls tries to address these issues and, especially, the seeming equivalence between the secular and the religious by means of the distinction he draws in *Political Liberalism* between political and comprehensive doctrines.[52] This is not the place for a lengthy treatment of the extended and complex set of arguments Rawls presents there, but a few relevant points are worth noting here.

[51] Smith, *Foreordained Failure*, 94, emphasis in original.

[52] John Rawls, *Political Liberalism* (New York: Columbia University Press, 1996).

Put simply, Rawls wants to argue, as against the equivalence tacitly asserted by Smith, that there is a qualitative or categorical distinction between religious belief systems and what he calls political liberalism. The former, along with certain forms of liberalism, are what he calls comprehensive doctrines, worldviews, or belief systems that, in my own terms, are concerned with and seek to address absolute and ultimate questions. In a diverse society such as ours we face an ineradicable pluralism of such worldviews, none of which can predominate:

> Religious and philosophical doctrines express views of the world and of our life with one another, severally and collectively, as a whole. Our individual and associative points of view, intellectual affinities, and affective attachments, are too diverse, especially in a free society, to enable those doctrines to serve as the basis of lasting and reasoned political agreement. Different conceptions of the world can reasonably be elaborated from different standpoints and diversity arises in part from our distinct perspectives.[53]

Political liberalism, by contrast, recognizes this "reasonable pluralism" and seeks to provide some way in which adherents of these diverse and often conflicting comprehensive doctrines can live together in the same society. Here is Rawls, at length:

> Political liberalism is not a form of Enlightenment liberalism, that is, a comprehensive liberal and often secular doctrine founded on reason and viewed as suitable for the modern age now that the religious authority of Christian ages is said to be no longer dominant. Political liberalism has no such aims. It takes for granted the fact of reasonable pluralism of comprehensive doctrines, where some of those doctrines are taken to be nonliberal and religious. The problem of political liberalism is to work out a political conception of political justice for a constitutional democratic regime that a plurality of reasonable doctrines, both religious and nonreligious, liberal and nonliberal, may freely endorse, and so freely live by and come to understand its virtues. Emphatically it does not aim to replace comprehensive doctrines, religious or nonreligious, but intends to be equally distinct from both and, it hopes, acceptable to both.[54]

Rawls' central claim, on which his case stands or falls, is that political liberalism is indeed equally distinct from both religious and nonreligious comprehensive doctrines. It "aims for a political conception of justice as a freestanding view. It offers no specific metaphysical or epistemological

[53] Rawls, *Political Liberalism*, 58.
[54] Rawls, *Political Liberalism*, xl.

doctrine beyond what is implied by the political conception itself."[55] Political liberalism thus offers a political—as opposed to a comprehensive—conception of justice that Rawls calls "freestanding,"[56] the features of which are

> first, that it is a moral conception worked out for a specific subject, namely, the basic structure of a constitutional democratic regime; second, that accepting the political conception does not presuppose accepting any particular comprehensive religious, philosophical, or moral doctrine; rather, the political conception presents itself as a reasonable conception for the basic structure alone; and third, that it is not formulated in terms of any comprehensive doctrine but in terms of certain fundamental ideas viewed as latent in the public political culture of a democratic society.[57]

To put this point more prosaically, imagine a street on which we find several houses. In one house the residents speak German; in another they speak English; in another they speak French; in still another the speak Chinese; in yet another they speak Spanish; and so forth. The question is, what does everyone speak at the block party? One answer is that everyone speaks the language, or a derivative of such a language, of one of the houses, for there is no other language to speak. Another answer, however, is that there is indeed a language distinct from and not derivative from the languages of all of the individual houses.

Where Smith's casual assertion of the identical epistemological status of religious and secular claims implicates the first answer, Rawls' purported distinction between political liberalism and comprehensive doctrines implicates the second.[58] "One of the deepest distinctions between conceptions of justice," Rawls says, "is between those that allow for a plurality of reasonable though opposing comprehensive doctrines each with its own conception of the good, and those that hold that there is but one such conception to be recognized by all citizens who are fully reasonable and rational."[59] Taking the former position, political liberalism "supposes

[55] Rawls, *Political Liberalism*, 10. Thus, in Rawlsian terms, the argument of the radical approach to Establishment Clause jurisprudence is that any political order necessarily embodies a comprehensive doctrine.

[56] At xliv Rawls states, "A political conception of justice is what I call freestanding . . . when it is not presented as derived from, or as part of, any comprehensive doctrine. Such a conception of justice in order to be a moral conception must contain its own intrinsic normative and moral ideal."

[57] Rawls, *Political Liberalism*, 175.

[58] "Secularism" as a philosophy would be, for Rawls, itself a comprehensive doctrine. If political liberalism is secular in some sense, then, it means it is in a sense different from that of a comprehensive doctrine. See chap. 6 *infra*.

[59] Rawls, *Political Liberalism*, 134.

that there are many conflicting reasonable comprehensive doctrines with their conceptions of the good, each compatible with the full rationality of human persons, so far as that can be ascertained with the resources of a political conception of justice."[60] Against that background, Rawls tries to argue, contrary to what Smith maintains, that there is no preferred position:

> We try, so far as we can, neither to assert nor to deny any particular comprehensive religious, philosophical, or moral view, or its associated theory of truth and the status of values. Since we assume each citizen to affirm some such view, we hope to make it possible for all to accept the political conception as true or reasonable from the standpoint of their own comprehensive view, whatever it may be.[61]

Yet, in fairness to Smith, we do indeed find a preferred position in Rawls, but Rawls maintains that such a preferred position—remember, the phrase is Smith's—is, because it is not a comprehensive doctrine, not the same as a preferred religious position. In Rawls' words,

> Even though political liberalism seeks common ground and is neutral in aim, it is important to emphasize that it may still affirm the superiority of certain forms of moral character and encourage certain moral virtues. Thus, justice as fairness includes an account of certain political virtues—the virtues of fair social cooperation such as the virtues of civility and tolerance, of reasonableness and the sense of fairness (IV:5-7). The crucial point is that admitting these virtues into a political conception does not lead to the perfectionist state of a comprehensive doctrine.[62]

The political conception of justice, in other words, is indeed a moral conception, but it is freestanding and remains distinct from any comprehensive doctrine.

> Thus, if a constitutional regime takes certain steps to strengthen the virtues of toleration and mutual trust, say by discouraging various kinds of religious and racial discrimination (in ways consistent with liberty of conscience and freedom of speech), it does not thereby become a perfectionist state of the kind found in Plato or Aristotle, nor does it establish a particular religion as in the Catholic and Protestant states of the early modern period. Rather, it is taking reasonable measures to strengthen the forms of thought and feeling that sustain fair social cooperation between its citizens regarded as free and

[60] Rawls, *Political Liberalism*, 135.
[61] Rawls, *Political Liberalism*, 150.
[62] Rawls, *Political Liberalism*, 194.

> equal. This is very different from the state's advancing a particular comprehensive doctrine in its own name.[63]

Again, a political conception of justice is political and not comprehensive, for Rawls, in that it does not and need not take a position on absolute and ultimate questions.

However, in Smith's favor we see Rawls noting that it is indeed not the case that "anything goes" under a political conception of justice. "The principles of any reasonable political conception must impose restrictions on permissible comprehensive views, and the basic institutions those principles require inevitably encourage some ways of life and discourage others, or even exclude them altogether."[64] More problematically, Rawls writes,

> Nevertheless, in affirming a political conception of justice we may eventually have to assert at least certain aspects of our own comprehensive religious or philosophical doctrine (by no means necessarily fully comprehensive). This will happen whenever some insists, for example, that certain questions are so fundamental that to insure their being rightly settled justifies religious strife. The religious salvation of those holding a particular religion, or indeed the salvation of a whole people, may be said to depend on it. At this point we may have no alternative but to deny this, or to imply its denial and hence to maintain the kind of thing we had hoped to avoid.[65]

I do not claim to grasp Rawls' argument in all of its subtlety, but it is difficult to avoid concluding from this passage that the political conception of justice may not be as fully freestanding as Rawls wants and needs to claim.[66] He at least appears to come perilously close here to softening that

[63] Rawls, *Political Liberalism*, 195.

[64] Rawls, *Political Liberalism*, 195.

[65] Rawls, *Political Liberalism*, 152.

[66] Rawls is certainly alert to this issue. At 190 he writes, "Historically one common theme of liberal thought is that the state must not favor any comprehensive doctrines and their associated conception of the good. But it is equally a common theme of critics of liberalism that it fails to do this and is, in fact, arbitrarily biased in favor of one or another form of individualism." His argument, nevertheless, is that there remains a fundamental distinction between the substantive conceptions of the good that we find in comprehensive doctrines and the substantive conception of the good that we find in political liberalism. The domain of the political, in other words, is sui generis.

For Rawls, being reasonable involves the idea of reciprocity—any particular comprehensive doctrine must extend to other comprehensive doctrines those rights that it claims for itself; not to do so would be unreasonable. Yet there are comprehensive doctrines that do not agree to disagree; but, for Rawls, not to be reasonable and agree to disagree is to reject the basic principle of democratic society, which is that every person has an equal right to his freedoms. Thus, in *Political Liberalism*, 152, Rawls either misspeaks or else undermines his whole case when he says that at such times we may

necessary hard-and-fast distinction between political liberalism and comprehensive doctrines. If that is indeed the case, then we would appear to be back at the theoretical dead end to which Smith wants to point.

Yet, curiously, there would seem to be at least one profound implication of the claim for the inescapability of preferred positions in matters of religious freedom, an implication about which Smith is silent. Recall this statement by Smith already noted earlier:

> Indeed, a theory derived from the preferred position might as accurately be called a theory of "official orthodoxy" or of religious or secular "establishment." The theory in essence asserts (or assumes) that government should operate in accordance with the standards and values of some religious or secular orthodoxy and should grant dissenters the freedom to deviate from the orthodoxy only insofar as the orthodoxy itself allows.[67]

As I noted, for Smith the preferred position necessarily becomes the de facto establishment that serves as the baseline for the range of possible religious freedom. For all that Smith advances for why theory is problematic, the question arises, does our constitutional system itself constitute an establishment of religion? That is, given his rejection of the possibility of neutrality as a matter of theory, is Smith thereby committed to the proposition that any political order is necessarily and unavoidably the establishment, the institutionalization, of a particular set of religious values? If so, then he will find himself in interesting company, in that he becomes committed, like Feldman and Rushdoony, to the proposition that the fundamental question regarding religion in America is not *whether* there should be an establishment of religion; rather, the question is always which religion will be the established religion.

Smith's argument against theory, then, appears to play into the positions of both the left and the right that any political order is necessarily and unavoidably the establishment or institutionalization of a particular set of religious values. Yet if a preferred position, in Smith's terms, is unavoidable, then could the preference for a secular establishment, one

---

have to recur to our own comprehensive doctrine, because core to his argument is the claim that political liberalism is a political, not comprehensive, liberalism. Society can legitimately constrain those who are not reasonable. It would be irrational for you to claim the right to impose your comprehensive doctrine if you have the power (a majority) because that licenses someone else to do that to you under other circumstances.

This goes back to the premise in the Declaration, that all men are created equal. If that is the basic premise of the polity, then everyone has an equal right to his or her freedoms, including religious freedom. To claim priority for your own religion, to deny someone that right, is to say that you have a right that he or she does not and thus is to violate this principle of equal rights and thus to deny the basic premise of our polity.

[67] Smith, *Foreordained Failure*, 74.

which would allow for a greater rather than lesser range of religious practices and values, itself provide the best prudential decision that we could advocate? For example, according to Kathleen Sullivan, "The bar against an establishment of religion entails the establishment of a civil order—the culture of liberal democracy—for resolving public moral disputes."[68] Such a culture, she admits, "may well function as a belief system with substantive content, rather than a neutral and transcendent arbiter among other belief systems."[69] Nevertheless, as we saw in the case of Rawls, she maintains that not all belief systems are *ex definitio* religious: "Even if the culture of liberal democracy is a belief system comparable to a religious faith in the way it structures knowledge, it simply does not follow that it is the equivalent of a religion for political and constitutional purposes."[70] Smith, indeed, is critical of Sullivan:

> Sullivan accurately describes the consequences of privileging a secular position; the question is whether this position can plausibly be characterized by the term *religious freedom*. How is Sullivan's secular establishment different with regard to religious freedom than religious establishments have been?[71]

The answer to his question is the prudential claim that a secular establishment would allow for the reasonable pluralism of competing comprehensive doctrines, in Rawls' terms, better than would a clearly religious establishment committed to certain absolute or ultimate truths.

The prudential question, in other words, is whether one side would allow room for another. For example, in the controversial matter of abortion, a prochoice regime allows someone to be personally prolife—as in the bumper sticker, "Against Abortion? Don't Have One"—whereas a prolife regime does not allow someone to be personally prochoice. To be sure, a prochoice regime does not allow the prolifer her or his goal of prohibiting abortion, and thus prevents her or him from realizing her or his particular values, but we have to maintain the common-sense distinction between aggression and self-defense here.[72] That is, if country X seeks to invade or otherwise take over country Y and bend it to its will, the resistance of country Y, while frustrating the aims of country X, counts as self-defense and ordinarily does not count as aggression itself against country X. Similarly, if Brown believes that everyone should subscribe to

[68] Kathleen M. Sullivan, "Religion and Democracy," in *The Bill of Rights in the Modern State*, ed. Geoffrey R. Stone and Richard A. Epstein (Chicago: University of Chicago Press, 1992), 198.

[69] Sullivan, "Religion and Democracy," 199.

[70] Sullivan, "Religion and Democracy," 200.

[71] Smith, *Foreordained Failure*, 74.

[72] These are not the most felicitous terms, but they will have to suffice for now.

his religious beliefs and that the government should officially establish his religion, the resistance of Black to this cannot count as Black's forcing *his* beliefs on Brown.

The very notion of religious freedom is based upon the concept of equality: you have a right to your religious beliefs that is equal to my right to my own religious beliefs. If this is indeed the case, then certainly the notion of religious freedom involves a commitment to a determinate value or set of values; it is not "neutral." However, in the case where Brown argues that his own religious beliefs entail the rejection of religious freedom for those who do not subscribe to his beliefs, his argument amounts to the claim that other-believers do not have an equal right to their beliefs; it would be a rejection of the concept of equality. Yet we would appear to be committed to saying that the necessary condition of Brown's making such an argument is the concept of equality he wants to reject. That is, Brown relies on an equality of right to hold his beliefs and argue for them insofar as he expects us to listen to his arguments, and that expectation presupposes *our* belief that Brown has a right to make them. If Brown were to argue that, given the truth of his beliefs, there can be no equality of right to one's beliefs because no one has the right to be wrong—error and sin have no rights—we would have to address such a claim in terms of the presupposition of equality of right that Brown necessarily makes when advancing his beliefs.

At bottom here, the question is, are all preferred positions equal? If we are left, as Smith suggests, with any theory constituting or relying upon a preferred position, then do we have good reasons for preferring one "preferred position" to all the others? That seems to be Sullivan's argument for the notion of a secular establishment, and it underlies my argument for secularism—or, more precisely, secularity[73]—in my claim that a secular political order allows for the widest range, if not for absolutely all, of possible religious beliefs and traditions. To be sure, no establishment, as Smith accurately explains, can allow room for any and all possible religious beliefs and practices, but we make a prudential decision in favor of an establishment that allows for the widest range of them. There may be no neutral theory of religious freedom, but it would follow from Smith's argument that we have to understand the United States to be the institutionalization of a particular theory of religious freedom that we could construct from a careful examination of our history and traditions. Smith appears to point in this direction at the end of his discussion:

> The framers did not enact into law any substantive version of religious freedom, nor does "reason" produce general or "principled" answers to questions

[73] See chap. 7 *infra*.

> about religious freedom. But it is at least imaginable that a full-blooded "historical" (not "originalist" in a positivist sense) approach might be more fruitful. Americans *have*, after all, developed and maintained beliefs about religious freedom; and even if those beliefs were not consciously enacted into positive law at the time of the founding, they have influenced and been embodied in our practices and traditions. Perhaps a historical approach could distill these different, developing beliefs and traditions into a usable law of religious freedom—or even, conceivably, into some modest but usable principles—that would be "constitutional" not in the standard positivist sense or in the theoretical or natural law sense, but rather in the sense of being "constitutive" of our political community.[74]

Understanding the United States to be the institutionalization of a particular theory of religious freedom that we could construct from a careful examination of our history and traditions suggests the possibility of a theoretical position between (1) those who want a purely neutral theory and (2) those who want some theory other than *our* institutionalized theory.

Perhaps there can be no pure theory in an abstract, Platonist sense (and Smith's critique of the possibility of a single principle of religious freedom is a critique of a Platonist approach to theory), but there can be a more pragmatic or prudential notion of theory as that which allows us to make sense of our experience. In other words, if a priori theory is impossible, an inductive theory is not. At the outset of his theoretical argument against the possibility of theory, Smith makes this important statement:

> In acknowledging a variety of versions of religious freedom, we can still insist that some opinions about the proper scope of religious freedom are more attractive, or more rationally defensible, than others. . . . This disagreement, however, merely entails the familiar sort of debate about whose arguments are stronger or whose position is more attractive or plausible. There is little to be gained by trying to frame the debate as one about who really perceives the true meaning of "the principle of religious freedom."[75]

I would suggest that this statement is not so much an encapsulation of a theoretical argument against theory as it is a prudential argument *for* theory. The guiding value, what gives this sense, is the commitment to religious freedom, not religion. If no principle of religious freedom is theoretically pure, we can at least posit that a principle of religious freedom that allows for a wider rather than a narrower range of religious freedom is to be preferred.

Despite the denial of the distinction between the religious and the secular, there is in fact a secular version of this argument in political

[74] Smith, *Foreordained Failure*, 123, emphasis in original.
[75] Smith, *Foreordained Failure*, 11.

theory. Rushdoony's claim that the state is an establishment of religion itself rests, as we saw in the preceding chapter, on two premises: first, that law is an expression of morality, that morality derives inescapably from religion, and that law therefore is an expression of religion; and second, that any political-legal order rests on and expresses a public orthodoxy, and that orthodoxy is at bottom religious. The latter premise appears most prominently in the work of Willmoore Kendall. Challenging the liberal idea of neutrality through a critique of John Stuart Mill, Kendall writes in *The Conservative Affirmation*,

> The open society, they [Mill's disciples] never weary of telling us, must see to it that all doctrines start out equal in the market-place of ideas; for society to assign an advantaged position to these doctrines rather than those would be tantamount to suppressing those. Society, therefore, can have no orthodoxy, no public truth, no standard, upon whose validity it is entitled to insist; outside its private homes, its churches, and perhaps its non-public schools, it cannot, therefore, indoctrinate; *all* questions are for it open questions, and must publicly be treated as open.[76]

The question Kendall poses, however, is, "How open can a society be and still remain open to all?"[77] In fact, he continues,

> Mill's proposals have as one of their tacit premises a false conception of the nature of society, and are, therefore, unrealistic on the face of them. They assume that society is, so to speak, a debating-club, devoted above all to the pursuit of truth, and capable therefore of subordinating itself—and all other considerations, all other goods, all other goals—to that pursuit.[78]

Yet society is committed not to the disinterested pursuit of truth, he argues, but to a specific truth or set of truths. A society cannot endure unless substantive commitments trump mere process:

> But we know that society is not a debating-club—all our experience of society drives the point home to us—and that, even if it were a debating-club, the chances of its adopting the pursuit of truth as its supreme good are negligible. Societies, alike by definition and according to the teaching of history, cherish a whole series of goods—among others, their own self-preservation, the *living* of the truth they believe themselves to embody already, and the communication of that truth (pretty much intact, moreover) to future generations, their religion, etc.—which they are likely to value as much as or

[76] Willmoore Kendall, *The Conservative Affirmation* (Chicago: Regnery Gateway, 1985), at 106, emphasis in original.
[77] Kendall, *Conservative Affirmation*, 111.
[78] Kendall, *Conservative Affirmation*, 112.

> more than the pursuit of truth, and *ought* to value as much as or more than the pursuit of truth, because these are preconditions of the pursuit of truth.[79]

Similarly, Frederick Wilhelmsen argues that "the proposition that a society—a political society—must abstract itself from all questions concerning the ultimate can only be entertained by a naïve rationalism that fails to see that men can live and act together only if they are bound together by code and custom, myth and legend, sculpture and song—all bespeaking some common confrontation of the Absolute."[80]

The other premise of the radical Establishment Clause question is that morality derives inescapably from religion, and that law therefore is an expression of religion. Underlying this premise is the assumption that all morality is essentially religious in nature.[81] It is the claim that no political-legal order is value free, that all values are ultimately religious in nature or are grounded in religious commitments, and thus that every political-legal order constitutes an establishment of religion. As Laura Underkuffler writes,

> The implementation of the idea that government cannot establish one religion in preference to others (the "equality of sects") has been relatively easy, at least in principle, when the religious nature of the competing ideologies is something on which we can agree. Thus, government cannot establish Protestantism to the exclusion of Catholicism, or Judaism to the exclusion of Islam, and the idea that this is a "Christian nation" is decidedly passé. More difficult problems have arisen when what are generally believed to be secular beliefs are characterized as religious ones, triggering claims that secular nature is, in fact, religious-sect favoritism, or when government's

[79] Kendall, *Conservative Affirmation*, 112–13, emphasis in original. Kendall ties his idea of an orthodoxy explicitly to religion elsewhere: The conservative assumes, he says, "that any viable society has an orthodoxy—a set of fundamental beliefs, implicit in its way of life, that it cannot and should not and, in any case, will not submit to the vicissitudes of the market place. He assumes, again with the tradition, that no society can survive—or should survive—without foundations driven deep in religious belief. And he assumes, with the authors of the Declaration of Independence, that no good society can be conceived that does not regard itself as moving through History . . . under God, ultimately therefore under a law whose source is the divine will, for a purpose that lies outside History." Willmoore Kendall, "Three on the Line," *National Review*, August 31, 1956, 179–81, 191, emphasis in original.

[80] Frederick D. Wilhelmsen, "My Doxy Is Orthodoxy," *National Review*, May 22, 1962, 365–66, 366.

[81] A possible complementary but different assumption is the more instrumental claim that morality can have no force without a religious foundation and the threat of divine sanction. See Fyodor Dostoevksy, *The Brothers Karamazov*: "'But what will become of men then?' I asked him, 'without God and immortal life? All things are lawful then, they can do what they like?'" (http://www.online-literature.com/dostoevsky/brothers_karamazov/73/, retrieved 8-12-10).

> secular nature is itself challenged as a violation of religion/non-religion equal-treatment guarantees. Claims of the last type are particularly intractable, as a theoretical matter. Since government must necessarily establish something—whether religious or nonreligious—through its choices of principles and practices, equal treatment of religion and nonreligion is, in this sense, impossible to achieve.[82]

In response, we can agree that to speak of law may well be—or even is necessarily—to speak of a moral vision, but to speak of morality is not necessarily to speak of religion. To say that any political system is committed to an orthodoxy or a certain set of values is not to say, without the premise that all values are essentially religious in nature, that it is committed to a certain set of religious beliefs.[83] All religions are belief systems, but it is a logical error to claim that, therefore, all belief systems are religions.

Indeed, as William Galston recognizes in *Liberal Purposes* and John Rawls recognizes in *Political Liberalism*,[84] a liberal political order certainly embodies a set of value commitments; there is no value-free political order. The liberal state, Galston argues, cannot "be properly understood as 'neutral' in any of the senses in which that term is currently employed. Like every other human community, it embraces a view of the human good that favors certain ways of life and tilts against others."[85] The liberal political order is committed to the value of an equal right to individual freedom, including religious freedom; it is committed to the idea that what is important is who decides, who makes the choices, and not what decision or choices are made. One could argue that it is possible or even necessary to have a political orthodoxy—e.g., our public schools teach the value of liberal democracy rather than monarchy or aristocracy—but

[82] Laura S. Underkuffler, "Through a Glass Darkly: Van Orden, McCreary, and the Dangers of Transparency in Establishment Clause Jurisprudence," *First Amendment Law Review* 5 (2006): 59, 60–61, footnotes omitted.

[83] Perhaps we simply find ourselves in a theoretical as well as moral and political impasse at this point: we either agree that all values are essentially religious in nature or we do not. Any political order is and involves the legitimation of certain values, but whether or not those values are or include religious values is the question. Nevertheless, my argument here is that from the standpoint of the Constitution, as distinct from some particular moral theory, the existence of the religion clauses, by singling out religion from what is not religion, necessarily presupposes that while all religious values are values, not all values are religious.

[84] William A. Galston, *Liberal Purposes: Goods, Virtues, and Diversity in the Liberal State* (New York: Cambridge University Press, 1991); and Rawls, *Political Liberalism*.

[85] Galston, *Liberal Purposes*, 3. He characterizes the "bare essentials" of his thesis as this: "Liberalism cannot, as many contemporary theorists suppose, be understood as broadly neutral concerning the human good. It is rather committed to a distinctive conception of the human good, a conception that undergirds the liberal conception of social justice" (18).

that is not the same thing as saying that there is a religious orthodoxy. The liberal polity is an institutionalization of an agreement to disagree, which itself is a substantive principle that excludes or at least disadvantages those who will not agree to disagree. Nevertheless, though perhaps intractable as a theoretical matter, as Underkuffler noted above, we can transcend the theoretical difficulty or even impossibility of a truly neutral set of value commitments, which Rushdoony exploits in service of his theological commitments, by a prudential choice. Even if a political-legal order necessarily establishes or institutionalizes an orthodoxy or some set of religious values and beliefs, some such values and beliefs allow for more diversity and autonomy than others.

In other words, put succinctly, the orthodoxy of liberalism allows for more heterodoxy than does the orthodoxy of religion, and for that reason, given the initial commitment to an equal right to individual freedom, the public orthodoxy of a liberal political order is preferable to the public orthodoxy of a religious political order. If we grant the proposition that a political-legal order always embodies an orthodoxy, then, as a matter of prudential and not theoretical judgment, on balance we prefer the orthodoxy that allows a greater rather than a lesser amount of individual freedom. One can admit that we do not have a choice between a government that represents, institutionalizes, or establishes a set of value commitments and a government that does not represent, institutionalize, or establish a set of value commitments, but we can still maintain that our task is to structure government around a set of value commitments that themselves allow the widest range and greatest diversity of other value commitments. The latter would be the concept of the liberal state. To say that the liberal polity is an institutionalization of an agreement to disagree is itself is a substantive principle, because it excludes those who will not agree to disagree. A liberal polity is thus not value free. Seeing the political-legal order as an institutionalization of an agreement to disagree based upon a commitment to the equal right of individual freedom allows for a broader range of diversity and individual autonomy than does viewing the political-legal order as the institutionalization of the word of God.

When we acknowledge that our choice is not between a political-legal order that establishes an orthodox set of values and one that does not, this prudential move, in turn, allows for establishing an orthodox set of values that allows for the widest range and greatest diversity of value commitments. Though perhaps not theoretically satisfying, this prudential approach is the best that we can do. It means, regarding religion, that the focus of the religion clauses is the protection not of religion but of religious freedom.[86] The question, of course, is how the religion clauses do that, and it is to their operation that we now turn.

[86] In an article titled "A Transformative Theory of Religious Freedom: Promoting the Reasons for Rights" (*Political Theory* 38, no. 2 [2010]: 187–213), Corey Brettschneider argues that "any robust conception of religious freedom will find itself at odds with some existing religious beliefs" and that "defenders of religious freedom should favor a role for the state in seeking to change some religious beliefs." He continues, "In particular, I suggest that the state has an interest in actively promoting the shared values of free and equal citizenship—values that are rightly understood to underlie the rights of religious freedom" (188). More specifically, he writes, "Some religious practices and religious beliefs are at odds with the principle that citizens should be allowed to practice their religion and to believe what they wish free of state actions. These beliefs are rightly condemned and discouraged by the legitimate state" (190). I agree with the first part of each of these statements, for each first part makes the distinction between protecting religion and protecting religious freedom that I advance here. Brettschneider reiterates this distinction thusly: "The example [of *Church of the Lukumi Babalu Aye v. Hialeah*, 508 U.S. 520 (1993)] reveals a principle of religious freedom might itself conflict with existing religious beliefs" (191).

However, the other part of Brettschneider's two statements cited here is troublesome. It is one thing to say that "the state has an interest in actively promoting the shared values of free and equal citizenship," for that is in fact our political and constitutional culture, taught to children as early as elementary school through respect and even reverence for founding documents such as the Declaration of Independence and the Constitution. It is quite different to say that certain religious beliefs "are rightly condemned and discouraged by the legitimate state." As he reads *Lukumi*, Brettschneider writes, "The Lukumi principle demands that when religious views oppose the ideal of religious freedom itself—for example, because they demand the imposition of their views on nonbelievers—the state must challenge the beliefs in question" (198). As thus stated, this comes perilously close to legitimating a critique or even attack on religious freedom in the name of religious freedom. To avoid that uncomfortable possibility, I would suggest instead that the state must play defense rather than offense. That is, government must defend religious freedom against religious beliefs and practices that threaten religious freedom, but government must not go on the offensive and actively seek out and condemn such religious beliefs and practices that do not immediately threaten religious freedom. This approach does not eliminate the orthodoxy discussed at the end of this chapter, but instead reaffirms the argument that in the absence of a theoretical solution to the paradoxical orthodoxy of religious freedom, all we have is the prudential solution that opts for more religious freedom over less religious freedom when there is no such thing as pure or complete religious freedom.

Chapter 5

The Concept of Coercion in Establishment Clause Jurisprudence

It is customary to begin a discussion of the Establishment Clause of the Constitution with a lament about the problematic state of jurisprudence in this important and controversial constitutional field. The typical claim we encounter holds that Establishment Clause doctrine is inconsistent or confusing at best, if not incoherent and contradictory at worst. As long ago as 1985, then–Associate Justice Rehnquist argued in *Wallace v. Jaffree*, "[I]n the 38 years since Everson our Establishment Clause cases have been neither principled nor unified."[1] This was particularly evident, he said, in school-related cases:

> For example, a State may lend to parochial school children geography textbooks that contain maps of the United States, but the State may not lend maps of the United States for use in geography class. A State may lend textbooks on American colonial history, but it may not lend a film on George Washington, or a film projector to show it in history class. A State may lend classroom workbooks, but may not lend workbooks in which the parochial school children write, thus rendering them nonreusable. A State may pay for bus transportation to religious schools but may not pay for bus transportation from the parochial school to the public zoo or natural history museum for a field trip. A State may pay for diagnostic services conducted in the parochial school but therapeutic services must be given in a different building; speech and hearing "services" conducted by the State inside the sectarian school are forbidden, . . . but the State may conduct speech and hearing diagnostic testing inside the sectarian school. Exceptional parochial school students may receive counseling, but it must take place outside of the parochial school, such as in a trailer parked down the street. A State may give cash to a parochial school to pay for the administration of state-written

[1] *Wallace v. Jaffree*, 472 U.S. 38 (1985), at 107 (dissenting opinion). See also Justice Scalia's view of Establishment Clause jurisprudence in n. 11 and its relevant text in chap. 4 *supra*.

> tests and state-ordered reporting services, but it may not provide funds for teacher-prepared tests on secular subjects. Religious instruction may not be given in public school, but the public school may release students during the day for religion classes elsewhere, and may enforce attendance at those classes with its truancy laws.[2]

By 2006, two decades later, nothing seemed to have changed. Among scholars, this example is representative of the usual criticism:

> Few areas of U.S. Supreme Court interpretation have attracted such strong and universal criticism as the Court's Establishment Clause jurisprudence. Over the half century that the Court has been deciding cases under the Clause, its muddled and inconsistent decisions have confounded scholars, lower courts, and at times, even members of the Court itself. So far, this tangled body of doctrine has resisted every attempt to bring clarity, predictability, and coherence to the constitutional standard for evaluating state action under the Clause.[3]

According to Steven Gey, one of the most interesting commentators on the constitutional and political theory of religion-clause jurisprudence, "It is by now axiomatic that the Supreme Court's Establishment Clause jurisprudence is a mess—both hopelessly confused and deeply contradictory."[4] If we are to have any hope of overcoming this problem, an attempt to clarify the contested and confusing state of Establishment Clause jurisprudence must begin with a recurrence to and restatement of first principles. My purpose in this chapter is not to propose a new test for deciding cases, but to begin to identify and unpack the substantive principle embodied in the Establishment Clause that would underlie any such test. The first element of that principle involves the concept of coercion, typically associated with a free-exercise rather than establishment violation. This chapter seeks to explore the way the Court has used the concept of coercion and to develop a richer version that can explain how and why an establishment violation affects religious freedom.

Such first principles are both formal and substantive in nature. Formal principles have to do with the logic of constitutional interpretation, of which there are two dimensions. First, we do well to recall the distinction between statutory construction and constitutional interpretation, which is the distinction between application and authority. The central issue in statutory construction is always the question of how a given statute

[2] *Wallace v. Jaffree*, at 110–11, footnotes and internal case citations omitted.

[3] Cynthia V. Ward, "Coercion and Choice under the Establishment Clause," *University of California-Davis Law Review* 39 (2006): 1621, at 1623, footnotes omitted.

[4] Steven G. Gey, "Reconciling the Supreme Court's Four Establishment Clauses," *University of Pennsylvania Journal of Constitutional Law* 8 (2006): 725, at 725.

applies to the facts of a given situation. For example, a central question in the case of *Grove City College v. Bell*, 465 U.S. 555 (1984), is whether and how Title IX's prohibition on sex discrimination applied to Grove City College athletics and to the institution in general. The assumption in statutory construction is that the government has the authority to pass the statute in question, and that the only real question is how it applies to the fact pattern at issue. The central issue in constitutional interpretation, on the other hand, is precisely the question of whether the government has the authority to pass a particular statute (or undertake a particular action) in the first place. The authority question goes to the political theory of the American constitutional order. The United States is a liberal democracy, which, as we have seen, means majorities rule, but not over everything. Our particular form of liberal democracy is our constitutional democracy, for it is the Constitution that determines the dividing line between what majorities may legitimately decide and what decisions are reserved to the individual. The Constitution does this, we saw earlier, by means of the Bill of Rights, which places certain rights beyond the reach of electoral majorities in the political process. The authority question in an Establishment Clause case, therefore, is whether government—national, state, or local—has the authority to legislate (in its legislative capacity) or act (in its executive capacity) on a particular matter that potentially respects an establishment of religion.

The second formal principle requiring reconsideration has to do with the nature of constitutional reasoning. Criticism of the state of Establishment Clause jurisprudence ordinarily focuses upon the various tests the Supreme Court has used to determine whether there is an establishment violation in a particular case: the *Lemon* test, the endorsement test, the coercion test, and what we might call the tradition test.[5] Legal scholars and the justices themselves typically attack and defend the validity of these tests as the fundamental normative standards of appropriate constitutional reasoning. Such tests function in Establishment Clause cases as elements of what I elsewhere have called the American constitutional syllogism.[6] That syllogism constitutes the basic structure

[5] According to Steven Gey, "[T]here are ten different doctrinal standards for applying the Establishment Clause that have been embraced by one or more Justices currently on the Court." "Vestiges of the Establishment Clause," *First Amendment Law Review* 5 (2006): 1, at 36. These are, in his words: the *Lemon* test, the endorsement test (Justice O'Connor), a broad coercion test (Justice Kennedy), a narrow coercion test (Justice Scalia), a formal-neutrality test, a substantive-neutrality test, a disincorporation theory (Justice Thomas), nonpreferentialism (Chief Justice Rehnquist), a divisiveness test, and ad hoc analysis.

[6] Dennis J. Goldford, *The American Constitution and the Debate over Originalism* (New York: Cambridge University Press, 2005), Introduction.

of constitutional reasoning as to the question of whether government has the authority under the Constitution to do what it wishes to do:

P_1: If X is contrary to the Constitution, then X is null and void.

P_2: X is indeed contrary to the Constitution.

C: X is null and void.

X here is any law or other act of government, and P_1 reflects the status of the Constitution as fundamental law, anterior and superior to ordinary law or other acts of government. P_2 represents the actual determination in a given instance of the constitutionality of X. Thus, in the case of the Establishment Clause, the syllogism runs as follows:

P_1: If X is contrary to the Establishment Clause, then X is null and void.

P_2: X is indeed contrary to the Establishment Clause.

C: X is null and void.

While important, however, this does not get us very far yet. Everyone agrees that an act of government in its legislative or executive capacity contrary to the Establishment Clause is unconstitutional, but how do we determine P_2? That is, how do we determine that an act of government is indeed contrary to the Establishment Clause?

This is where the conventional tests enter the picture, for the tests of an Establishment Clause violation are themselves actually part of what we can consider a subsyllogism to which P_2 is the conclusion:

P_1: If X is contrary to the Establishment Clause, then X is null and void.

$P_{1.1}$: If X fails test Q, then X is contrary to the Establishment Clause

$P_{1.2}$: X fails test Q; therefore,

P_2: X is indeed contrary to the Establishment Clause.

C: X is null and void.

The key issue here, of course, is our warrant for $P_{1.1}$: if X fails test Q, then X is contrary to the Establishment Clause. What determines that test Q, as opposed to test R or S or T, is the proper test? How do we know, in other words, which test—the *Lemon* test, the endorsement test, the coercion test, the tradition test, or perhaps some other test—adequately expresses the meaning of the Establishment Clause? To answer that key question, it is necessary to make the logically prior and absolutely fundamental determination of what constitutes the central principle at the heart of the Establishment Clause. In his *Wallace* critique of the *Lemon* test, Justice

Rehnquist writes, "The three-part test represents a determined effort to craft a workable rule from a historically faulty doctrine; but the rule can only be as sound as the doctrine it attempts to service."[7] Independently of whether or not we agree with Justice Rehnquist's rejection of the *Lemon* test, his broader theoretical point is fundamental: the rule—i.e., the test—can be only as sound as the principle it represents and serves. The question is, given the prohibitory nature of the Establishment Clause, what is the central nonestablishment principle? The absence of consensus on that central principle generates the ongoing disputes over what test satisfactorily registers the existence or nonexistence of an establishment violation.

The lack of consensus on the central principle at stake in Establishment Clause jurisprudence and the consequent confusion therein, I suggest, reflect two problems, the first of which I categorize as a problem of political theory, and the second of which I categorize as a problem of constitutional theory. The political-theory problem is the longstanding issue of the source of norms and principles: do we derive these from reason or from tradition? As applied to the Establishment Clause, the question is, do traditional religious practices determine the constitutional validity of the test for an establishment violation, or does the test for an establishment violation determine the constitutional validity of traditional religious practices? For example, Justice Anthony Kennedy writes in *Allegheny County*, "I take it as settled law that, whatever standard the Court applies to Establishment Clause claims, it must at least suggest results consistent with our precedents and the historical practices that, by tradition, have informed our First Amendment jurisprudence."[8] On the other hand, he argues, "A test for implementing the protections of the Establishment Clause that, if applied with consistency, would invalidate longstanding traditions cannot be a proper reading of the Clause."[9]

Citing this very statement by Justice Kennedy, Justice Antonin Scalia prefaces his dissenting opinion in *Lee v. Weisman* with this same emphasis on tradition:

> In holding that the Establishment Clause prohibits invocations and benedictions at public school graduation ceremonies, the Court—with nary a mention that it is doing so—lays waste a tradition that is as old as public school graduation ceremonies themselves, and that is a component of an even more longstanding American tradition of nonsectarian prayer to God at public celebrations generally.[10]

[7] *Wallace v. Jaffree*, at 107 (dissenting opinion).
[8] *Allegheny County v. Greater Pittsburgh* ACLU, 492 U.S. 573 (1989), at 669.
[9] *Allegheny County*, at 670.
[10] *Lee v. Weisman*, 505 U.S. 577 (1992), at 631–32.

The problem, he states succinctly in that dissent, is this: "Our Religion Clause jurisprudence has become bedeviled (so to speak) by reliance on formulaic abstractions that are not derived from, but positively conflict with, our long-accepted constitutional traditions."[11] Likewise, dissenting in *McCreary County v. ACLU of Kentucky*, Scalia argues, "[T]he Court's oft repeated assertion that the government cannot favor religious practice is false." The reason, he maintains, is the normative status of traditional practices. Scalia thus concludes, "Acknowledgment of the contribution that religion has made to our Nation's legal and governmental heritage partakes of a centuries-old tradition. . . . Display of the Ten Commandments is well within the mainstream of this practice of acknowledgment."[12]

Such appeals to tradition raise in constitutional language a fundamental question of political theory. On the one hand, does an Establishment Clause test determine what is normative in our traditions? Implicitly providing an affirmative answer that that question, Justice Sandra Day O'Connor, for example, writes in *Allegheny County*, "Historical acceptance of a practice does not in itself validate that practice under the Establishment Clause if the practice violates the values protected by that clause, just as historical acceptance of racial or gender based discrimination does not immunize such practices from scrutiny under the Fourteenth Amendment."[13] On the other hand, do our traditions determine what counts as the normative Establishment Clause test? This, clearly, is the position Scalia takes in his *Lee* and *McCreary* dissents. For Justice O'Connor, then, the test for an establishment violation determines the constitutional validity of traditional religious practices; for Justice Scalia, traditional religious practices determine the constitutional validity of the test for an establishment violation. In terms of political theory, we find here the contrast between liberal and conservative modes of political reasoning about sources of normative standards parallel to the contrast in constitutional reasoning between norms "implicit in the concept of ordered liberty" and "principles of justice so rooted in the traditions and conscience of our people as to be ranked as fundamental."[14] The appeal to the concept of ordered liberty is an appeal to reason, whereas the appeal to principles of justice rooted

[11] *Lee v. Weisman*, at 644.

[12] *McCreary County*, 545 U.S. 844 (2005), at 906.

[13] *Allegheny County*, at 630.

[14] *Palko v. Connecticut*, 302 U.S. 319 (1937), at 325 (citing *Snyder v. Massachusetts*, 291 U.S. 97 [1934]). The Establishment Clause of course limits Congress (and, according to Justice Clarence Thomas and some conservative legal scholars, limits Congress alone and not the states) independently of the Due Process Clause of the Fourteenth Amendment under examination in *Palko*, but the political-theory issue of reason vs. tradition, stated here in *Palko* terms, is always fully at issue in Establishment Clause interpretation at any level.

in the traditions and conscience of the American people is, obviously, an appeal to tradition. One explanation for the lack of consensus on the central principle at stake in Establishment Clause jurisprudence, therefore, is the lack of consensus on the source of normative standards to which we are to appeal. Our political-theory problem in Establishment Clause jurisprudence is that we are faced with normative differences over which source of normative standards is, if you will, normative. To the extent that the Constitution provides the arena and terminology of our fundamental arguments of political principle, the lack of consensus on the central principle at stake in Establishment Clause jurisprudence may well be a permanent consequence of our political differences.

We thus find that we have transitioned from the domain of formal principle to that of substantive principle, that is, to the question of what constitutes the central principle at the heart of the Establishment Clause. The lack of consensus on that central principle generates the ongoing disputes over what test satisfactorily determines the presence or absence of an Establishment Clause violation. Referring to the various tests, Gey writes, "The problem lies in the Court's unwillingness to settle on a comprehensive (and comprehensible) theory of the Establishment Clause. No set of standards will make sense unless those standards are informed by some notion of what they are supposed to accomplish."[15] Indeed, avoiding the question of what substantive principle underlies the Establishment Clause allows or even causes circularity problems. Justice Kennedy's *Allegheny* statement—"A test for implementing the protections of the Establishment Clause that, if applied with consistency, would invalidate longstanding traditions cannot be a proper reading of the Clause"[16]—suggests that, on the one hand, the test is supposed to determine whether there is an Establishment Clause violation, but, on the other, the presence or absence of such a violation apparently determines what legitimately counts as a test. Additionally, the norm of privileging tradition in this manner, thereby making it the proper test, cannot be justified by tradition itself.[17]

If Gey is correct, then why is the Court unwilling "to settle on a comprehensive (and comprehensible) theory of the Establishment Clause"? The reason he offers is that "members of the Court are deeply conflicted about what any of these standards are supposed to achieve."[18] What, in

[15] Gey, "Reconciling," at 783.

[16] *Allegheny County*, at 670.

[17] That is a problem in classical conservatism. Someone like Edmund Burke might wish to prefer the wisdom embodied in tradition to the speculations of abstract reason (see Burke, *Reflections on the Revolution in France* [Indianapolis: Hackett Publishing, 1987]), but the preference for tradition cannot be justified on the basis of tradition itself. Reason unavoidably sneaks back into the discussion.

[18] Gey, "Reconciling," at 730.

other words, is the purpose of the Establishment Clause in particular and of the religion clauses in general? At the most abstract level, that purpose, affirmed by justices on all sides of particular religion-clause issues, is the protection of religious freedom. In *Allegheny County*, cited above, Justice Kennedy writes, "The freedom to worship as one pleases without government interference or oppression is the great object of both the Establishment and the Free Exercise Clauses."[19] Concurring in *Abington v. Schempp*, Justice Goldberg states that these two clauses are complementary means to the same end: "The basic purpose of the religion clause of the First Amendment is to promote and assure the fullest possible scope of religious liberty and tolerance for all and to nurture the conditions which secure the best hope of attainment of that end."[20] Likewise concurring in *Abington*, Justice Brennan writes of "the role of the Establishment Clause as co-guarantor, with the Free Exercise Clause, of religious liberty. The Framers did not entrust the liberty of religious beliefs to either clause alone."[21] Writing for the Court in *Abington*, Justice Clark holds that the two religion clauses "overlap" in their protection of religious freedom, stating that the Free Exercise Clause "recognizes the value of religious training, teaching and observance and, more particularly, the right of every person to freely choose his own course with reference thereto, free of any compulsion from the state."[22] Though dissenting in *Abington*, Justice Stewart writes, "What our Constitution indispensably protects is the freedom of each of us, be he Jew or Agnostic, Christian or Atheist, Buddhist or Freethinker, to believe or disbelieve, to worship or not worship, to pray or keep silent, according to his own conscience, uncoerced and unrestrained by government."[23]

Even Justice Douglas, whose statement in his 1952 opinion for the Court in *Zorach v. Clauson* that "[w]e are a religious people whose institutions presuppose a Supreme Being"[24] is routinely cited by those asserting a close connection between government and religion, writes of religious freedom in his next two sentences: "We guarantee the freedom to worship as one chooses. We make room for as wide a variety of beliefs and creeds as the spiritual needs of man deem necessary."[25] Later, dissenting in *McGowan v. Maryland* in 1961, Justice Douglas repeats his idea of

[19] *Allegheny County* at 660, Kennedy (dissenting in part).

[20] *Abington School District v. Schempp*, 374 U.S. 203 (1963), at 305 (Goldberg concurring, joined by Justice Harlan).

[21] *Abington*, at 256 (Brennan, concurring).

[22] *Abington*, at 222.

[23] *Abington*, at 320 (Stewart, dissenting).

[24] *Zorach v. Clauson*, 343 U.S. 306 (1952), at 313.

[25] *Zorach v. Clauson*.

religious foundations but once again reemphasizes the priority of religious freedom:[26]

> But those who fashioned the First Amendment decided that if and when God is to be served, His service will not be motivated by coercive measures of government. "Congress shall make no law respecting an establishment of religion, or prohibiting the free exercise thereof"—such is the command of the First Amendment made applicable to the State by reason of the Due Process Clause of the Fourteenth. This means, as I understand it, that if a religious leaven is to be worked into the affairs of our people, it is to be done by individuals and groups, not by the Government. This necessarily means, first, that the dogma, creed, scruples, or practices of no religious group or sect are to be preferred over those of any others; second, that no one shall be interfered with by government for practicing the religion of his choice; third, that the State may not require anyone to practice a religion or even any religion; and fourth, that the State cannot compel one so to conduct himself as not to offend the religious scruples of another. The idea, as I understand it, was to limit the power of government to act in religious matters, not to limit the freedom of religious men to act religiously nor to restrict the freedom of atheists or agnostics.[27]

The significance of this argument, however, is not just that it is a brief in defense of religious freedom. It is, I submit, the claim advanced here that the religion clauses protect religious freedom and not religion itself.

Justice Douglas' fourth point—"that the State cannot compel one so to conduct himself as not to offend the religious scruples of another"—illustrates this distinction between protecting religion and protecting religious freedom. An attempt to protect religion could include, for example, the criminalization of blasphemy. According to section 36 of the Irish Defamation Act of 2009,

> (1) A person who publishes or utters blasphemous matter shall be guilty of an offence and shall be liable upon conviction on indictment to a fine not exceeding 25,000.
>
> (2) For the purposes of this section, a person publishes or utters blasphemous matter if—
>
> (a) he or she publishes or utters matter that is grossly abusive or insulting in relation to matters held sacred by any religion,

[26] "The institutions of our society are founded on the belief that there is an authority higher than the authority of the State; that there is a moral law which the State is powerless to alter; that the individual possesses rights, conferred by the Creator, which government must respect." *McGowan v. Maryland*, 366 U.S. 420 (1961), at 563 (Douglas, dissenting).

[27] *McGowan*, at 563–64, internal references omitted.

thereby causing outrage among a substantial number of the adherents of that religion, and

(b) he or she intends, by the publication or utterance of the matter concerned, to cause such outrage.[28]

An older blasphemy law is apparently still in force in Indonesia, the purpose of which is summarized in a report in the April 17, 2010, *Jakarta Post*:

> The rationale behind the 1965 Blasphemy Law is to maintain religious orthodoxy; to guarantee that the established religious teachings and dogma are secure; to protect religious doctrines from new or different understandings. Any group deviating from the orthodox would be called a "sect" and subject to blasphemy charges and persecution. No religious interpretation would be allowed beyond the orthodox interpretation.[29]

If Justice Douglas is correct, then the Establishment Clause prohibits the criminalization of blasphemy. The First Amendment, he says, "admonishes government to be interested in allowing religious freedom to flourish—whether the result is to produce Catholics, Jews, or Protestants, or to turn the people toward the path of Buddha, or to end in a predominantly Moslem nation, or to produce in the long run atheists or agnostics."[30]

Of course, one could argue that the best way to protect religion is in fact not to protect it directly, that protecting the freedom of religion indirectly protects religion, as illustrated by the vibrancy and diversity of religious denominations and activity in the United States. What is thereby protected is not religion considered as an institution and practice or a set of institutions and practices, but rather the individual's right to determine his or her own religious beliefs, affiliations, and practices. This ratifies the point that the purpose of the religion clauses is to protect religious freedom rather than religion, for protecting religion rather than religious freedom amounts to protecting the religion of the majority. The focus on the individual here is crucial: the possessor of religious freedom is not the majority understood as a group, for what else could the religion clauses be—"Congress shall make no law respecting an establishment of religion, or prohibiting the free exercise thereof"—but a limitation on the freedom

[28] Irish Defamation Act of 2009 (http://www.oireachtas.ie/documents/bills28/acts/2009/a3109.pdf, retrieved 4-16-10). Such blasphemous matter is subject to seizure, according to section 37. To be sure, section 36 also provides that the defendant may prove that "a reasonable person would find genuine literary, artistic, political, scientific, or academic value in the matter to which the offence relates."

[29] Ahmad Najib Burhani, "Religious Orthodoxy and the Blasphemy Law," *Jakarta Post*, April 17, 2010 (http://www.thejakartapost.com/news/2010/03/18/religious-orthodoxy-and-blasphemy-law.html, retrieved 4-16-10).

[30] *McGowan*, at 564.

of the majority to act as a group in pursuit of its own religious interests. That religious freedom is an individual freedom means that religious freedom is that of the individual against the demands and values of the religious majority. That is the logic that underlies the conventional distinction between separationism and accommodationism.

The second problem leading to the lack of consensus on the central principle at stake in Establishment Clause jurisprudence, I noted earlier, is a matter of constitutional theory. This problem is the difficulty the Supreme Court and legal commentators have had in solving a theoretical puzzle at the heart of religion-clause jurisprudence: precisely how does an Establishment violation limit or otherwise impinge upon freedom of religion? If we take as our premises the proposition that those who wrote and ratified the language of the First Amendment knew what they were doing, and the proposition that the purpose of the religion clauses is to protect religious freedom, then clearly the presence of the two clauses implies that religious freedom can be infringed or limited in two ways: it can be infringed or limited by a denial of the free exercise of religion, and it can be infringed or limited by an establishment of religion. As Justice O'Connor writes in the *McCreary* case,

> The First Amendment expresses our Nation's fundamental commitment to religious liberty by means of two provisions–one protecting the free exercise of religion, the other barring establishment of religion. They were written by the descendents of people who had come to this land precisely so that they could practice their religion freely. Together with the other First Amendment guarantees–of free speech, a free press, and the rights to assemble and petition–the Religion Clauses were designed to safeguard the freedom of conscience and belief that those immigrants had sought. They embody an idea that was once considered radical: Free people are entitled to free and diverse thoughts, which government ought neither to constrain nor to direct.[31]

It is almost tautologically clear that when government limits the free exercise of religion it limits religious freedom. In a Free Exercise situation, the government criminalizes or otherwise sanctions some action I want to undertake on religious grounds, whether it is having several spouses,[32] operating my business on a Sunday,[33] wearing a yarmulke while in Air Force uniform,[34] smoking peyote,[35] or engaging in other such actions.

[31] O'Connor, *McCreary County*, at 881–82 (concurring).
[32] *Reynolds v. United States*, 98 U.S. 145 (1878).
[33] *Braunfeld v. Brown*, 366 U.S. 599 (1961).
[34] *Goldman v. Weinberger*, 475 U.S. 503 (1986).
[35] Employment Division, *Oregon Department of Human Resources v. Smith*, 494 U.S. 872 (1990).

Why, then, does the Constitution contain two religion clauses? In other words, if the overarching purpose of the religion clauses, acknowledged by almost all commentators, is the singular goal of guaranteeing religious freedom, why do we find in the First Amendment two religion clauses rather than just one? The answer to that question tells us something important about the nature of religious freedom in the American political order in general, and about the Establishment Clause in particular.

One way of coming to understand the duality of the religion clauses is, of course, through a historical approach. We know that both houses of Congress considered several versions of the clauses before reaching the text we know today.[36] On June 8, 1789, Madison proposed this amendment to be inserted in the Constitution between clauses 3 and 4 of article I, section 9: "The civil rights of none shall be abridged on account of religious belief or worship, nor shall any national religion be established, nor shall the full and equal rights of conscience be in any manner, or on any pretext, infringed." On August 15 the House Committee of the Whole altered this to read, "No religion shall be established by law, nor shall the equal rights of conscience be infringed." During the course of debate that day, this language itself was changed to say, Congress "shall make no laws touching religion, or infringing the rights of conscience." Finally, on August 20, the text was amended again to read, "Congress shall make no law establishing religion or to prevent the free exercise thereof, or to infringe the rights of conscience."

The Senate began debate on this and other amendments on September 2, through the period ending September 9. After rejecting three versions of a religion-clause amendment,[37] the Senate altered the House amendment to read, "Congress shall make no law establishing articles of faith or a mode of worship, or prohibiting the free exercise of religion." The House, however, refused to accept this language, but agreed to a conference committee to try to find wording acceptable to both chambers.

[36] The historical discussion that follows is based on Louis Fisher, *Religious Liberty in America: Political Safeguards* (Lawrence: University Press of Kansas, 2002), 54–56; Philip B. Kurland and Ralph Lerner, eds., *The Founders' Constitution*, vol. 5 (Chicago: University of Chicago Press, 1987), 93–94; and Leonard W. Levy, *The Establishment Clause: Religion and the First Amendment*, 2nd ed., rev. (Chapel Hill: University of North Carolina Press, 1994). For a detailed summary of the legislative history of the religion clauses with good references to sources, see http://candst.tripod.com/tnppage/basic4a.htm (retrieved 8-18-07).

[37] Those rejected versions were "Congress shall make no law establishing one religious sect or society in preference to others," "Congress shall not make any law infringing the rights of conscience, or establishing any religious sect or society," and "Congress shall make no law establishing any particular denomination of religion in preference to another." Levy, *Establishment Clause*, 81.

Facing determined refusal by the House to agree to the Senate version, the Senate conferees finally agreed to accept the House version providing it read, "Congress shall make no law respecting an establishment of religion, or prohibiting the free exercise thereof." With the House's approval of this wording, the Senate voted on September 25 to accept what has become the present text of the religion clauses.

This very brief summary of the drafting of the religion clauses indicates the historical development of the text we have come to know. However, following Justice Joseph Story's admonition that "[n]othing but the text itself was adopted by the people,"[38] we have to ask why the duality of the religion clauses makes sense. In other words, there are two different ways of approaching understanding the duality of the religion clauses. One is the historical approach, which explains how we happened to come up with two clauses; the second is the theoretical question: why does it make sense that there are two clauses? The latter question is the one of interest here. On the premise that we do and ought to interpret the Constitution as a principled document, then we need to explain the duality of the religion clauses not just in terms of the brute facticity of historical accident but in theoretical terms as elements of a coherent principle.

I begin very simply by setting out a proposition that states the obvious but nevertheless tells us something quite significant about the religion clauses as constitutional guarantors of religious freedom. Taking the text seriously, as we should, and assuming that those who drafted and ratified the clauses knew what they were doing, we have to conclude from the text that the duality of the clauses implies that religious freedom can be infringed in two ways: government can infringe religious freedom by laws prohibiting the free exercise of religion, religious beliefs, or religious practices, and government can infringe religious freedom by laws respecting the establishment of religion, religious beliefs, or religious practices.[39] Yet this formulation, while true, merely raises the central question: how do Establishment Clause issues differ from Free Exercise Clause issues? The appearance of two clauses instead of one in the text of the Constitution suggests that the guarantee that there will be free exercise of religion and

[38] Joseph Story, *Commentaries on the Constitution of the United States* (1833), http://www.lonang.com/exlibris/story/sto-305.htm (retrieved 8-22-07), bk 3, chap. 5, §406.

[39] Accepting the longstanding argument of the Supreme Court the Fourteenth Amendment has incorporated the religion clauses and made them applicable against the states, I refer here simply to government in general instead of specifying the federal or state governments. In short order I shall address the claim that the Establishment Clause is purely a jurisdictional measure, leaving religion in the hands of the states and free from any federal legislation, that as such cannot logically be incorporated into the Fourteenth Amendment.

the guarantee that there will not be anything respecting an establishment of religion,[40] while each a necessary condition of religious freedom, are not each on its own a sufficient condition of religious freedom. The text suggests that if our goal is to protect the freedom of religion, then we need both a guarantee of the free exercise of religion and a guarantee against anything respecting an establishment of religion. The two guarantees together are both necessary and sufficient conditions of religious freedom in the American political-legal system.

So, again, how do Establishment Clause issues differ from Free Exercise Clause issues? We could say by way of distinguishing the two that the central meaning of the Free Exercise Clause is that rejection of a particular religion, religious belief, or religious practice cannot be a condition of full participation in American citizenship, while the central meaning of the Establishment Clause is that affirmation of or adherence to a particular religion, religious belief, or religious practice cannot be a condition of full participation in American citizenship. That is, for anyone to be an American citizen, government can neither require her or him to reject nor require her or him to accept a particular religion, religious belief, or religious practice. We could say also that the meaning of the prohibition on establishment is that government should not favor religion in general, nor any religion or religious beliefs and practices in particular, while the meaning of the free-exercise requirement is that government should not disfavor religion in general, or any religion or religious beliefs and practices in particular. Governmental disfavor toward religion is clearly a threat to religious freedom, but what the prohibition on governmental favor toward religion suggests is that a fundamental threat to religious freedom can be religion itself. In other words, the Constitution protects not religion, but religious freedom.[41]

Recall, however, the well-known admonition by Chief Justice Warren Burger about the religion clauses: "The Court has struggled to find a neutral course between the two Religion Clauses, both of which are cast

[40] I use the perhaps awkward phrase "the guarantee that there will not be anything respecting an establishment of religion" to indicate that the constitutional protection is broader than a guarantee that there will not be an establishment of religion. The First Amendment states in part, "Congress shall make no law respecting an establishment of religion," not "Congress shall make no law establishing religion."

[41] Those in contemporary American politics who seek a greater accommodation of religion by government—not to mention those who more radically question the legitimacy of the concept of separation of church and state—thus would appear to be more sympathetic to the view that the Constitution protects religion. Those who oppose greater accommodation and support the separation of church and state as traditionally understood would appear to be more sympathetic to the view that the Constitution protects religious freedom.

in absolute terms, and either of which, if expanded to a logical extreme, would tend to clash with the other."[42] Particularly in view of comments in Supreme Court opinions that the clauses often overlap, or, if pushed far enough, even run into each other, how distinct are the clauses from each other? Justice O'Connor's endorsement test, for example, is normally considered to be a test for an Establishment Clause violation, yet her formulation of it includes the claim that government cannot send a message of disapproval, which would seem, as a case of governmental disfavor, to be a Free Exercise rather than Establishment issue.[43]

Along those lines, consider the flag-salute cases of the 1940s. The circumstances at issue in *Minersville v. Gobitis* were stated by the Court as follows:

> Lillian Gobitis, aged twelve, and her brother William, aged ten, were expelled from the public schools of Minersville, Pennsylvania, for refusing to salute the national flag as part of a daily school exercise. The local Board of Education required both teachers and pupils to participate in this ceremony. The ceremony is a familiar one. The right hand is placed on the breast and the following pledge recited in unison: "I pledge allegiance to my flag, and to the Republic for which it stands; one nation indivisible, with liberty and justice for all." While the words are spoken, teachers and pupils extend their right hands in salute to the flag. The Gobitis family are affiliated with "Jehovah's Witnesses," for whom the Bible as the Word of God is the supreme authority. The children had been brought up conscientiously to believe that such a gesture of respect for the flag was forbidden by command of scripture.[44]

The children here were required to participate in a civil—as opposed to religious—ceremony their parents held to be contrary to their religious beliefs, and were penalized for refusing to do so. A similar situation obtained in *West Virginia v. Barnette*:

> Appellees, citizens of the United States and of West Virginia, brought suit in the United States District Court for themselves and others similarly situated asking its injunction to restrain enforcement of these laws and regulations against Jehovah's Witnesses. The Witnesses are an unincorporated body teaching that the obligation imposed by law of God is superior to that of laws enacted by temporal government. Their religious beliefs include a

[42] *Walz v. Tax Commission*, 397 U.S. 664 (1970), at 669.

[43] "Endorsement sends a message to nonadherents that they are outsiders, not full members of the political community, and an accompanying message to adherents that they are insiders, favored members of the political community. Disapproval sends the opposite message." Justice Sandra Day O'Connor, *Lynch v. Donnelly*, 465 U.S. 668 (1984), at 688 (concurring).

[44] *Minersville School District v. Gobitis*, 310 U.S. 586 (1940), at 592, footnote omitted.

> literal version of Exodus, Chapter 20, verses 4 and 5, which says: "Thou shalt not make unto thee any graven image, or any likeness of anything that is in heaven above, or that is in the earth beneath, or that is in the water under the earth; thou shalt not bow down thyself to them nor serve them." They consider that the flag is an "image" within this command. For this reason they refuse to salute it. Children of this faith have been expelled from school and are threatened with exclusion for no other cause. Officials threaten to send them to reformatories maintained for criminally inclined juveniles. Parents of such children have been prosecuted and are threatened with prosecutions for causing delinquency.[45]

The penalty here is certainly clear. Now, consider the factual circumstances in *Lee v. Weisman*, the case having to do with prayer at a graduation ceremony:

> Deborah Weisman graduated from Nathan Bishop Middle School, a public school in Providence, at a formal ceremony in June, 1989. She was about 14 years old. For many years, it has been the policy of the Providence School Committee and the Superintendent of Schools to permit principals to invite members of the clergy to give invocations and benedictions at middle school and high school graduations. Many, but not all, of the principals elected to include prayers as part of the graduation ceremonies. Acting for himself and his daughter, Deborah's father, Daniel Weisman, objected to any prayers at Deborah's middle school graduation, but to no avail. The school principal, petitioner Robert E. Lee, invited a rabbi to deliver prayers at the graduation exercises for Deborah's class. Rabbi Leslie Gutterman, of the Temple Beth El in Providence, accepted.[46]

Contrary to the circumstances of the flag-salute cases, in *Lee* the student's participation in the graduation ceremony was voluntary. Ms. Weisman was not required to attend the ceremony to receive her diploma, nor was she subject to any legal penalties for refusing not to participate, as was the case in the *Gobitis* and *Barnette*.[47]

These references to the flag-salute and the graduation-prayer cases provide the foundation for questioning further our initial concern with the distinction between Free Exercise and Establishment issues. In all three of these cases we find a situation in which an individual confronts the dilemma of participating in a school-based ceremony or ritual that, so each claimed, violates in some sense his or her religious convictions.

[45] *West Virginia v. Barnette*, 319 U.S. 624 (1943), at 630.

[46] *Lee v. Weisman*, at 581.

[47] Much of the argument in Lee, particularly that between Justices Kennedy and Scalia, concerns the question as to whether Ms. Weisman was subject to coercion in some sense. That issue is what we address as this chapter proceeds.

The puzzling dimension of this is that *Gobitis* and *Barnette* are considered Free Exercise cases, whereas *Lee v. Weisman* is considered an Establishment case. To be sure, in *Lee* the school was sponsoring an allegedly religious ceremony, while in the flag-salute cases the schools were sponsoring an apparently civic ritual. Nevertheless, from the perspective of the Jehovah's Witnesses the latter was in effect a religious ceremony and one that was contrary to their own religious beliefs, which was Ms. Weisman's claim in the later case. In what sense, then, do we conceptualize *Gobitis* and *Barnette* as Free Exercise cases and *Lee* as an Establishment case?

The usual constitutional question when the Free Exercise Clause is at issue is, how strong or compelling must the government's reason for prohibiting the action in question be in order to override the presumption of Free Exercise protection?[48] Prior to 1990, the Court took it for granted that for such a fundamental right as religious freedom the government's reason must be not just rational or important, but compelling: "It is basic that no showing merely of a rational relationship to some colorable state interest would suffice; in this highly sensitive constitutional area, '[o]nly the gravest abuses, endangering paramount interests, give occasion for permissible limitation.'"[49] By contrast, in *Employment Division v. Smith*, the Court backs away from the compelling-interest standard, holding that the *Sherbert* test, according to which "governmental actions that substantially burden a religious practice must be justified by a compelling governmental interest,"[50] should not be applied to "a neutral, generally applicable regulatory law that compelled activity forbidden by an individual's religion."[51] Either way, the religious-freedom issue in Free Exercise situations is clear: I want to do X, or I claim that my religious belief obligates and requires me to do X, but the government prohibits me from doing X. Free Exercise situations are relatively uncomplicated as a matter of constitutional theory, though there can be some theoretical difficulty in

[48] Recall this statement by the Supreme Court in *Reynolds v. United States*:

> Laws are made for the government of actions, and while they cannot interfere with mere religious belief and opinions, they may with practices. Suppose one believed that human sacrifices were a necessary part of religious worship, would it be seriously contended that the civil government under which he lived could not interfere to prevent a sacrifice? Or if a wife religiously believed it was her duty to burn herself upon the funeral pile of her dead husband, would it be beyond the power of the civil government to prevent her carrying her belief into practice? (98 U.S. 145 (1878), at 166)

The central Free Exercise Clause question is not *whether* government may impinge upon the free exercise of religion, but *when*—under what conditions—it may do so.

[49] *Sherbert v. Verner*, 374 U.S. 398 (1963), at 407, citing *Thomas v. Collins*, 323 U.S. 516 (1945), at 530.

[50] *Employment Division v. Smith*, at 883.

[51] *Employment Division v. Smith*, at 880.

that they depend upon a distinction between belief and conduct and the assumption that they are separable.[52]

In an Establishment Clause situation, on the other hand, the religious-freedom question is much less clear. How does government limit or infringe upon my religious freedom when it does something respecting an establishment of religion? If the government taxes me to support religious institutions and the propagation of religious beliefs, particularly those of others but perhaps my own as well, then the government impinges upon my religious freedom by forcing me to do something I do not want to do. That is clear enough. But how does it affect my religious freedom for government to sponsor religious displays directly or to create conditions through the structured context of the public school environment in which individuals engage in religious activities such as moments of silence and prayer at graduation exercises or football games?[53] That is not so clear. Recalling that law, in at least one of its functions, makes us do what we do not want to do and prohibits us from doing what we do want to do, perhaps we might say that Free Exercise cases are ones in which the law prohibits us from doing what we do want to do (to have multiple spouses, to be open for business on Sunday, to smoke peyote), while Establishment Clause cases are ones in which the law makes us do what we do not want to do (to pay taxes to someone else's religious institution, to attend mandatory worship services, to have to make a choice between sitting through graduation prayer and not attending the ceremony).

What the foregoing sentence suggests, however, is that we have to deal with the concept of coercion when we try to understand the constitutional dimension of religious freedom in America. After all, if being legally able to do want we want to do and to refrain from doing what we do not want to do regarding religious matters constitutes the (most abstract) structure of religious freedom, then we have to contend with the fact that the opposite of freedom is coercion.[54] The concept of coercion raises two

[52] Following the *Reynolds* reasoning, the Court states in *Cantwell v. Connecticut* that the idea of free exercise of religion in the First Amendment "embraces two concepts, freedom to believe and freedom to act. The first is absolute but, in the nature of things, the second cannot be." 310 U.S. 296 (1940), at 304.

[53] In order, see, for example, *Lynch v. Donnelly*, 465 U.S. 668 (1984), *Wallace v. Jaffree*, 472 U.S. 38 (1985), *Lee v. Weisman*, 505 U.S. 577 (1992), and *Santa Fe Independent School District v. Doe*, 530 U.S. 290 (2000).

[54] Hence the famous paradox of freedom in book I, chapter 7 of Rousseau's *Social Contract*: "In order then that the social compact may not be an empty formula, it tacitly includes the undertaking, which alone can give force to the rest, that whoever refuses to obey the general will shall be compelled to do so by the whole body. This means nothing less than that he will be forced to be free; for this is the condition which, by giving each citizen to his country, secures him against all personal

central questions in religion-clause analysis. First, what counts as coercion? Is it a thin, narrowly defined concept that includes relatively little, or is it a thicker, more broadly defined concept that includes a range of phenomena beyond those included within the thinner concept? Second, is coercion strictly a necessary characteristic of free-exercise violations and not of establishment violations, or do the latter raise the question of coercion as well? Recall my contention earlier that if the purpose of the religion clauses is to protect religious freedom, then clearly the presence of the two clauses implies that religious freedom can be infringed or limited in two ways: it can be infringed or limited by a denial of the free exercise of religion, and it can be infringed or limited by an establishment of religion. Religious freedom, in other words, requires both a prohibition of denials of free exercise and a prohibition of anything respecting a religious establishment. This suggests that an Establishment violation involves coercion, but then how do we distinguish that violation from a free-exercise violation? If the purpose of the religion clauses is to protect religious freedom,[55] and if the opposite of freedom is coercion, it is more difficult to understand the coercion found in an establishment case than in a free-exercise case.

---

dependence." Jean-Jacques Rousseau, *The Social Contract*, translated by G. D. H. Cole (http://www.constitution.org/jjr/socon_01.htm#007, retrieved 8-10-06). The standard objection to this paradox is that if we are free, we are not being forced, and if we are forced, we are not free.

[55] "The freedom to worship as one pleases without government interference oppression is the great object of both the Establishment and the Free Exercise Clauses." Justice Kennedy in *Allegheny*, at 660. In *Cantwell v. Connecticut*, the Court states at 218–19 that the religious freedom guaranteed by the religion clauses "forestalls compulsion by law of the acceptance of any creed or the practice of any form of worship. Freedom of conscience and freedom to adhere to such religious organization or form of worship as the individual may choose cannot be restricted by law. On the other hand, it safeguards the free exercise of the chosen form of religion. Thus, the Amendment embraces two concepts—freedom to believe and freedom to act. The first is absolute but, in the nature of things, the second cannot be." In *Wallace v. Jaffree*, Justice O'Connor states at 68, "Although a distinct jurisprudence as enveloped each of these Clauses, their common purpose is to secure religious liberty. . . . On these principles the Court has been and remains unanimous." Professor Carl Esbeck writes, "There is near universal agreement on the starting point: the overarching purpose of the First Amendment is to secure religious freedom, for persons of faith or none, and for religious organizations." Carl H. Esbeck, "A Restatement of the Supreme Court's Law of Religious Freedom: Coherence, Conflict, or Chaos?" *Notre Dame Law Review* 70 (1995): 581, at 592. Professor Noah Feldman argues more specifically that "the Establishment Clause was born, like many other elements of the Bill of Rights, out of a desire to protect the individual from coercion at the hands of the state." Noah Feldman, "From Liberty to Equality: The Transformation of the Establishment Clause," *California Law Review* 90 (2002): 673, at 675.

The difficulty, of course, lies in sorting out the answers to these strands of the concept of coercion. In a 1986 article, then-Professor Michael W. McConnell, relying on his understanding of James Madison, argues that "compulsion is not just an element, it is the essence of an establishment."[56] Similarly, in his dissenting opinion in *Allegheny County v. Greater Pittsburgh ACLU*, Justice Anthony Kennedy sets out what has come to be known as the coercion test:

> The ability of the organized community to recognize and accommodate religion in a society with a pervasive public sector requires diligent observance of the border between accommodation and establishment. Our cases disclose two limiting principles: government may not coerce anyone to support or participate in any religion or its exercise; and it may not, in the guise of avoiding hostility or callous indifference, give direct benefits to religion in such a degree that it in fact "establishes a [state] religion or religious faith, or tends to do so." Lynch v. Donnelly, 465 U.S., at 678. These two principles, while distinct, are not unrelated, for it would be difficult indeed to establish a religion without some measure of more or less subtle coercion, be it in the form of taxation to supply the substantial benefits that would sustain a state-established faith, direct compulsion to observance, or governmental exhortation to religiosity that amounts in fact to proselytizing.[57]

Finally, Justice Scalia, dissenting in *Lee v. Weisman*, refers to coercion as "a hallmark of historical establishments of religion."[58] We will return to McConnell, Kennedy, and Scalia momentarily, but suffice it to say at this point that some commentators argue that Kennedy in *Allegheny* and Scalia generally employ such a narrow concept of coercion that it would give a pass to all sorts of government practices and laws that, broadly speaking, we consider to be Establishment violations.[59] Thus one alternative is to detach the concept of coercion from the essence of an Establishment violation because it is too narrow; coercion would be not a necessary and sufficient feature of an Establishment violation, as Kennedy and Scalia would have it, but instead a sufficient but not necessary feature of such a violation.

[56] Michael W. McConnell, "Coercion: The Lost Element of Establishment," *William and Mary Law Review* 27 (1986): 933, at 937.

[57] *Allegheny*, at 660–61.

[58] *Lee v. Weisman*, at 640.

[59] See, e.g., Steven G. Gey, "Religious Coercion and the Establishment Clause," *University of Illinois Law Review* (1994): 463, arguing at 465 that "coercion theory radically departs from existing attitudes about the role of government, the parameters of individual autonomy, and the nature of religion." Specifically, he maintains at 493 that "the narrow definition of coercion imposes almost no limit whatsoever on government-sponsored religious activity. Adopting this version of the coercion standard would rob the Establishment Clause of almost all its power."

By contrast, my purpose in this chapter is to develop a concept of coercion that is a broader or thicker—yet still determinate—concept than its advocates have employed. If I can do so, then we would have another option for Establishment Clause analysis beyond the alternatives of adopting a narrow concept of coercion or rejecting the concept of coercion as a necessary feature of that analysis. Borrowing from considerations on the concept of power, I suggest as my thesis that an Establishment Clause violation is indeed necessarily a matter of coercion, but coercion understood in its implicit rather than its overt dimension. Kennedy, that is, was correct to focus on coercion, but his concept was too thin. I will make this argument about the concept of coercion by introducing three further concepts: the concept of civic identity, the concept of religious identity, and, somewhat inelegantly, the concept of government's "taking a position" on the truth or worth of religion. The general theory I am proposing, therefore, has two central components: first, a broader, more inclusive concept of coercion; and second, as we will see in the next chapter, a concept I am calling position taking, the idea that nonestablishment means that government is not supposed to take a position on the truth or worth of religion, religious beliefs, religious values, or religious practices.

In *Lemon v. Kurtzman*, the Court addresses the question of the constitutionality of state aid to church-related elementary and secondary schools. With regard to the consistency of such aid with the Establishment Clause, Chief Justice Burger, writing for the majority, sets out the three prongs of what has come to be called, after the case at hand, the *Lemon* test:

> Every analysis in this area must begin with consideration of the cumulative criteria developed by the Court over many years. Three such tests may be gleaned from our cases. First, the statute must have a secular legislative purpose; second, its principal or primary effect must be one that neither advances nor inhibits religion . . . ; finally, the statute must not foster "an excessive government entanglement with religion."[60]

Despite the apparent clarity and precision of these three prongs, however, for many commentators and members of the Court the *Lemon* test turned out to be, in practice, a bit of a lemon.[61] Analytically, suffice it to say that the central or core meaning of the Establishment Clause suggested by the *Lemon* test is the concept of strict neutrality among religions and between religion and nonreligion. In essence, the first prong mandates that the

[60] *Lemon v. Kurtzman*, 403 U.S. 602 (1971), at 612–13, internal case references omitted.

[61] For purposes of my argument in this chapter, neither criticism from various members of the Court nor the massive literature the *Lemon* test has generated need be cited here.

purpose of a statute be neutral with regard to religion, the second prong mandates that the effect of a statute be neutral with regard to religion, and the third prong's attempt to separate government and religion into different domains also suggests the concept of neutrality. Beyond the critique of strict neutrality both on and off the Court,[62] the principal problems with *Lemon* can be categorized as the question of determining evidence of statutory purpose (text of the statute, intentions and motivations of legislators) and the question of whether there is indeed a neutral space a statute can occupy between advancing and inhibiting religion.[63]

In her well-known effort to clarify the *Lemon* test, Justice Sandra Day O'Connor sets out what she called the endorsement test in the case of *Lynch v. Donnelly*:

> The Establishment Clause prohibits government from making adherence to a religion relevant in any way to a person's standing in the political community. Government can run afoul of that prohibition in two principal ways. One is excessive entanglement with religious institutions, which may interfere with the independence of the institutions, give the institutions access to government or governmental powers not fully shared by nonadherents of the religion, and foster the creation of political constituencies defined along religious lines. The second and more direct infringement is government endorsement or disapproval of religion. Endorsement sends a message to nonadherents that they are outsiders, not full members of the political community, and an accompanying message to adherents that they are insiders, favored members of the political community. Disapproval sends the opposite message.[64]

O'Connor seeks here, after subscribing to the third prong of the *Lemon* test, to clarify the purpose and effects prong of *Lemon* by stating that a law

[62] See most recently, for example, the nonpreferentialist argument by Patrick M. Garry in "Religious Freedom Deserves More Than Neutrality: The Constitutional Argument for Nonpreferential Favoritism of Religion," *Florida Law Review* 57 (2005): 1. I discuss this briefly in chap. 6, n. 21. Steven Gey, in the article cited above, makes this interesting argument about *Lemon*: "Contrary to the usual criticism of *Lemon*, the problem is not that the terms of Lemon mean too little; the problem is that the terms of *Lemon* mean too much. An honest application of the *Lemon* test would require a far more rigorous separation of church and state than a majority of the current Supreme Court is willing to enforce. This does not mean the test is flawed. Rather, the separation principle that gives the test meaning does not have the support necessary to provide courts applying *Lemon* with a consistent orientation." Gey, "Religious Coercion," at 470.

[63] This is analogous to the concept of a line in Euclidian geometry. By definition, as a series of points each of which has neither length nor width, a line has length but no width. Is the neutral space between advancing and inhibiting religion meaningful, or does it always dissolve into one of the two alternatives because, like Euclid's line, it has no width?

[64] *Lynch v. Donnelly*, at 687–88, internal case references omitted.

or act of government fails to pass Establishment Clause muster if it either endorses or disapproves of a particular religion.[65] That determination, she holds, must be made in terms of what a "reasonable observer"[66] would understand by the law or act of government. This approach, however, is criticized by Justice Kennedy in *Allegheny* as "flawed in its fundamentals and unworkable in practice," and thus a "most unwelcome addition" to Establishment Clause jurisprudence.[67] Taking his stand, as we saw earlier, on the normativity of tradition, Kennedy writes, "Either the endorsement test must invalidate scores of traditional practices recognizing the place religion holds in our culture, or it must be twisted and stretched to avoid inconsistency with practices we know to have been permitted in the past, while condemning similar practices with no greater endorsement effect simply by reason of their lack of historical antecedent. Neither result is acceptable."[68]

The most effective indication of an Establishment Clause violation, according to Kennedy, is thus not endorsement but rather the presence of coercion. As cited above, he writes,

> The ability of the organized community to recognize and accommodate religion in a society with a pervasive public sector requires diligent observance of the border between accommodation and establishment. Our cases disclose two limiting principles: government may not coerce anyone to support or participate in any religion or its exercise; and it may not, in the guise of avoiding hostility or callous indifference, give direct benefits to religion in such a degree that it in fact "establishes a [state] religion or religious faith, or tends to do so." Lynch v. Donnelly, 465 U.S., at 678. These two principles, while distinct, are not unrelated, for it would be difficult indeed to establish a religion without some measure of more or less subtle coercion, be it in the form of taxation to supply the substantial benefits that would sustain a state-established faith, direct compulsion to observance, or governmental exhortation to religiosity that amounts in fact to proselytizing.[69]

[65] "The purpose prong of the *Lemon* test asks whether government's actual purpose is to endorse or disapprove of religion. The effect prong asks whether, irrespective of government's actual purpose, the practice under review in fact conveys a message of endorsement or disapproval. An affirmative answer to either question should render the challenged practice invalid." O'Connor, *Lynch v. Donnelly*, at 690. This test, too, has spawned an enormous critical literature, beyond the scope of this chapter.

[66] *Allegheny*, at 631 and 635.

[67] *Allegheny*, at 669 and 668.

[68] *Allegheny*, at 674.

[69] *Allegheny*, at 660–61. As Steven Gey characterizes Kennedy's position, "The definition of coercion that Justice Kennedy employs in his Allegheny opinion is the very narrow, common understanding of the term. Under this definition, coercion occurs only when a person is compelled by force or threat to do something that he or she would not otherwise do." Gey, "Religious Coercion," at 494. Therefore, "If government

The coercion test is preferable, as Kennedy sees it, both because prohibitions on religious coercion fall within traditional American practices and because it is a sharper, cleaner, more distinct concept than endorsement. Nevertheless, he leaves a certain ambiguity in his *Allegheny* statement insofar as he pairs coercion with a second principle. There is at least an apparent precision to the statement that "government may not coerce anyone to support or participate in any religion or its exercise," but the recitation of the separate—even if related—principle that government "may not, in the guise of avoiding hostility or callous indifference, give direct benefits to religion in such a degree that it in fact 'establishes a [state] religion or religious faith, or tends to do so,'" suggests that a coercion test does not cover the full domain of Establishment Clause violations. Regarding the crèche and the menorah at issue in *Allegheny*, Kennedy writes,

> There is no suggestion here that the government's power to coerce has been used to further the interests of Christianity or Judaism in any way. No one was compelled to observe or participate in any religious ceremony or activity. Neither the city nor the county contributed significant amounts of tax money to serve the cause of one religious faith. The creche and the menorah are purely passive symbols of religious holidays. Passersby who disagree with the message conveyed by these displays are free to ignore them, or even to turn their backs, just as they are free to do when they disagree with any other form of government speech.[70]

Yet despite this claim that the freedom to ignore or turn one's back on a religious symbol amounts to evidence for a lack of coercion, Kennedy also argues,

> Symbolic recognition or accommodation of religious faith may violate the Clause in an extreme case. I doubt not, for example, that the Clause forbids a city to permit the permanent erection of a large Latin cross on the roof of city hall. This is not because government speech about religion is per se suspect, as the majority would have it, but because such an obtrusive year-round

---

action endorsing another religion has not changed an individual religious practitioner's religious behavior, then there has been no coercion. Indications that members of the religious minority have felt excluded or offended by the government's religious speech are irrelevant." Gey, "Religious Coercion," at 499.

[70] *Allegheny*, at 664. Similarly, in *Van Orden v. Perry*, 545 U.S. 677 (2005), at 695, Justice Thomas writes in favor of this narrow version of the coercion test: "In no sense does Texas compel petitioner Van Orden to do anything. The only injury to him is that he takes offense at seeing the monument as he passes it on his way to the Texas Supreme Court Library. He need not stop to read it or even to look at it, let alone to express support for it or adopt the Commandments as guides for his life. The mere presence of the monument along his path involves no coercion and thus does not violate the Establishment Clause."

> religious display would place the government's weight behind an obvious effort to proselytize on behalf of a particular religion.[71]

Why can a passerby not simply ignore or turn her or his back on this large Latin cross? After all, he holds, "Absent coercion, the risk of infringement of religious liberty by passive or symbolic accommodation is minimal."[72] If such a display is for Kennedy indeed an Establishment Clause violation, then either his concept of coercion is in fact not a necessary feature of such a violation, or else the concept of coercion is more complex than he takes it to be in his analysis in *Allegheny*.

My own argument is that the latter alternative is the better one, and that Kennedy's language in places implicitly points us in that direction. Consider his statement, above, of the two principles of Establishment Clause violation: "direct compulsion" is clearly coercion, but the phrase, "governmental exhortation to religiosity that amounts in fact to proselytizing"—like his other reference above to "plac[ing] the government's weight behind an obvious effort to proselytize on behalf of a particular religion"—and the phrase, "more or less subtle coercion," suggest a concept of coercion that is more than, or not limited to, the idea of direct compulsion. This, in fact, is the direction in which Kennedy's majority opinion in *Lee v. Weisman* moves, sparking Scalia's angry dissent. *Lee*, as is well known, has to do with the constitutionality of prayers at a middle-school graduation, and the Court declared them an Establishment Clause violation. What is significant for our purpose here is Kennedy's hesitantly expressed sense that the concept of coercion involves more than Scalia's idea of "coercion of religious orthodoxy and of financial support by force of law and threat of penalty."[73] Kennedy, however, writes, "Even for those students who object to the religious exercise, their attendance and participation in the state-sponsored religious activity are, in a fair and real sense, obligatory, though the school district does not require attendance as a condition for receipt of the diploma."[74] He refers to "subtle coercive pressure in the elementary and secondary public schools,"[75] and to holdings in *Engel v. Vitale*[76] and *Abington v. Schempp*[77] that "prayer exercises in public schools carry a particular risk of indirect coercion."[78] At greater length, Kennedy writes,

[71] *Allegheny*, at 661 (footnote omitted).
[72] *Allegheny*, at 662.
[73] *Lee v. Weisman*, at 640.
[74] *Lee v. Weisman*, at 586.
[75] *Lee v. Weisman*, at 592.
[76] *Engel v. Vitale*, 370 U.S. 421 (1962).
[77] *Abington*.
[78] *Lee v. Weisman*, at 592. Kennedy went on to say that the public and peer pressure

> There was a stipulation in the District Court that attendance at graduation and promotional ceremonies is voluntary. Petitioners the United States, as amicus, made this a center point of the case, arguing that the option of not attending the graduation excuses any inducement or coercion in the ceremony itself. The argument lacks all persuasion. Law reaches past formalism. And to say a teenage student has a real choice not to attend her high school graduation is formalistic in the extreme. True, Deborah could elect not to attend commencement without renouncing her diploma; but we shall not allow the case to turn on this point. Everyone knows that, in our society and in our culture, high school graduation is one of life's most significant occasions. A school rule which excuses attendance is beside the point. Attendance may not be required by official decree, yet it is apparent that a student is not free to absent herself from the graduation exercise in any real sense of the term "voluntary," for absence would require forfeiture of those intangible benefits which have motivated the student through youth and all her high school years.[79]

Clearly, Kennedy was trying in *Lee* to recognize coercion in the real world, so to speak, even if he could not articulate his concept precisely,[80] prompting Scalia's criticism that "[t]he Court's argument that state officials have 'coerced' students to take part in the invocation and benediction at graduation ceremonies is, not to put too fine a point on it, incoherent."[81]

Despite Scalia's typically blunt comment, Kennedy's unsatisfactory attempt to articulate coherently a "thick" concept of coercion, in contrast to Scalia's "thin" concept, can be said to track a subtle development in Michael McConnell's thinking about the concept of coercion. As noted above, in "Coercion: The Lost Element of Establishment," McConnell argues that compulsion is "the essence of an establishment." Because, in his words, "[i]t is difficult to see . . . how an establishment could exist in the absence of some form of coercion,"[82] the problems with the *Lemon* test stem from the fact that it fails to recognize this point. McConnell states,

---

on students to stand silently and respectfully "though subtle and indirect, can be as real as any overt compulsion" (at 593), which drew Scalia's snide reference to Freud in his dissent at 642.

[79] *Lee v. Weisman*, at 594–95 (internal citations omitted).

[80] Perhaps, like Justice Potter Stewart in the obscenity cases, he knows it (coercion) when he sees it. See Stewart's concurring opinion in *Jacobellis v. Ohio*, 378 U.S. 184 (1964), at 197.

[81] *Lee v. Weisman*, at 636. Much earlier, in the school-prayer case of *Engel v. Vitale*, Justice William Douglas takes a similarly thin view of the concept of coercion: "[T]here is no element of compulsion or coercion in New York's regulation requiring that public schools be opened each day with the following prayer." At 438.

[82] McConnell, "Coercion," at 937.

> Doctrinally, renewed attention to coercion suggests that the Court's three-part test for an establishment of religion should be modified. A rule that forbids government actions with the purpose or effect of advancing religion fails to distinguish between efforts to coerce and influence religious belief and action, on the one hand, and efforts to facilitate the exercise of one's chosen faith, on the other.[83]

Yet McConnell, perhaps unknown even to himself, hints at the development of this position: after stating "that the courts are wasting their time when they draw nice distinctions about various manifestations of religion in public life that entail no use of the taxing power and have no coercive effect,"[84] he writes, "On the other hand, my analysis suggests that aid to religion must not be structured to influence or distort religious choice."[85] The idea here of a structure that influences or distorts religious choice is fundamental, as we will see shortly.

Without providing an explicit theoretical underpinning, though, McConnell nevertheless developed this idea further a few years later in "Religious Freedom at a Crossroads." The coercion test, he said,

> has the considerable virtue of returning to the historical purposes of the Establishment Clause, and it would redirect attention toward the actual effects of governmental power, rather than toward mere appearances. Perhaps more importantly, it would restore the symmetry between the Religion Clauses that was broken when the Court declared that coercion was an element of the violation of the Free Exercise Clause but not of the Establishment Clause.[86]

However, referring back to his 1986 article cited in the paragraph immediately above, he now voices second thoughts about the coercion test:

> One of the first articles I wrote on the Religion Clauses criticized the Court for its unexplained dicta that coercion was not an element of an establishment violation. I therefore take some satisfaction in seeing renewed interest in coercion as an aspect of the establishment analysis. But if I had it to do over again, I would take pains to emphasize that the concept of "coercion" cannot, in itself, supply a standard for distinguishing between establishments and nonestablishments, and that *it is vital to understand the concept of coercion broadly and realistically*.[87]

[83] McConnell, "Coercion," at 940, footnote omitted.

[84] McConnell, "Coercion," at 939, footnote omitted.

[85] McConnell, "Coercion," at 940.

[86] Michael McConnell, "Religious Freedom at a Crossroads," *University of Chicago Law Review* 59 (1992): 115, at 158.

[87] McConnell, "Religious Freedom," at 158, emphasis added, footnote omitted.

While McConnell was writing this just before the *Lee v. Weisman* decision was announced, his reference here to a broad and realistic concept of coercion anticipated Kennedy's position in that case. Indeed, continuing from the point at which the previous citation ended, McConnell assesses the *Lee* issues in this way:

> For example, the Court is now being urged to adopt the coercion test in a case involving a public prayer at a junior high school graduation ceremony. I would have thought that gathering a captive audience is a classic example of coercion; participation is hardly voluntary if the cost of avoiding the prayer is to miss one's graduation. Equally seriously, it appears that the content of the prayer was subject to indirect governmental control, which is a species of coercion. For the Court to embrace the coercion test in this form would be a small step back toward permitting the government to indoctrinate children in the favored civil religion of nondenominational theism.[88]

The upshot of this analysis is that McConnell too, like Kennedy, suggests in this article a thicker concept of coercion than Scalia's idea of the "force of law and threat of penalty."[89] The latter concept, in other words, is not a sufficiently "broad and realistic concept of coercion," but we need a more precise articulation of the theoretical underpinnings of such a concept.

The difficulty, of course, lies in sorting this out, and it is complicated by the Court's disconnection of the concept of establishment from the concept of coercion in its early religion-clause cases in order to distinguish free-exercise and establishment violations. While free-exercise cases certainly raise contentious issues, they seem to me to be, relative to establishment cases, uncomplicated theoretically even if they raise difficult value questions. The core free-exercise issue, as we saw earlier, is the question of when government may legitimately prohibit the free exercise of religion (for almost no one argues that the First Amendment absolutely bars prohibition of free exercise), which spawns the subordinate questions of what test the government must pass—compelling state interest, rational basis—if it is to overcome a presumption in favor of free exercise, and whether the contested abridgement must be intentional or just an effect of an otherwise valid government action. I do not wish to underestimate the seriousness of free-exercise issues, but my contention is that establishment issues seem to raise particularly difficult and knotty theoretical problems with regard to coercion. In particular, if the purpose

[88] McConnell, "Religious Freedom," at 158–59, footnotes omitted.

[89] He warns—his own word—that "an emphasis on coercion could tend toward acquiescence in more subtle forms of governmental power" (McConnell, "Religious Freedom," at 159), but this simply registers his dissatisfaction with the thinner concept of coercion.

of the religion clauses is to protect religious freedom,[90] and if the opposite of freedom is coercion, it is more difficult to understand the coercion found in an establishment case than in a free-exercise case. After all, aside from its enabling or empowering function,[91] law involves prohibiting someone from doing what he or she does want to do or forcing someone to do what he or she does not want to do. The Court has recognized this coercion easily in free-exercise cases but has had difficulty explaining it in establishment-clause cases. The Court pointed to this distinction most famously in *Engel v. Vitale*:

> Although these two clauses may, in certain instances, overlap, they forbid two quite different kinds of governmental encroachment upon religious freedom. The Establishment Clause, unlike the Free Exercise Clause, does not depend upon any showing of direct governmental compulsion and is violated by the enactment of laws which establish an official religion whether those laws operate directly to coerce nonobserving individuals or not. This is not to say, of course, that laws officially prescribing a particular form of religious worship do not involve coercion of such individuals. When the power, prestige and financial support of government is placed behind a particular religious belief, the indirect coercive pressure upon religious minorities to conform to the prevailing officially approved religion is plain. But the purposes underlying the Establishment Clause go much further than that. Its first and most immediate purpose rested on the belief that a union of government and religion tends to destroy government and to degrade religion.[92]

Following this logic, the Court in *Abington v. Schempp* states, "[I]t is necessary in a free exercise case for one to show the coercive effect of the enactment as it operates against him in the practice of his religion. The distinction between the two clauses is apparent—a violation of the Free Exercise Clause is predicated on coercion, while the Establishment Clause violation need not be so attended."[93] Thus, whereas coercion is both a necessary and sufficient condition of bringing a free-exercise claim, it is not necessary to an establishment claim,[94] but we are hard pressed to explain what it might mean to say that it is sufficient. The Court's reference in *Engel* to "indirect coercive pressure" is not crystal

[90] "The freedom to worship as one pleases without government interference or oppression is the great object of both the Establishment and the Free Exercise Clauses." Justice Kennedy in *Allegheny*, at 660.

[91] See H. L. A. Hart, *The Concept of Law*, 2nd ed. (Oxford: Oxford University Press, 1997), chap. 3, "The Variety of Laws."

[92] *Engel v. Vitale*, at 430–31.

[93] *Abington*, at 223.

[94] "Although our precedents make clear that proof of government coercion is not necessary to prove an Establishment Clause violation," writes Justice Blackmun in his *Allegheny* concurrence at 604, "it is sufficient."

clear, but it suggests a perhaps inchoate sense that something more is going on here than what the usual understanding of coercion emphasizes, a sense that later became explicit in the arguments of Kennedy and McConnell that we examined above.

What, then, is that "something more" in the concept of coercion that makes it thicker rather than thinner? To begin to provide an answer, the first point to note is that if we agree that the religion clauses together stand for the affirmation of religious freedom, then the denial of such freedom means that someone is forced—coerced—to do something he or she does not want to do, or prohibited from doing something he or she does want to do. At the level of common sense, consequently, the point of guaranteeing religious freedom is to protect people, through both the Establishment Clause and the Free Exercise Clause, against the denial of that freedom.[95] People are not to be subject to coercion in matters of religion. Given that baseline, my argument is that, similar to what Peter Bachrach and Morton Baratz called the two faces of power,[96] the "something more" in the concept of coercion is the fact that coercion has two dimensions, overt and implicit. Understanding this distinction is not a matter of simply looking for a definition, but because we want to understand coercion the way the ordinary, nonphilosophical person would understand it; in fact, a quick look at ordinary-language usage will point us toward the theoretical underpinnings we want. According to the *Oxford English Dictionary*, to coerce is "to constrain or restrain (a voluntary or moral agent) by the application of superior force, or by authority resting on force; to constrain to compliance or obedience by forceable means; 'to keep in order by force' (J.)."[97] Now, if we think of *Lee v. Weisman*, then in terms of the descriptions of coercion here, it is clear,

[95] "The freedom to worship as one pleases without government interference or oppression," Kennedy writes at 660 in *Allegheny*, "is the great object of both the Establishment and Free Exercise Clauses." Similarly, Blackmun states, "The First Amendment encompasses two distinct guarantees—the government shall make no law respecting an establishment of religion or prohibiting the free exercise thereof—both with the common purpose of securing religious liberty." *Allegheny*, at 605.

[96] Peter Bachrach and Morton S. Baratz, "Two Faces of Power," *American Political Science Review* 56 (1962): 947–52. The analysis of the concept of power has a long history in political science, sociology, and philosophy. See, e.g., Thomas J. Anton, "Power, Pluralism, and Local Politics," *Administrative Science Quarterly* 7, no. 4 (1963): 425–57, a classic article distinguishing between the way political scientists and sociologists conceive power. In *Power: A Radical View*, 2nd ed. (Houndmills, U.K.: Palgrave Macmillan, 2005), Steven Lukes distinguishes a "third face" of power, and, discussing the work of Michel Foucault, Peter Digeser adds another in "The Fourth Face of Power," *The Journal of Politics* 54, no. 4 (1992): 977–1007. For my more limited purposes here, however, the idea of two faces of power will suffice.

[97] "Coerce," def. 1, *OED*.

as Scalia argued, that there was nothing coercive about having students sit or stand respectfully during a graduation prayer. Nevertheless, the idea of constraining to compliance or obedience contains the germ of the thicker concept of coercion we seek, a germ we find in the *OED*'s definition of coercion: "constraint, restraint, compulsion; the application of force to control the action of a voluntary agent."[98] The phrase "to control the action of a voluntary agent" suggests that to coerce someone is, put succinctly, either to make his or her choice or to make him or her choose. Specifically, coercion occurs when the government makes me do something *and* when it puts me in the position of having to decide that I have to do something; government can make a choice for me, or it can make me make a choice.[99] The former dimension of coercion is overt and consists, in a sense, of the denial of choice, while the latter dimension is implicit and consists of the structuring of choice.

It is true, however, that the phrase "denial of choice" as a central feature of coercion can and often does obfuscate an important trait of a coercive situation. According to Michael Bayles, in a case of what he calls dispositional coercion, "one man (the agent) threatens another (the victim) with a sanction if the latter fails to act as requested."[100] This accords with our conventional understanding of coercion, but Bayles adds this contention: "A victim of dispositional coercion always has a choice. He can either do as told, or do something else and receive a sanction."[101] If this is true, then it threatens the viability of my distinction between overt and implicit coercion, for all coercion would involve the structuring of choice I attribute to the latter. Recall a classic story about comedian Jack Benny:

> Jack Benny, the well-known American entertainer from long ago, used to joke self-deprecatingly about his frugality. Once, he told of walking down a New York street late at night when he suddenly felt cold, hard metal pointing into his back and a gruff voice barked, "Your money or your life!" When he didn't immediately respond, the gun at his back pressed deeper into his flesh and the voice from behind became more menacing, "Your money or your life!" Benny replied, "I'm thinking, I'm thinking."[102]

[98] "Coercion, def. 1, *OED*.

[99] Consider the situation in the film *Sophie's Choice* regarding which of Sophie's children should live or die. The German officer did not make her choice—he made her choose; he did not coerce Sophie to give up one child in particular, but rather forced her to choose which child to give up. The former is certainly a case of coercion, but the latter surely is as well.

[100] Michael D. Bayles, "A Concept of Coercion," in *Coercion*, ed. J. Roland Pennock and John W. Chapman (Chicago: Aldine-Atherton, 1972), 16–29, 17.

[101] Bayles, "Concept of Coercion," 18.

[102] Yossy Goldman, "Your Money or Your Life?" Chadbad.org. http://www.chabad.org/parshah/article.asp?AID=156189 (retrieved 7-27-06).

This story certainly fits Bayles' account and a more recent account of the dynamics of coercion. According to Michael Rhodes,

> The notion that coercion does not involve a choice being made by the coerced agent is nonsensical, yet pervasive. With genuine instances of coercion, expressions such as "so and so was forced to surrender his wallet" are entirely misleading if "forced" is understood to imply an absence of free will or choice. A gunman relies upon the victim's capacity for choice when attempting coercion, and assumes that the victim will choose his life over his wallet.[103]

People may indeed be too quick to say, "I was forced to do X," or "I was coerced to do X." We can argue that at a certain level, given a choice between two options, one of which is an evil (giving up one's money) and the other of which no reasonable person would do in ordinary circumstances (giving up one's life rather than surrendering one's wallet or purse), we can understand why people would say they had no choice, or were forced to do X. But that should not obscure cases in which people are given alternatives between two evils and the coercion is not that they are made to choose one or the other, but rather that they are made to choose at all. As Bernard Gert states, "A man acts freely if and only if he acts voluntarily and does not do so because of any unreasonable incentives. A man who acts voluntarily, but only because of some unreasonable incentives, does not act freely."[104] The reason the Jack Benny story is funny is that he considers as two reasonable alternatives what no normal person would consider as such. There may well be choice in the situation of surrendering one's money or one's life, but there is a meaningful difference between choice between two reasonable alternatives and choice between a reasonable and an unreasonable alternative.[105] No one wants—would choose—to be faced with the latter, and being put into that situation must count as an instance of coercion despite the fact that the victim has a choice. "To be deprived of freedom," Gert contends, "it is sufficient that one be threatened with unreasonable incentives."[106]

Consider, for example, the way we experience the constraints of chess. Imagine a situation in which my opponent moves her knight into a position from which it threatens both my queen and my rook. Prior to

[103] Michael R. Rhodes, "The Nature of Coercion," *Journal of Value Inquiry* 34 (2000): 369–81, at 370.

[104] Bernard Gert, "Coercion and Freedom," in Pennock and Chapman, *Coercion*, 30–48, 32.

[105] Recall Aristotle's discussion of voluntary and involuntary actions in the case of the necessity of throwing goods overboard in a storm in bk 3, chap. 3 of *Nicomachean Ethics*. http://classics.mit.edu/Aristotle/nicomachaen.3.iii.html (retrieved 5-17-11).

[106] Gert, "Coercion and Freedom," 39.

my opponent's move neither piece was immediately threatened and I was free to move them or not to move them in accordance with my own strategy. If she had moved her knight into a different position and threatened my queen alone, she would have forced me to move my queen to safety (assuming for the sake of argument that such a move was available to me). In the present situation, however, her move has put me into the position of having to choose, that is, of having to make a choice as to which piece I have to sacrifice. She does not choose which piece to take; I have that choice. Nevertheless, phenomenologically speaking—that is, from the standpoint of the way I experience the position into which her move has put me—I certainly have the sense of being coerced despite the fact that I still choose which piece to lose. My point, therefore, is that when my queen is threatened my opponent has coerced me overtly, for she has left me no choice—I have to move my queen—but when her knight threatens both my queen and my rook, she has coerced me implicitly—she has forced me to choose.[107]

This implicit dimension of coercion is, I would argue, the second face of coercion and the one that provides the theoretical grounding for the concept of coercion that both Kennedy and McConnell were in effect articulating. For example, to Justice Scalia, as long as there is neither civil

[107] This dimension of coercion appears also, I suggest, in the experience people have when they receive something in the mail regarding a subscription or other such financial arrangement and are required to "opt out" if they choose to refuse the offer. The commonplace sense of irritation and even violation people express in that circumstance indicates their resentment toward what is arguably a form of coercion. Choosing to receive a particular product or service is one thing; having to opt out of receiving it is another. The "default" in the former case is my free will; the "default" in the latter case is the will of the seller—hence, a form of coercion. We see this in the statement of facts in *McCollum v. Board of Education*, 333 U.S. 203 (1948), with Justice Black writing for the Court at 209: "Classes were conducted in the regular classrooms of the school building. Students who did not choose to take the religious instruction were not released from public school duties; they were required to leave their classrooms and go to some other place in the school building for pursuit of their secular studies. On the other hand, students who were released from secular study for the religious instructions were required to be present at the religious classes. Reports of their presence or absence were to be made to their secular teachers." The default here is clearly religion because it was students who did not take religious instruction who had to leave their regular classrooms. Similarly, in *Abington*, Justice Clark writing for the Court at 205 stated, "The Commonwealth of Pennsylvania by law, 24 Pa. Stat. 15-1516, as amended, Pub. Law 1928 (Supp. 1960) Dec. 17, 1959, requires that 'At least ten verses from the Holy Bible shall be read, without comment, at the opening of each public school on each school day. Any child shall be excused from such Bible reading, or attending such Bible reading, upon the written request of his parent or guardian.'" This is another opt-out system, making the religious exercises the default and those not choosing religious instruction to be the exception.

nor criminal penalty for not participating in some sort of government-sponsored or -endorsed religious activity (prayer in the classroom, at a school graduation, at a school football game) or not being required to look at a Ten Commandments monument, then there is no coercion. Justice Douglas argues in the *Engel v. Vitale* school-prayer case that "there is no element of compulsion or coercion" involved in reciting the Regents' prayer:

> The prayer is said upon the commencement of the school day, immediately following the pledge of allegiance to the flag. The prayer is said aloud in the presence of a teacher, who either leads the recitation or selects a student to do so. No student, however, is compelled to take part. The respondents have adopted a regulation which provides that "Neither teachers nor any school authority shall comment on participation or non-participation . . . nor suggest or request that any posture or language be used or dress be worn or be not used or not worn." Provision is also made for excusing children, upon written request of a parent or guardian, from the saying of the prayer or from the room in which the prayer is said. A letter implementing and explaining this regulation has been sent to each taxpayer and parent in the school district. As I read this regulation, a child is free to stand or not stand, to recite or not recite, without fear of reprisal or even comment by the teacher or any other school official.[108]

Legal compulsion is distinct from social compulsion, but legal compulsion can structure circumstances that allow for or even encourage social compulsion. Regarding the *McCollum* release-time case, for example, Bruce Dierenfield notes, "To reach her goal of 100 percent participation, Terry McCollum's fifth-grade teacher pressured him to join. When he refused, the teacher banished him to a tiny room next to the teacher's toilet and then to the hall, where he was teased and given a steady diet of 'black eyes, bloody noses, and welts.'"[109] Referring to one of the *Engel* litigants, Dierenfield writes, "In school the Lyons children endured continual taunts and threats because they remained silent during the prayer."[110] As late as 1993, in the *Santa Fe* case about prayer before high school football games, according to Dierenfield, "The Santa Fe School District had crossed the church-state line numerous times before this latest dust-up. Fourth graders who refused to recite a Protestant prayer were denied lunch. Teachers had pressured their students to attend evangelical

[108] *Engel v. Vitale*, at 438. Note the default here and in the *McCollum* release-time case: those who did not want to participate in the religious ritual or lessons had to leave the room or otherwise ask to be excused.

[109] Bruce J. Dierenfield, *The Battle over School Prayer: How Engel v. Vitale Changed America* (Lawrence: University Press of Kansas, 2007), 53.

[110] Dierenfield, *Battle*, 138–39.

revival meetings."[111] So much of the Court's discussion of coercion in religion cases misses this human side of the matter.[112] Was all this school policy? No, so there was no overt coercion. Did school policy create the circumstances that enabled this kind of coercion to occur? Yes, and this was implicit coercion.

Indeed, I would hypothesize that coercion appears in its overt form in free-exercise cases, whereas it appears in both its overt and implicit forms in establishment cases. After all, one obvious problem with placing coercion at the core of an Establishment Clause violation is this: if coercion is a necessary feature of both establishment and free-exercise violations, then what remains of the difference between the two clauses and the two types of violation? In the words of Douglas Laycock, one of our most thoughtful scholars of religion-clause jurisprudence,

> Coercing citizens to support a religion in which they do not believe will often, and arguably always, violate the Free Exercise Clause. If the Establishment Clause were also confined to coercion, it would be redundant. This redundancy in the coercion interpretation is textual support for the belief that the Establishment Clause goes beyond coercion, and therefore that noncoercive support of religion is an establishment.[113]

In *Allegheny* Justice O'Connor, too, cautions against making the Free Exercise Clause redundant by making coercion a necessary feature of an establishment violation:

[111] Dierenfield, *Battle*, 209.

[112] For a more recent example, see the story of the experience of the Dobrich family of Delaware, the only Jews in their small town. When they and others asked the Indian River district school board to replace overtly Christian prayers with others that were more generic and less exclusionary, they encountered anger and threats from the local community. Neela Banerjee, "Families Challenging Religious Influence in Delaware Schools," *The New York Times*, July 29, 2006 (http://www.nytimes.com/2006/07/29/us/29delaware.html?_r=1&scp=2&sq=Dobrich&st=nyt&oref=slogin, retrieved 6-13-08). The Dobriches, in the words of a local talk-radio host, should "[s]top interfering with our traditions, stop interfering with our faith and leave our country the way we knew it to be." According to a local businessman, "If they feel singled out, they should find another school or excuse themselves from those functions. It's our way of life." Banerjee, "Families Challenging." Classmates of the Dobrich son, Alex, called him "Alex the Jew" and "Jew boy." Mrs. Dobrich was told, "'If you want people to stop calling him 'Jew boy,' you tell him to give his heart to Jesus.' Immediately afterward, the Dobriches got threatening phone calls." Banerjee, "Families Challenging."

[113] Douglas Laycock, "Religious Liberty as Liberty," *Journal of Contemporary Legal Issues* 7 (1996): 313, at 339–40. Interestingly, however, at 314 he states, "Religious liberty does not view religion as a good thing to be promoted, nor as a dangerous force to be contained." I would argue precisely the opposite: religion is both good and dangerous, and that is why the Constitution contains, respectively, the Free Exercise Clause and the Establishment Clause.

> An Establishment Clause standard that prohibits only "coercive" practices or overt efforts at government proselytization . . . , but fails to take account of the numerous more subtle ways that government can show favoritism to particular beliefs or convey a message of disapproval to others, would not, in my view, adequately protect the religious liberty or respect the religious diversity of the members of our pluralistic political community. Thus, this Court has never relied on coercion alone as the touchstone of Establishment Clause analysis. . . . To require a showing of coercion, even indirect coercion, as an essential element of an Establishment Clause violation would make the Free Exercise Clause a redundancy.[114]

Also in *Allegheny*, Justice David Souter argues that the various religion-clause precedents "simply cannot . . . support the position that a showing of coercion is necessary to a successful Establishment Clause claim," due to the fact that "a literal application of the coercion test would render the Establishment Clause a virtual nullity."[115] The argument behind all such claims, however, seems to be this: the concept of coercion has a singular dimension that is clear, precise, sharp, and limited; since the core of a Free Exercise Clause violation is coercion, to put coercion at the core of an Establishment Clause violation is to render one or the other clause redundant; therefore, coercion cannot be at the core of—a necessary feature of—an Establishment Clause violation. On the other hand, if the concept of coercion has a second dimension, then the two clauses could rest on coercion in different ways.

Once we acknowledge—or at least stipulate for the sake of argument—that coercion can be both overt or implicit rather than just overt, the question obviously arises, what is the nature of coercion in Free Exercise Clause and Establishment Clause cases? The former group, as I suggested earlier, appears to be relatively simple: in Free Exercise cases government prevents us from doing something religious we want to do—e.g., have multiple wives or smoke peyote[116]—or forces us to do something we do not want to do—e.g., salute the flag.[117] Each type of coercion is what I would consider overt coercion, in that by law or other type of action government is essentially making our choice for us, that is, imposing a decision against our will. Coercion—overt coercion—is

[114] *Allegheny*, at 628–29, internal citations omitted.

[115] *Allegheny*, at 620 and 621.

[116] *U.S. v. Reynolds*, 98 U.S. 145 (1879) and *Employment Division v. Smith*.

[117] *Minersville School District v. Gobitis* and *West Virginia State Board of Education v. Barnette*. In the latter case, students were allowed to opt out of participation in the flag salute, but the opt-out solution presumes the legitimacy of the ritual and makes it the default and the objecting students the rejecters. The students were thus forced into a choice.

thus both a necessary and sufficient condition of a Free Exercise case. An Establishment Clause violation can involve overt coercion in this sense too, exemplified most obviously by being forced to pay a tax to support an established religion that is not our own or to attend mandatory religious services that are not our own. Here too, overt coercion can be a sufficient condition of an establishment case, as the *Engel* citation above noted.[118] Yet if we can agree that there is indeed an establishment violation if a person has to pay taxes to support a religion or attend services not his or her own, why is it coercion for someone to see a government-sponsored religious display, as in *Allegheny*, or to have to sit and listen to prayer, as in *Lee v. Weisman*? That is, how does it affect my religious freedom for government to sponsor religious displays directly or to create conditions through the structured context of the public school environment in which individuals engage in religious activities such as moments of silence and prayer at graduation exercises or football games? The answer to this question will enable us to identify the core meaning of the Establishment Clause, and it is to this argument that we now turn.

[118] See the text at n. 98 *supra*.

Chapter 6

The Concept of Position Taking in Establishment Clause Jurisprudence

The political significance of the religion clauses comes into play most directly with the Establishment Clause. The Free Exercise Clause is important principally regarding the individual, having to do with the individual's liberty in matters of private religious belief and practice. It thus speaks to the question of what government is required to do—respect the religious freedom of American citizens. The Free Exercise Clause thus speaks to the question of religious freedom in an obvious and explicit manner. The Establishment Clause, on the other hand, speaks to the question of what government is required not to do, with the consequence that its role in the protection of religious freedom is a trickier and more complex issue than we find with the Free Exercise Clause. The Establishment Clause, in particular, raises the issue of the public place, role, and status of religion, which goes to the heart of the question as to the meaning of the religion clauses to the nature of the American political order, the central question of this book.

Surveying the similarities and distinctions between rights protected against federal infringement by the Bill of Rights and rights protected against state infringement by the Due Process Clause of the Fourteenth Amendment, Justice Benjamin Cardozo writes in *Palko v. Connecticut*, "The line of division may seem to be wavering and broken if there is a hasty catalogue of the cases on the one side and the other. Reflection and analysis will induce a different view. There emerges the perception of a rationalizing principle which gives to discrete instances a proper order and coherence."[1] Such a "rationalizing principle which gives to discrete instances a proper order and coherence" is precisely what the jurisprudence of the Establishment Clause of the First Amendment has lacked

[1] *Palko v. Connecticut*, 302 U.S. 319 (1937), at 325.

since the *Everson* decision some sixty years ago.[2] Indeed, it is customary to begin an essay on the Establishment Clause in the First Amendment to the U.S. Constitution with a lament about the problematic state of jurisprudence in this important and controversial constitutional field. The typical claim we encounter holds that Establishment Clause doctrine is inconsistent or confusing at best, or even incoherent and contradictory at worst. We lack a "rationalizing principle," to use Cardozo's term, because of our ongoing disagreement as to the central principle at the core of the Establishment Clause. For example, with very rare exceptions, we know in our constitutional bones that direct government funding of a church's facilities and operations violates the Establishment Clause, whereas we do not similarly know that government sponsorship of a clearly religious display does also. We disagree about what principle would cover both sets of circumstances, among many others, clearly and coherently. Moreover, given the prohibitory nature of the clause—"Congress shall make no law respecting an establishment of religion"—determining and coming to a consensus on the central principle of the Establishment Clause is possibly complicated by the fact that any such principle is in fact a nonestablishment principle.

As we saw in the previous chapter, one traditional solution to the problem of determining the central principle at the core of the Establishment Clause is tradition. Appeals to tradition as the governing interpretive norm partake of one of two norms Cardozo notes in his *Palko* discussion of his "rationalizing principle" cited earlier: "The right to trial by jury and the immunity from prosecution except as the result of an indictment may have value and importance. Even so, they are not of the very essence of a scheme of ordered liberty. To abolish them is not to violate a 'principle of justice so rooted in the traditions and conscience of our people as to be ranked as fundamental.'"[3] Contrary to an appeal to "the very essence of a scheme of ordered liberty" or to what is "implicit in the concept of ordered liberty," an appeal to what we might call reason or political or even moral theory, the appeal to the "traditions and conscience of our people" would appear to provide a bulwark against the dangers of abstract reason in the concreteness of historical tradition.

Nevertheless, there are at least four difficulties with the appeal to tradition for a determination of the central principle at the core of the Establishment Clause. First, how do we determine what counts as a tradition? How long does a practice have to occur before we label it a tradition? The litigation over the Ten Commandments display struck down in 2005 in *McCreary v. ACLU of Kentucky*, for example, began in November 1999

[2] *Everson v. Board of Education*, 330 U.S. 1 (1947).
[3] *Palko*, at 325, internal references omitted.

after the display was first created in the summer of 1999, whereas the Ten Commandments monument sustained in 2005 in *Van Orden v. Perry* had stood on state capitol grounds for forty years prior to litigation. Second, we need the ability to distinguish between good traditions and bad traditions; almost no one would argue that any tradition is by definition good. We have or used to have all sorts of traditions in American society, such as Independence Day celebrations, St. Patrick's Day revelries, discrimination, and lynching, but we would not necessarily consider all of them to be good or legitimate. The concept of tradition itself would not enable us to make these distinctions between good and bad traditions. Third, any practice that we might come to consider a tradition would seemingly reflect the wishes of a majority, while, as we noted in chapter 1, the idea of a right of religious freedom underlying both religion clauses entails a protection of a minority against the wishes of a majority. Fourth and finally, the appeal to tradition, if we are to avoid begging the question, cannot itself be justified by an appeal to tradition. We cannot rely on tradition for the reason that we have a tradition of doing so.

All four difficulties necessarily drive us back to the other interpretive norm Cardozo noted, namely, the idea of what is "implicit in the concept of ordered liberty," an appeal to what we might call reason or political or even moral theory. We need a theory, in other words, to enable us to identify, sort through, and justify competing traditions. Still, if the concept of tradition is problematic, one might recur to the notion of original intent to provide the fundamental nonestablishment principle we seek. Here too, however, we need a theory. Leaving aside the familiar complexities of the originalism debate,[4] we find that advocates of grounding a principle of nonestablishment in original intent either lack the courage of their convictions or still require the very enterprise of theory the appeal to original intent is supposed to eliminate. For example, as we have seen, Justice Joseph Story famously states,

> Probably at the time of the adoption of the constitution, and of the amendment to it, now under consideration, the general, if not the universal, sentiment in America was, that Christianity ought to receive encouragement from the state, so far as was not incompatible with the private rights of conscience, and the freedom of religious worship. An attempt to level all religions, and to make it a matter of state policy to hold all in utter indifference, would have created universal disapprobation, if not universal indignation.[5]

[4] See Dennis J. Goldford, *The American Constitution and the Debate over Originalism* (New York: Cambridge University Press, 2005).

[5] Joseph Story, "Commentaries on the Constitution 3:§1868," in *The Founders' Constitution* (http://press-pubs.uchicago.edu/founders/documents/amendI_religions69.html, retrieved 3-23-08).

That said—considering it appropriate for government to favor and foster Christianity as opposed to other religions—he goes on to argue that "the duty of supporting religion, and especially the Christian religion, is very different from the right to force the consciences of other men, or to punish them for worshipping God in the manner, which, they believe, their accountability to him requires."[6] Nevertheless, as we have seen earlier, he continues,

> The real object of the amendment was, not to countenance, much less to advance Mahometanism, or Judaism, or infidelity, by prostrating Christianity; but to exclude all rivalry among Christian sects, and to prevent any national ecclesiastical establishment, which should give to an hierarchy the exclusive patronage of the national government.[7]

If Story is correct that the original intent of the Establishment Clause was not to "countenance, much less to advance" Islam or Judaism, to mention only these two religions, then advocates of original intent either (1) lack the courage to maintain this view today, (2) need to show that Story is simply wrong in his history, or (3) must avail themselves of a constitutional theory that will explain why Islam and Judaism are indeed to be "countenanced."

Justice Scalia in essence takes the third tack when he writes in *McCreary*, "The three most popular religions in the United States, Christianity, Judaism, and Islam—which combined account for 97.7% of all believers—are monotheistic."[8] He includes Islam and Judaism with Christianity as monotheistic religions and argues that government may favor monotheistic over non-monotheistic religions: "With respect to public acknowledgment of religious belief, it is entirely clear from our Nation's historical practices that the Establishment Clause permits this disregard of polytheists and believers in unconcerned deities, just as it permits the disregard of devout atheists."[9] Justice Stevens, by contrast, argues at length in *Van Orden v. Perry*, the companion case to *McCreary*, that Scalia has his history wrong:

> The original understanding of the type of "religion" that qualified for constitutional protection under the Establishment Clause likely did not include those followers of Judaism and Islam who are among the preferred "monotheistic" religions Justice Scalia has embraced in his *McCreary County* opinion. The inclusion of Jews and Muslims inside the category of

[6] Story, *Commentaries*, §1870.

[7] Story, *Commentaries*, §1871.

[8] Scalia, *McCreary County, Kentucky, et al. v. American Civil Liberties Union of Kentucky, et al.*, 545 U.S. 844 (2005), at 894.

[9] *McCreary*, at 893.

> constitutionally favored religions surely would have shocked Chief Justice Marshall and Justice Story. Indeed, Justice Scalia is unable to point to any persuasive historical evidence or entrenched traditions in support of his decision to give specially preferred constitutional status to all monotheistic religions. Perhaps this is because the history of the Establishment Clause's original meaning just as strongly supports a preference for Christianity as it does a preference for monotheism. Generic references to "God" hardly constitute evidence that those who spoke the word meant to be inclusive of all monotheistic believers; nor do such references demonstrate that those who heard the word spoken understood it broadly to include all monotheistic faiths. Justice Scalia's inclusion of Judaism and Islam is a laudable act of religious tolerance, but it is one that is unmoored from the Constitution's history and text, and moreover one that is patently arbitrary in its inclusion of some, but exclusion of other (*e.g.*, Buddhism), widely practiced non-Christian religions. Given the original understanding of the men who championed our "Christian nation"—men who had no cause to view anti-Semitism or contempt for atheists as problems worthy of civic concern—one must ask whether Justice Scalia "has not had the courage (or the foolhardiness) to apply [his originalism] principle consistently."[10]

Yet if Scalia is correct, he comes perilously close to the argument of Judge Roy Moore, the famous "Ten Commandments Judge" from Alabama: "By leaving religion undefined, the Court has opened the door to the erroneous assumption that, under the Establishment Clause, religion could include Buddhism, Hinduism, Taoism, and whatever might occupy in man's life a place parallel to that filled by God, or even Secular Humanism, which might be defined as man's belief in his own supremacy and sufficiency."[11]

What serious judge, lawyer, or commentator is going to argue in twenty-first-century America that Buddhism, Hinduism, and Taoism, to name just those three faiths, do not count as religion within the meaning of the Establishment Clause? All we could conclude is that an originalist like Scalia is wrong about the relevant original intent, or that originalism itself is wrong as an interpretive approach, or else that he needs a constitutional theory to explain why polytheistic faiths do count as religion within the meaning of the Establishment Clause. Principle, therefore, is essential, and especially so if we are to make sense of coercion in Establishment Clause cases. If we think we lock the front door to avoid the danger of working with an abstract principle that might have at best only a tenuous connection with political and constitutional reality, such a principle

[10] Stevens (dissenting), *Van Orden v. Perry*, 545 U.S. 667 (2005), at 729.

[11] Roy S. Moore, "Religion in the Public Square," *Cumberland Law Review* 29 (1998): 347, at 356–57, footnote omitted.

always comes in through the back door to show up, however implicitly, in our arguments.

To be sure, in *Kiryas Joel v. Grumet*, Justice Sandra Day O'Connor sounds a cautionary warning against just such a project for the Establishment Clause. "It is always appealing," she writes, "to look for a single test, a Grand Unified Theory that would resolve all the cases that may arise under a particular Clause." However, she concludes, "Experience proves that the Establishment Clause, like the Free Speech Clause, cannot easily be reduced to a single test. There are different categories of Establishment Clause cases, which may call for different approaches," and "Any test that must deal with widely disparate situations risks being so vague as to be useless."[12] O'Connor's warning, then, is that no single test adequately covers the full range of circumstances that arise under the Establishment Clause. Professor Thomas C. Berg summarizes the two principal approaches of legal scholars sympathetic to O'Connor's argument:

> Perhaps disheartened by the Court's repeated failures, a number of writers have concluded that at least at present, there is no single viable principle or approach available for courts to use to decide cases under the Religion Clauses. In their weakest form, such views suggest merely that courts for now should look case by case at a wide variety of factors, rather than try to set forth a comprehensive constitutional doctrine of religious freedom. In stronger forms, however, such views suggest that no coherent account of religious freedom is possible or even desirable under the conditions of American religious and political life; and that courts ought to step aside and let church-state issues be resolved through the mechanisms of political decision-making.[13]

Nevertheless, against such views Berg maintains that "in the area of church and state, there are good reasons to try to discipline results by theory as much as possible, and acceptable theories are available."[14] Apart from the question of what theories Berg considers acceptable, as a philosophical matter I subscribe to his contention that any test necessarily presupposes a theory or principle. "Underlying any specific tests," Berg writes, "must be a deeper set of principles or values. These are necessary to determine what the content of different tests will be, and even to decide what the categories are that call for different tests."[15] Professor

[12] *Kiryas Joel v. Grumet*, 512 U.S. 687 (1994), O'Connor (concurring opinion), at 718, 720, and 718.

[13] Thomas C. Berg, "Religion Clause Anti-Theories," *Notre Dame Law Review* 72 (1997): 603, at 693–94.

[14] Berg, "Religion Clause Anti-Theories," at 694.

[15] Berg, "Religion Clause Anti-Theories," at 697. However, we see that, as in the

Robert Sedler, like Justice O'Connor, recognizes the complexity of Establishment Clause adjudication, but argues that "there are four components to the law of the Establishment Clause: (1) an overriding principle; (2) three operational principles; (3) a number of subsidiary doctrines; and (4) the Court's precedents in the five major areas of Establishment Clause litigation."[16] We see that, as in the position to which Berg and I subscribe, Sedler too considers as the first component of Establishment Clause adjudication "an overriding principle," which he maintains is the principle of complete official neutrality.[17] What is important here is not so much Sedler's particular conception of the overriding principle, but rather his view of the function of an overriding principle in what he calls the law of the Establishment Clause:

> The overriding principle of complete official neutrality toward religion is as close as the Court is likely to come in formulating an underlying theory as to the meaning of the Establishment Clause and its function in our constitutional system. In view of this overriding principle, the Court has in effect said that the function of the Establishment Clause in our constitutional system is to promote complete official neutrality toward religion. In theory, the constitutionality of any governmental action involving religion depends on whether or not that action is consistent with this overriding principle. This overriding principle, of course, does not provide much guidance in determining whether or not a particular governmental practice involving religion violates the Establishment Clause. This is the function of the other components of the "law of the Establishment Clause." Nonetheless, the development and application of the other components of the "law of the Establishment Clause" are informed by the overriding principle of complete official neutrality toward religion.[18]

Thus, while an overriding principle by itself rarely if ever could serve as an adjudicatory calculus that would operate automatically, it is, I submit, a necessary precondition of the intelligibility and coherence of Establishment Clause jurisprudence.

What, then, is the central principle—actually, a nonestablishment principle—at the core of the Establishment Clause? Any suitable

---

position to which Berg and I subscribe, Sedler lists as the first component of Establishment Clause adjudication "an overriding principle."

[16] Robert A. Sedler, "Understanding the Establishment Clause: The Perspective of Constitutional Litigation," *Wayne Law Review* 43 (1997): 1317, at 1338.

[17] For Sedler, "The overriding principle of the Establishment Clause is that the Establishment Clause commands complete official neutrality toward religion. The government cannot favor religion over non-religion, and it cannot favor one religion over another." Sedler, "Understanding the Establishment Clause," at 1338–39, footnote omitted.

[18] Sedler, "Understanding the Establishment Clause," at 1340–41, footnotes. omitted.

candidate, I suggest, must accord with the overarching premise that government may neither require a citizen to affirm adherence to a particular religion, religious belief, or religious practice (hence, the Establishment Clause), nor require a citizen to reject adherence to a particular religion, religious belief, or religious practice (hence, the Free Exercise Clause). In other words, government may not require us to adhere to a religion that is not our own, and government may not prohibit us from adhering to a religion that is our own. Given this premise, my argument is that we find the central principle at the core of the Establishment Clause an understated contention by Justice Blackmun in his opinion for the Court in *Allegheny*: "The Establishment Clause, at the very least, prohibits government from appearing to take a position on questions of religious belief or from 'making adherence to a religion relevant in any way to a person's standing in the political community.'"[19] The latter clause reflects Justice O'Connor's endorsement test, which I will discuss *infra*; it is the former clause that is crucial.

The essential principle of the Establishment Clause—what I advance as the central prohibitory principle at the core of the Establishment Clause—is this: government shall not, either by law or by any other form of action, take a position, or do anything that amounts to taking a position, on the truth or the worth of (1) religion in general, (2) particular religious beliefs and values, or (3) particular religious practices. This tripartite set of categories refers, first, to the truth or worth of religion in general (e.g., government declares that a religion is true, or encourages citizens to believe that religion is a good thing); second, to the truth or worth of particular religious beliefs (e.g., government declares that the parting of the Red Sea or the resurrection and divinity of Jesus of Nazareth is a matter of historical fact, or that we cannot get to heaven without subscribing to certain religious beliefs) and values (e.g., government supports celibacy, asceticism, etc. for distinctly religious reasons); and third, to the truth or worth of particular religious practices (government declares something to the effect that prayer is good for us, or that we should engage in faith healing, or that the bread and wine in Christian communion actually are [or, alternatively, merely represent] the body and blood of Christ). The intelligibility of the Establishment Clause necessarily rests on the proposition that it is possible for government to take no position regarding the truth or worth of religion in general, particular religious beliefs and values, and particular religious practices.

[19] *Allegheny County v. Greater Pittsburgh ACLU*, 492 U.S. 573 (1989), at 594, citing O'Connor in *Lynch v. Donnelly*, 465 U.S. 668 (1984), at 687.

With varying degrees of emphasis and deliberateness, some constitutional commentators have noted this principle. Douglas Laycock, for one, conceptualizes the Establishment Clause in this manner:

> Religious liberty does not constitute America as a Christian Nation, nor does it establish a "secular moral order." These too are equal and opposite errors. Each assumes that on the most fundamental religious questions, the Constitution has taken a position. But the core point of religious liberty is that the government does not take positions on religious questions—not in its daily administration, not in its laws, and not in its Constitution either.[20]

Referring to both theistic and nontheistic beliefs, he argues, "Government should be neutral among these beliefs, endorsing none of them and taking no position on the truth or value of any of them."[21] Christopher Eisgruber and Lawrence Sager write, "By its very definition, disestablishment requires the government to abstain from promulgating official versions of religious doctrine."[22] Similarly, in an article defending the *Lemon* test's secular-purpose requirement, Andrew Koppelman focuses on what I am calling the concept of position taking. At the core of the

[20] Douglas Laycock, "Religious Liberty as Liberty," *Journal of Contemporary Legal Issues* 7 (1996): 313, at 313.

[21] Laycock, "Religious Liberty," at 331. Contrast this to the argument by Patrick M. Garry in "The Democratic Aspect of the Establishment Clause: A Refutation of the Argument That the Clause Serves to Protect Religious or Nonreligious Minorities," *Mercer Law Review* 59 (2008): 595: "The Framers' principal concern in drafting the Establishment Clause was to ensure equality among religions, not between religion and nonreligion. They did not think that the government should adopt a position of being areligious or certainly anti-religious. To the contrary, they believed that government had a duty to affirmatively support religion." At 617, footnotes omitted. Garry argues that the Establishment Clause is a majoritarian provision rather than a minority-rights provision, in that "it protects both the ability of groups of individuals to form religious organizations and the freedom of each religious organization to assert a voice reflective of the size of that organization's constituency in the public arena. Essentially, the Establishment Clause allows religious majorities to act freely, without the government inhibiting or discriminating against those chosen associations and without the government imposing a state-mandated religion on society." At 623. The problem, Garry maintains, is that "the Court's Establishment Clause doctrines primarily affect the practices and public speech rights of society's dominant religions. However, by restricting these religions from interacting with the public sector, the ability of the members of those religions to publicly advance their notions of truth is severely limited." At 620, footnote omitted. There is a difference, however, between limiting the ability of religious people to publicly advance their notions of truth and limiting their ability to do so via the agency and institutions of government. The latter is the focus of my argument about position taking.

[22] Christopher L. Eisgruber and Lawrence G. Sager, "The Supreme Court's Hands-Off Approach to Religious Doctrine: Does It Matter What Religion Is?" *Notre Dame Law Review* 84 (2009): 807, at 812, footnote omitted.

Establishment Clause, he writes, is the principle that "government may not declare religious truth":[23]

> Present [secular-purpose] doctrine already allows for what the doctrine's critics most value: state recognition of the distinctive value of religion. The state is already free to recognize the uniqueness of religion as a human concern, and the law does so by treating religion as something special in a broad range of legislative and judicial actions. What the state may not do—what the doctrine properly forbids it to do—is declare any particular religious doctrine to be the true one, or enact laws that clearly imply such a declaration of religious truth.[24]

Government, in other words, is not in the theology business; it is not a theological institution, in contrast to, for example, the Roman Catholic Congregation for the Doctrine of the Faith.[25] As Koppelman writes, "What the state may not do—what the doctrine properly forbids it to do—is declare any particular religious doctrine to be the true one, or enact laws that clearly imply such a declaration of religious truth."[26]

Michael Perry too articulates a version of this principle that government may not take a position in religious matters. In a lengthy but apt paragraph he writes,

[23] Andrew Koppelman, "Secular Purpose," *Virginia Law Review* 88 (2002): 87, at 89.

[24] Koppelman, "Secular Purpose," at 88. He continues, "An easy example is a statute that required public schools to post the Ten Commandments in every classroom, and thereby instructed students in 'the religious duties of believers: worshipping the Lord God alone, avoiding idolatry, not using the Lord's name in vain, and observing the Sabbath Day.' The purpose of the law, plain on its face, was to proclaim a certain idea of religious truth. That purpose was religious, not secular. The law could not have been upheld without permitting government to declare religious truth." At 89, footnote omitted. Koppelman goes on to link the requirement of neutrality, among religions and between religion and nonreligion, to the prohibition on what I call position taking.

[25] "Art. 48—The proper duty of the Congregation for the Doctrine of the Faith is to promote and safeguard the doctrine on faith and morals in the whole Catholic world; so it has competence in things that touch this matter in any way." http://www.vatican.va/holy_father/john_paul_ii/apost_constitutions/documents/hf_jp-ii_apc_19880628_pastor-bonus-roman-curia_en.html#CONGREGATIONS (retrieved 4-4-07).

[26] Koppelman, "Secular Purpose," at 88. See also Gerard V. Bradley, "Religion at a Public University," *William and Mary Law Review* 49 (2008): 2217, at 2243: "The Founders took the possibility of religious truth seriously. They put 'sectarian' matters outside the competence of government, but they did not thereby denigrate them. They stipulated a sort of mental discipline for lawmakers. By and large they held that such matters were propositions: assertions that could be either true or false. The First Amendment meant that the truth or falsity of such matters had to be put aside in civil affairs; the First Amendment neither stipulated nor supposed that the truth or falsity of these things existed. The First Amendment said that the validity of these propositions was beyond the competence of public authority."

> [T]he central point of the free exercise and non-establishment norms, taken together, is that government may not make judgments about the value or disvalue—the truth value, the moral value, the social value—of religions or religious practices or religious (theological) tenets as such (i.e., as religious). Government has no such power, and government may not arrogate to itself any such power. . . . No matter how much some persons might prefer one or more religions, government may not take any action based on the view that the preferred religion or religions are, as religion, better along one or another dimension of value than one or more other religions or than no religion at all. So, for example, government may not take any action based on the view that Christianity, or Roman Catholicism, or the Fifth Street Baptist Church, is, as a religion or a church, closer to the truth than one or more other religions or churches or than no religion at all—or, if not necessarily closer to the truth, at least a more authentic reflection of the religious history and culture of the American people.[27]

And, finally, even Justice Kennedy, in his *Allegheny* dissent, cited the argument in *Epperson v. Arkansas* that government "must be neutral in matters of religious theory, doctrine, and practice,' and 'may not aid, foster, or promote one religion or religious theory against another or even against the militant opposite."[28]

This concept of position taking appears implicitly and explicitly in comments by both James Madison and Court opinions. In his *Memorial and Remonstrance against Religious Assessments*, cited frequently if not constantly by commentators, Madison states,

> 4. Because, the bill violates that equality which ought to be the basis of every law, and which is more indispensable, in proportion as the validity or expediency of any law is more liable to be impeached. If "all men are by nature equally free and independent," all men are to be considered as entering into Society on equal conditions; as relinquishing no more, and therefore retaining no less, one than another, of their natural rights. Above all are they to be considered as retaining an "equal title to the free exercise of Religion according to the dictates of conscience." Whilst we assert for ourselves a freedom to embrace, to profess and to observe the Religion which we believe to be of divine origin, we cannot deny an equal freedom to those whose minds have not yet yielded to the evidence which has convinced us. If this freedom be abused, it is an offence against God, not against man: To God, therefore, not to men, must an account of it be rendered. As the bill violates equality

[27] Michael J. Perry, *Religion in Politics: Constitutional and Moral Perspectives* (New York: Oxford University Press, 1997), 14–15. See also Michael J. Perry, "Freedom of Religion in the United States: Fin de Siecle Sketches," *Indiana Law Journal* 75 (2000): 295.

[28] *Allegheny*, at 656–57, citing *Epperson v. Arkansas*, 393 U.S. 97 (1968), at 103–4.

> by subjecting some to peculiar burdens; so it violates the same principle, by granting to others peculiar exemptions.[29]

The principle in this passage of an "equal title to the free exercise of religion" implies, I suggest, that the purpose of the Establishment Clause is to prevent the government from putting its weight or favor on the side of a particular religion, because governmental position taking would violate this fundamental equality of religious freedom. For government to take a position on the worth, not to mention the truth, of religion in general or of a particular religion would be to disrespect, to denigrate, the equal right others have to religious beliefs of their own. The government's declaration of my religious truth would amount to a declaration that your religious "truth" is false.

So, too, various opinions in cases before the Court reflect the concept of position taking. In *Cantwell v. Connecticut*, for example, the Court rejects the notion of a government official having the power to determine what is or is not religious:

> It will be noted, however, that the Act requires an application to the secretary of the public welfare council of the State; that he is empowered to determine whether the cause is a religious one, and that the issue of a certificate depends upon his affirmative action. If he finds that the cause is not that of religion, to solicit for it becomes a crime. He is not to issue a certificate as a matter of course. His decision to issue or refuse it involves appraisal of facts, the exercise of judgment, and the formation of an opinion. He is authorized to withhold his approval if he determines that the cause is not a religious one. Such a censorship of religion as the means of determining its right to survive is a denial of liberty protected by the First Amendment and included in the liberty which is within the protection of the Fourteenth.[30]

[29] Text drawn from the version appended by Justice Rutledge to his dissenting opinion in Everson, at 66.

[30] *Cantwell v. Connecticut*, 310 U.S. 296 (1940), at 305. As we saw earlier, in *Church of Lukumi Babalu Aye v. City of Hialeah*, 508 U.S. 520 (1993), at 541–42, the Court rejects this argument as contrary to the Establishment Clause: "The chaplain of the Hialeah Police Department told the city council that Santeria was a sin, 'foolishness,' 'an abomination to the Lord,' and the worship of 'demons.' He advised the city council: 'We need to be helping people and sharing with them the truth that is found in Jesus Christ.' He concluded: 'I would exhort you . . . not to permit this Church to exist.'" Nevertheless, though government is not to be in the business of determining what counts as a religion, it cannot avoid doing that at times—e.g., the IRS always deals with the question of what counts as a religion for tax purposes. On the other hand, if the Establishment Clause's purpose is merely to ensure that government may not act preferentially toward a favored religion while it legitimately aids all religions equally, that certainly puts government in the business of determining what is a legitimate religion. The Methodists, Catholics, Jews, etc. are "religions," but is Wicca or, as the previous citation about the Lukumi raised the question, is Santeria?

Similarly, writing in *Engel v. Vitale*, Justice Black states,

> By the time of the adoption of the Constitution, our history shows that there was a widespread awareness among many Americans of the dangers of a union of Church and State. These people knew, some of them from bitter personal experience, that one of the greatest dangers to the freedom of the individual to worship in his own way lay in the Government's placing its official stamp of approval upon one particular kind of prayer or one particular form of religious services. . . . The First Amendment was added to the Constitution to stand as a guarantee that neither the power nor the prestige of the Federal Government would be used to control, support or influence the kinds of prayer the American people can say.[31]

The rejection of the idea of an "official stamp of approval upon one particular kind of prayer or one particular form of religious services" implicates the concept of position taking. In *Abington v. Schempp* Justice Clark holds that the Establishment Clause stemmed from "the teachings of history that powerful sects or groups might bring about a fusion of governmental and religious functions or a concert or dependency of one upon the other to the end that official support of the State or Federal Government would be placed behind the tenets of one or of all orthodoxies."[32] The Establishment Clause prohibits this, he says, and such a prohibition means that government may not take a position on the "tenets of one or of all orthodoxies." In other words, to Clark, the Establishment Clause

---

As a result of this problem, Winnifred Fallers Sullivan argues we cannot possibly protect religious freedom as religious because we cannot successfully define religion: "A fundamental definitional ambiguity inheres in all religion cases. Whatever law is being applied in a particular case, whether statutory or constitutional, all religion cases in the United States require a finding that the activity in question qualifies as 'religion.' Such cases put courts in a difficult position. On the one hand, they are required by the use of the word 'religion' in statutes and the Constitution to inquire into its meaning, to draw lines between 'religion' and not-'religion.' On the other hand, there is much law in the United States saying that judges cannot enter into disputes regarding religious orthodoxy. The definition of religion for legal purposes in this country remains, as a result, profoundly unsettled." *The Impossiblity of Religious Freedom* (Princeton, N.J.: Princeton University Press, 2005), 29–30 (footnote omitted). Her position is, instead, this: "What is arguably impossible is justly enforcing laws granting persons rights that are defined with respect to their religious beliefs or practices. Forsaking religious freedom as a legally enforced right might enable greater equality among persons and greater clarity and self-determination for religious individuals and communities. Such a change would end discrimination against those who do not self-identify as religious or whose religion is disfavored" (8). The problem with such a solution is of course the existence of the religion clauses in the Constitution. They call for enforcement of a free-exercise right and, as I shall explain in the next chapter, a nonestablishment right.

[31] *Engel v. Vitale*, 370 U.S. 421 (1962), at 430.

[32] *Abington School District v. Schempp*, 374 U.S. 203 (1963), at 205.

"withdrew all legislative power respecting religious belief or the expression thereof."[33] In the same case Justice Douglas writes that the clause "is not limited to precluding the State itself from conducting religious exercises. It also forbids the State to employ its facilities or funds in a way that gives any church, or all churches, greater strength in our society than it would have by relying on its members alone."[34] The First Amendment, he says, "commands government to have no interest in theology or ritual."[35]

Other cases as well suggest at least an implicit concept of position taking. In *McGowan v. Maryland* Justice Frankfurter argues that "the long colonial struggle for disestablishment—the struggle to free all men, whatever their theological views, from state-compelled obligation to acknowledge and support state-favored faiths—made indisputably fundamental to our American culture the principle that the enforcement of religious belief as such is no legitimate concern of civil government."[36] His lengthier description of the Establishment Clause here implicitly employs the concept of position taking:

> The Establishment Clause withdrew from the sphere of legitimate legislative concern and competence a specific, but comprehensive, area of human conduct: man's belief or disbelief in the verity of some transcendental idea and man's expression in action of that belief or disbelief. Congress may not make these matters, as such, the subject of legislation, nor, now, may any legislature in this country. Neither the National Government nor, under the Due Process Clause of the Fourteenth Amendment, a State may, by any device, support belief or the expression of belief for its own sake, whether from conviction of the truth of that belief, or from conviction that by the propagation of that belief the civil welfare of the State is served, or because a majority of its citizens, holding that belief, are offended when all do not hold it.[37]

[33] *Abington*, at 222. He employs the same terminology with regard to the Free Exercise Clause, stating that "it withdraws from legislative power, state and federal, the exertion of any restraint on the free exercise of religion" (at 223–24, emphasis added). Compare Justice Clark's argument here that the Free Exercise Clause "has never meant that a majority could use the machinery of the State to practice its beliefs" (at 226) to the argument we have seen by Justice Scalia that "in the context of public acknowledgments of God there are legitimate competing interests: On the one hand, the interest of that minority in not feeling 'excluded'; but on the other, the interest of the overwhelming majority of religious believers in being able to give God thanks and supplication as a people, and with respect to our national endeavors. Our national tradition has resolved that conflict in favor of the majority." *McCreary*, at 844.

[34] *Abington*, at 229.

[35] *Abington*, at 564.

[36] *McGowan v. Maryland*, 366 U.S. 420 (1961), at 460.

[37] *McGowan v. Maryland*, at 465–66. Likewise, in *Texas Monthly, Inc. v. Bullock*, 489 U.S. 1 (1989), Justice Brennan writes at 8–9: "In proscribing all laws 'respecting an establishment of religion,' the Constitution prohibits, at the very least, legislation that constitutes an endorsement of one or another set of religious beliefs or of religion

Years earlier, Frankfurter had said, "The essence of the religious freedom guaranteed by our Constitution is therefore this: no religion shall either receive the state's support or incur its hostility. Religion is outside the sphere of political government."[38] In *U.S. v. Seeger* the Court dealt with the allowable grounds for a person subject to the military draft to invoke a claim to conscientious-objector status. Justice Clark, speaking for the Court, held that

> Congress, in using the expression "Supreme Being" rather than the designation "God," was merely clarifying the meaning of religious training and belief so as to embrace all religions and to exclude essentially political, sociological, or philosophical views. We believe that under this construction, the test of belief "in a relation to a Supreme Being" is whether a given belief that is sincere and meaningful occupies a place in the life of its possessor parallel to that filled by the orthodox belief in God of one who clearly qualifies for the exemption.[39]

The key holding for our purposes here was this: "The validity of what [one who claims conscientious-objector status] believes cannot be questioned. Some theologians, and indeed some examiners, might be tempted to question the existence of the registrant's 'Supreme Being' or the truth of his concepts. But these are inquiries foreclosed to Government."[40] The government, that is, may make a judgment as to the sincerity of the claimant's religious beliefs, but may not make a judgment as to—i.e., take a position on—the truth of the claimant's religious beliefs.[41]

Such statements by the Court, I suggest, are various ways of asserting the principle that government may not take a position, nor do anything

---

generally. It is part of our settled jurisprudence that 'the Establishment Clause prohibits government from abandoning secular purposes in order to put an imprimatur on one religion, or on religion as such, or to favor the adherents of any sect or religious organization.' *Gillette v. United States*, 401 U.S. 437, 450 (1971)."

[38] *West Virginia v. Barnette*, 319 U.S. 624 (1943), at 654 (dissenting).

[39] *United States v. Seeger*, 380 U.S. 163 (1965), at 165–66.

[40] *United States v. Seeger*, at 184.

[41] At the same time, *Seeger* asserts the special character of religious belief: it matters to the individual in a way that other beliefs, while enjoying free-speech protections, do not. The section of the statute at issue, Clark stated at 173, "excludes those persons who, disavowing religious belief, decide on the basis of essentially political, sociological or economic considerations that war is wrong and that they will have no part of it. These judgments have historically been reserved for the Government, and in matters which can be said to fall within these areas the conviction of the individual has never been permitted to override that of the state" (internal references omitted). Religion is indeed special; it, and not political, economic, sociological, or philosophical views, can provide the grounds for conscientious objection. Such views, as the argument here goes, are legitimately subject to the give-and-take of ordinary debate and to resolution through majority rule and electoral politics; religion and religious differences are not.

that amounts to taking a position, on the truth or worth of religion, religious beliefs and values, and religious practices. As Justice Jackson says in *Everson*,

> [T]he effect of the religious freedom Amendment to our Constitution was *to take every form of propagation of religion out of the realm of things which could directly or indirectly be made public business* and thereby be supported in whole or in part at taxpayers' expense. That is a difference which the Constitution sets up between religion and almost every other subject matter of legislation, a difference which goes to the very root of religious freedom and which the Court is overlooking today.[42]

This principle certainly stands as a rule for courts that they have no business making theological judgments. In the church-property dispute at issue in *Presbyterian Church v. Hull Church*, the Court states that "First Amendment values are plainly jeopardized when church property litigation is made to turn on the resolution by civil courts of controversies over religious doctrine and practice. . . . Because of these hazards, the First Amendment enjoins the employment of organs of government for essentially religious purposes."[43] This clearly echoes Justice Brennan's earlier argument in *Abington*, citing *Watson v. Jones*, that "the law knows no heresy," that "in order to give effect to the First Amendment's purpose of requiring on the part of all organs of government a strict neutrality toward theological questions, courts should not undertake to decide such questions."[44]

Nevertheless, what can we make of Justice Scalia's statement in *Van Orden v. Perry* that "there is nothing unconstitutional in a State's favoring religion generally, honoring God through public prayer and acknowledgement, or, in a nonproselytizing manner, venerating the Ten Commandments," or his position in *McCreary* that the Establishment Clause

[42] *Everson*, at 26 (dissenting), emphasis added.

[43] *Presbyterian Church v. Hull Church*, 393 U.S. 440 (1969), at 449. In an earlier case, *United States v. Ballard*, 322 U.S. 78 (1944), the Court held at 86 that freedom of thought "embraces the right to maintain theories of life and of death and of the hereafter which are rank heresy to followers of the orthodox faiths. Heresy trials are foreign to our Constitution. Men may believe what they cannot prove. They may not be put to the proof of their religious doctrines or beliefs." Furthermore, "The Fathers of the Constitution were not unaware of the varied and extreme views of religious sects, of the violence of disagreement among them, and of the lack of any one religious creed on which all men would agree. They fashioned a charter of government which envisaged the widest possible toleration of conflicting views. Man's relation to his God was made no concern of the state. He was granted the right to worship as he pleased, and to answer to no man for the verity of his religious views." *United States v. Ballard*, at 87.

[44] *Abington*, at 243.

permits an official preference for monotheism?[45] One response is to say that he grounds this statement on historical practice in America, but that such historical practice does not live up to the principle embodied in the Establishment Clause. A second is to ask whether Scalia's views on this issue are entirely consistent. In footnote 4 of his *McCreary* dissent he states,

> This is not to say that a display of the Ten Commandments could never constitute an impermissible endorsement of a particular religious view. The Establishment Clause would prohibit, for example, governmental endorsement of a particular version of the Decalogue as authoritative. Here the display of the Ten Commandments alongside eight secular documents, and the plaque's explanation for their inclusion, make clear that they were not posted to take sides in a theological dispute.[46]

This is curious. Scalia appears to think that it would be wrong for government to put up a sectarian version of the Ten Commandments and make a pronouncement that this version is the authoritative version, but putting up a sectarian version without such a pronouncement would apparently not be an unconstitutional endorsement. Yet the very choice of a particular version by itself amounts to a tacit endorsement of a sectarian version and thus violates the nonestablishment principle.[47] He stated in *Employment Division v. Smith*,

[45] *Van Orden*, at 692. Along these lines, surely one of the most ambiguous statements in religion-clause jurisprudence is Justice Douglas' assertion, discussed earlier, that "[w]e are a religious people whose institutions presuppose a Supreme Being." *Zorach v. Clauson*, 343 U.S. 306 (1952), at 313. What could this mean? After all, the divine right of kings presupposes a Supreme Being. Apparently the only place Douglas gave even a modicum of an explanation of his assertion was in his dissenting opinion in *McGowan v. Maryland*, at 562–63: "The institutions of our society are founded on the belief that there is an authority higher than the authority of the State; that there is a moral law which the State is powerless to alter; that the individual possesses rights, conferred by the Creator, which government must respect. The Declaration of Independence stated the now familiar theme: 'We hold these Truths to be self-evident, that all Men are created equal, that they are endowed by their Creator with certain unalienable Rights, that among these are Life, Liberty, and the Pursuit of Happiness.' And the body of the Constitution as well as the Bill of Rights enshrined those principles." Perhaps it is the theory of natural rights of the Declaration, and not some notion of the United States as a Christian nation, that undergirds Douglas' otherwise unexplained claim that our institutions presuppose a Supreme Being.

[46] *McCreary*, at 895.

[47] According to Paul Finkelman, "In addition to being religious in the most obvious sense of the term, any display of the Ten Commandments will inevitably favor one faith or one denomination over all others. . . . Jews, Catholics, Lutherans, and most Protestants differ in the way they number and organize the Commandments. These religions, and denominations within them, also differ in how they translate the Commandments from the original Hebrew into English. Thus, any display of

> The free exercise of religion means, first and foremost, the right to believe and profess whatever religious doctrine one desires. Thus, the First Amendment obviously excludes all "governmental regulation of religious beliefs as such." . . . The government may not compel affirmation of religious belief . . . , punish the expression of religious doctrines it believes to be false . . . , impose special disabilities on the basis of religious views or religious status . . . , or lend its power to one or the other side in controversies over religious authority or dogma.[48]

If any version of the Ten Commandments is inherently sectarian, then for government to choose one version to post would amount precisely to an act of "lend[ing] its power to one or the other side in controversies over religious authority or dogma"—and thus taking a position—which Scalia rejects in *Smith*.

One last and perhaps most important argument in favor of my thesis that the Establishment Clause means that government may not take a position on the truth or worth of religion in general, religious beliefs and values, or religious practices addresses the objection that by the very inclusion of the religion clauses in the First Amendment the Constitution has indeed taken a position on at least the worth of religion and religious belief, values, and practice. Relying on the distinction between Constitution and government parallel to that between fundamental law and ordinary law, that argument is this: the Constitution takes the position that religion is so important and central to people's lives—is of such fundamental and intimate worth to people—that *government* should not take a position on the truth or worth of religion and religious beliefs, values, and practices. The Constitution, in other words, takes a position on the importance of religion (not its truth or worth) by saying that government may take no position on religion, and does so in order to avoid placing people between the Scylla and Charybdis of their conscience and the law, of God and Caesar. There is a fundamental difference between government's saying that religion is important and government's recognizing

---

the Commandments is inherently sectarian, because it must choose a translation, ordering, and numbering system that will favor, or endorse one or more religions, and therefore disfavor other religions." "The Ten Commandments on the Courthouse Lawn and Elsewhere," *Fordham Law Review* 73 (2005): 1477, at 1478–79. This is an interesting and important article. Continuing, he writes, "Adherents to those faiths that accept the Ten Commandments do not agree on the numbering of the Commandments, the content of each Commandment, the translation of the Commandments, or even their meaning" (1485), with the consequence that "any ordering of the Commandments or translation of the original Hebrew text will reflect the position of one or more faiths and exclude that of other faiths" (1483).

[48] *Employment Division, Oregon Department of Human Resources v. Smith*, 494 U.S. 872 (1990), at 877, internal references omitted.

that people consider religion to be important; it is a difference between government's taking a position on the importance or validity of religion and government's respecting the position that individual citizens take on the importance or validity of religion.

The very wording of the Establishment Clause—"Congress shall make no law respecting an establishment of religion"—amounts to what I am calling the concept of position taking, for the Clause means that Congress is simply not to legislate on religious matters. The concept is hiding in plain sight here. When Steven Smith argues, as we saw in chapter 4, that the religion clauses taken as a whole are jurisdictional principles disempowering Congress in favor of the states from legislating on religious matters, he in effect supports my idea of position taking at least as applied to Congress.[49] Smith may be wrong as to his controversial claim that the religion clauses are jurisdictional principles only, but my concept of position taking suggests that what appears to be a formal, jurisdictional principle is actually a substantive principle. The religion clauses may be purely jurisdictional, but, if so, they are jurisdictional in the sense that they announce a substantive principle and apply or direct it to the federal government (Congress). We can tell that there is a substantive principle at stake there because we can look at various state bills of rights and find the same language, substituting the General Assembly or some such legislative body for Congress.[50] There is clearly a principle

[49] "If we ask, therefore, what principle or theory of religious liberty the framers and ratifiers of the religion clauses adopted, the most accurate answer is 'None.' They consciously chose not to answer the religion question, and they were able for the most part to avoid it (or at least thought they were) because of the way in which they answered the jurisdiction question—that is, by assigning the religious question to the states. This observation suggests that it is futile to try to extrapolate or reconstruct a principle or theory of religious liberty from the original meaning of the religion clauses. Those clauses quite simply were not based on any such principle or theory." Steven D. Smith, *Foreordained Failure: The Quest for a Constitutional Principle of Religious Freedom* (New York: Oxford University Press, 1995), 21.

[50] Consider these three examples:

> Alaska: article I, section 4. Freedom of Religion: "No law shall be made respecting an establishment of religion, or prohibiting the free exercise thereof."
>
> Iowa: article I, section 3: "The general assembly shall make no law respecting an establishment of religion, or prohibiting the free exercise thereof; nor shall any person be compelled to attend any place of worship, pay tithes, taxes, or other rates for building or repairing places of worship, or the maintenance of any minister, or ministry."
>
> South Carolina: article I, section 2: "The General Assembly shall make no law respecting an establishment of religion or prohibiting the free exercise thereof, or abridging the freedom of speech or of the press; or the right of the people peaceably to assemble and to petition the government or any department thereof for a redress of grievances."

at issue, but the question is simply, to what government or institution is the principle directed? The nonestablishment principle is something that can be incorporated, contrary to Justice Thomas' statement that the Establishment Clause makes no sense other than as a jurisdictional statement.[51] Moreover, even if initially limited to the federal government, that substantive principle became applicable to the states through the Fourteenth Amendment. Hence, the meaning of the Establishment Clause is that government—not just Congress—shall make no law respecting an establishment of religion, which is to say that the Constitution takes the substantive position that government is not to take a position on the truth or worth of religion.[52]

Thus, I suggest that there is substantial evidence in both Supreme Court decisions and the scholarly literature for my contention that the essential nonestablishment principle is that government shall not take a position, nor do anything that amounts to taking a position, on the truth or the worth of (1) religion in general, (2) particular religions or religious beliefs, or (3) particular religious practices. However, the fact that awkward phrases like "the essential nonestablishment principle" or "the essential principle of nonestablishment" or "the concept of position taking" grate on the ears is not merely a matter of style and literacy, but, instead, goes to the question of substantive meaning. The question is whether this concept of position taking is just another way of expressing Justice O'Connor's concept of endorsement or just another way of expressing what has come to be known as the concept of neutrality or equal treatment. Certainly there is an appearance of similarity: just as we say that government shall not take a position on the truth or worth of religion, religious beliefs and values, and religious practices, we could say that government must not endorse, or must be neutral regarding, the truth or worth of religion, religious beliefs and values, and religious practices.

These examples indicate that the language itself—"X shall make no law respecting an establishment of religion"—has meaning beyond merely a federalism or jurisdictional focus, because otherwise it would make no sense for the state to make such statements. These state provisions illustrate that there is a substantive principle asserted in the nonestablishment phrase, viz., that government shall not take a position on religion.

[51] See Justice Thomas' concurring opinion in *Elk Grove Unified School Dist. v. Newdow*, 542 U.S. 1 (2004).

[52] As Madison writes in *Memorial and Remonstrance,* "[I]n matters of Religion, no mans right is abridged by the institution of Civil Society and that Religion is wholly exempt from its cognizance" (The Founders' Constitution, amendment I [Religion], http://press-pubs.uchicago.edu/founders/documents/amendI_religions43.html, retrieved 12-3-10). This idea of being "exempt from its cognizance" is precisely the principle of not taking a position on the truth or worth of religion.

Nevertheless, I wish to advance two claims. First, the concept of position taking is not identical to O'Connor's concept of endorsement but rather is a broader and, I think, more objectively determinable concept that includes within it but extends beyond the concept of endorsement. Second, as used in the legal literature the concept of neutrality is highly problematic: the concept itself has become highly contested; in its contemporary, post-*Mitchell* incarnation,[53] the concept of neutrality is actually inconsistent with the uniqueness of religion that is recognized textually in the First Amendment; and, at least in some versions, the concept of neutrality creates precisely the governmental entanglement with religion that it is supposed to eliminate. I will argue that if we are to use the concept of neutrality at all, my concept of position taking is the best way to make sense of it. More broadly, I suggest that this concept of not taking a position on the truth or worth of religion, religious beliefs and values, and religious practices is what stands behind the contested notions of not just neutrality but of endorsement and the separation of church and state as well. The prohibition of an official government position on the truth or worth of religion, religious beliefs and values, and religious practices is what we mean by—what underlies—the idea of neutrality, nonendorsement, and separation of church and state.

In her well-known effort to clarify the *Lemon* test, Justice Sandra Day O'Connor sets out what she calls the endorsement test in the case of *Lynch v. Donnelly*:

> The Establishment Clause prohibits government from making adherence to a religion relevant in any way to a person's standing in the political community. Government can run afoul of that prohibition in two principal ways. One is excessive entanglement with religious institutions, which may interfere with the independence of the institutions, give the institutions access to government or governmental powers not fully shared by nonadherents of the religion, and foster the creation of political constituencies defined along religious lines. The second and more direct infringement is government endorsement or disapproval of religion. Endorsement sends a message to nonadherents that they are outsiders, not full members of the political community, and an accompanying message to adherents that they are insiders, favored members of the political community. Disapproval sends the opposite message.[54]

O'Connor seeks here, after subscribing to the third prong of the *Lemon* test, to clarify the purpose and effects prong of *Lemon* by stating that a law or act of government fails to pass Establishment Clause muster if it either

[53] *Mitchell v. Helms*, 530 U.S. 793 (2000).

[54] *Lynch v. Donnelly*, at 687–88, internal case references omitted.

endorses or disapproves of a particular religion.[55] That determination, she holds, must be made in terms of what a "reasonable observer"[56] would understand by the law or act of government. However, as a huge critical literature has indicated, the central theme of the endorsement test—the message of approval or disapproval—appears to focus upon the subjective reactions of the viewer or hearer of the religious message. In other words, the way to determine whether the government's statements or actions have endorsed a religion or religious message is to determine whether the individual observer feels like an outsider. An inquiry into whether government has sent a message of endorsement dissolves immediately into an inquiry into the personal feelings of the observer.[57]

By contrast, the concept of position taking I advance here is not identical to, not just another way of expressing, O'Connor's concept of endorsement, but is instead a broader and, I think, more objectively determinable concept that includes within it the concept of endorsement. The *Lemon* test and the endorsement test—and we recall that O'Connor introduced the latter to clarify the former—both operate in terms of both the purpose and effect of a government law or other such action. The problem is that the question of purpose raises evidentiary issues as to the significance of intentions and motivations,[58] while the question of effect, even considered from the standpoint of the reasonable observer, raises the issue of objectivity. On the other hand, if we say that government must refrain from taking a position on the truth or worth of religion, a religious belief, or a religious practice, we may be able to avoid questions of purpose and effect and simply whether the government law or act at issue does in fact take such a position. Interpretive disagreements will certainly occur, as they do in almost any situation, but asking what the governmental act does would appear to be less difficult than inquiring into its sponsors' motivations or into the personal reactions of individual observers.

[55] "The purpose prong of the *Lemon* test asks whether government's actual purpose is to endorse or disapprove of religion. The effect prong asks whether, irrespective of government's actual purpose, the practice under review in fact conveys a message of endorsement or disapproval. An affirmative answer to either question should render the challenged practice invalid." O'Connor, *Lynch v. Donnelly*, at 690. This test, too, has spawned an enormous critical literature, beyond the scope of this chapter.

[56] *Allegheny*, at 631 and 635.

[57] As we saw in chapter 5, the endorsement test was criticized by Justice Kennedy as "flawed in its fundamentals and unworkable in practice," and thus a "most unwelcome addition" to Establishment Clause jurisprudence. *Allegheny*, at 669 and 668.

[58] See, e.g., *Wallace v. Jaffree*, 472 U.S. 38 (1985). Did the motivation of certain Alabama legislators to reintroduce school prayer really invalidate a statute that contained the phrase "meditation or voluntary prayer" in its call for a mandatory moment of silence?

The concept of position taking, and the principle of not taking a position that flows from it, thus differs from the endorsement test in that it focuses on the governmental action or message rather than on the reaction of the observer. At the same time, just as O'Connor believes that the endorsement test helps us make more analytic sense of the *Lemon* test, I am suggesting that the concept of position taking helps us make more analytic sense of the endorsement test. The reason the endorsement test forbids government do anything that amounts to a religious endorsement or disapproval is that such endorsement or disapproval would violate the principle that government is not to do anything that amounts to taking a position on the truth or worth of religion, religious belief, or religious practice. In particular, despite O'Connor's vague reference to disapproval ("Disapproval sends the opposite message"), the usual focus of the endorsement test is on approval—endorsement. The non-position-taking principle more clearly forbids government not only from acting or speaking favorably toward a religious message but also from acting or speaking unfavorably toward such a message. Government simply may not take a position on the truth or worth of religion one way or another.

Why not, however, just call this concept of position taking what it might well appear to be—a concept of neutrality? Perhaps the conception of neutrality that comes closest to the idea of not taking a position is Douglas Laycock's idea of substantive neutrality, namely, "The religion clauses require government to minimize the extent to which it either encourages or discourages religious belief or disbelief, practice or non-practice, observance or nonobservance."[59] William Marshall argues that a "discernable pattern" of doctrinal consistency emerges from Establishment Clause case law, suggesting that "the Court has implicitly been guided by a general notion of equality—both equality between religions and between religion and nonreligion."[60] Robert Sedler, as we have seen, states, "The overriding principle of the Establishment Clause is that the Establishment Clause commands complete official neutrality toward religion. The government cannot favor religion over non-religion, and it cannot favor one religion over another."[61]

Professor Steven Green provides a nice summary of the development of neutrality theory:

[59] Douglas Laycock, "Formal, Substantive, and Disaggregated Neutrality toward Religion," *DePaul Law Review* 39 (1990): 993, at 1002.

[60] William P. Marshall, "What Is the Matter with Equality? An Assessment of the Equal Treatment of Religion and Nonreligion in First Amendment Jurisprudence," *Indiana Law Journal* 75 (2000): 193, at 196.

[61] Sedler, "Understanding the Establishment Clause," at 1338–39, footnote omitted.

> Although neutrality had been discussed as an instructive concept for non-establishment as far back as *Everson v. Board of Education*, the first modern Establishment Clause case, it was not until the mid-1980s that neutrality acquired an independent substantive meaning and later became determinative of outcomes. In 1981, the Court relied on equality principles to invalidate a state university policy of denying student religious groups the same access to facilities as was afforded to student secular groups. The Court reaffirmed that neutrality or equal treatment should prevail over separationist considerations in later access cases involving religious clubs in public schools and religious use of public forums and facilities.[62]

The difficulty, however, is that the concept of neutrality has become highly contested and problematic. In the first place, at least three different conceptions of the concept of neutrality have functioned as constituting or expressive of the general principle of the Establishment Clause. The first conception of neutrality appears famously in *Epperson v. Arkansas*, which we saw in chapter 3:

> Government in our democracy, state and national, must be neutral in matters of religious theory, doctrine, and practice. It may not be hostile to any religion or to the advocacy of no-religion; and it may not aid, foster, or promote one religion or religious theory against another or even against the militant opposite. The First Amendment mandates governmental neutrality between religion and religion, and between religion and nonreligion.[63]

Here is the concept of strict neutrality, the idea that government must be neutral between one religion and another (religion A, religion B, religion C, etc.) and between religion and nonreligion. Neutrality, on this conception, is the idea of a position for government to occupy between favoritism and hostility, the idea at the core of the second prong of the *Lemon* test: a statute's "principal or primary effect must be one that neither advances nor inhibits religion, Board of Education v. Allen, 392 U.S. 236, 243 (1968)."[64]

[62] Steven K. Green, "Locke v. Davey and the Limits to Neutrality Theory," *Temple Law Review* 77 (2004): 913, at 914, footnotes omitted. "Neutrality theory," he continues at 914–15, "reached its apex and position of dominance in *Mitchell v. Helms* (2000) and *Zelman v. Simmons-Harris* (2002), the latter decision upholding publicly funded vouchers for private religious schooling. It was in *Mitchell*, however, that a Court plurality raised neutrality to the sine qua non of constitutionality, writing that: if the government, seeking to further some legitimate secular purpose, offers aid on the same terms, without regard to religion, to all who adequately further that purpose . . . then it is fair to say that any aid going to a religious recipient only has the effect of furthering that secular purpose" (footnotes omitted).

[63] *Epperson v. Arkansas*, at 104, footnote omitted.

[64] *Lemon v. Kurtzman*, 403 U.S. 602 (1971), at 613.

The second conception of neutrality as the central principle of the Establishment Clause appears in then-Justice William Rehnquist's dissenting opinion in *Wallace v. Jaffree*:

> It would seem from this [foregoing] evidence that the Establishment Clause of the First Amendment had acquired a well-accepted meaning: it forbade establishment of a national religion, and forbade preference among religious sects or denominations. . . . The Establishment Clause did not require government neutrality between religion and irreligion nor did it prohibit the Federal Government from providing nondiscriminatory aid to religion. There is simply no historical foundation for the proposition that the Framers intended to build the 'wall of separation' that was constitutionalized in Everson.[65]

This conception of neutrality maintains the idea of governmental neutrality between one religion and another, but, as the concept of benevolent neutrality, it is a narrower or "thinner" conception in that it allows for governmental support of religion over nonreligion. The third conception of neutrality, narrower still, appears in the previously noted argument of Justice Scalia in *McCreary* that government may favor monotheistic over non-monotheistic religions. On this view government must be neutral between one monotheistic religion and another, but may favor monotheistic religions over polytheistic religions as well as atheism (nonreligion).

To say that the Establishment Clause mandates neutrality, therefore, does not answer the question of what conception of the concept of neutrality it mandates. Saying that the principle I advance—government may not take a position, or do anything that amounts to taking a position, on the truth or worth of religion, religious beliefs or values, or religious practices—is simply a neutrality principle obscures this variation among the possible conceptions of neutrality. At the same time, this principle would seem to be much more consistent with the first, broader or thicker conception of neutrality, for both the second and third conceptions clearly allow for government to take a position on the truth or worth of religion. At its most general, Establishment Clause jurisprudence revolves around the tension between the separationism of *Everson v. Board of Education*[66]

[65] *Wallace v. Jaffree*, 472 U.S. 38 (1985), at 106.

[66] "The 'establishment of religion' clause of the First Amendment means at least this: Neither a state nor the Federal Government can set up a church. Neither can pass laws which aid one religion, aid all religions, or prefer one religion over another. Neither can force nor influence a person to go to or to remain away from church against his will or force him to profess a belief or disbelief in any religion. No person can be punished for entertaining or professing religious beliefs or disbeliefs, for church attendance or non-attendance. No tax in any amount, large or small, can be levied to support any religious activities or institutions, whatever they may be called,

and the accommodationism of *Zorach v. Clauson*,[67] and the recurring theoretical assumption has been that the concept of neutrality is the solution to this tension.[68] Because there are at least three competing conceptions of neutrality in Establishment Clause jurisprudence, I suggest, it is not the concept of neutrality that explains the concept of position taking I advance, but rather the concept of position taking I advance is what explains the concept of neutrality.

Thus, we see that the concept of neutrality has been highly contested and problematic in the first place because at least three competing conceptions of it have functioned as the general principle of the Establishment Clause. According to Green,

> Neutrality is "a coat of many colors," the second Justice Harlan once remarked, and the concept is open to many interpretations. The Court used the term to represent quite distinct concepts—as a median between being pro-and anti-religious, as a synonym for "secular," and as a form of evenhanded treatment. One need only peruse the multiple opinions in Mitchell v. Helms, all offering divergent views of neutrality, to appreciate the confusion and division that exists over this concept.[69]

The concept of neutrality has been highly contested and problematic in a second way as well, one that concerns its function not as the general, overarching principle of the Establishment Clause but rather as a particular test of whether or not an Establishment Clause violation has occurred. On this understanding, neutrality means equality, equal treatment, or evenhandedness. For example, writing for the Court in *Rosenberger v. Rector*, Justice Kennedy argues that "the guarantee of neutrality is

---

or whatever form they may adopt to teach or practice religion. Neither a state nor the Federal Government can, openly or secretly, participate in the affairs of any religious organizations or groups and vice versa. In the words of Jefferson, the clause against establishment of religion by law was intended to erect 'a wall of separation between Church and State.'" *Everson*, at 15–16.

[67] "We are a religious people whose institutions presuppose a Supreme Being. We guarantee the freedom to worship as one chooses." *Zorach v. Clauson*, at 313.

[68] From the perspective of the distinction I have drawn between protecting religion and protecting religious freedom, one could also argue that separationism and accommodationism are not antithetical positions, that the best means to the end of accommodating religion is to separate church and state. In other words, we adopt the separation of church and state demanded by separationism not out of opposition to religion, but in support of religion—but support in an important, special sense. The religion clauses call for the separation of church and state, to put the case more precisely, in order to support not religion, but religious freedom. Thus, if the broad conception of neutrality appears to be unfavorable or even hostile to religion, the response must be that, while it is not hostile to religion, its purpose is to protect not religion per se but religious freedom.

[69] Green, "Locke v. Davey," at 935, footnotes omitted.

respected, not offended, when the government, following neutral criteria and evenhanded policies, extends benefits to recipients whose ideologies and viewpoints, including religious ones, are broad and diverse."[70] Subsequently, pointing to the changing conceptions of neutrality, Justice Souter contends in his dissenting opinion in *Mitchell v. Helms* that members of the Court

> have used the term in at least three ways in our cases, and an understanding of the term's evolution will help to explain the concept as it is understood today, as well as the limits of its significance in Establishment Clause analysis. "Neutrality" has been employed as a term to describe the requisite state of government equipoise between the forbidden encouragement and discouragement of religion; to characterize a benefit or aid as secular; and to indicate evenhandedness in distributing it.[71]

Writing for the Court in *Mitchell*, Justice Clarence Thomas advances the equal-treatment conception of neutrality:

> In distinguishing between indoctrination that is attributable to the State and indoctrination that is not, we have consistently turned to the principle of neutrality, upholding aid that is offered to a broad range of groups or persons without regard to their religion. If the religious, irreligious, and areligious are all alike eligible for governmental aid, no one would conclude that any indoctrination that any particular recipient conducts has been done at the behest of the government.[72]

The key idea here is that neutrality involves the government's treating religion and nonreligion alike, treating religion the same way it treats nonreligious or secular organizations and programs. Souter's criticism of this conception of neutrality as equal treatment is that the Court has moved from a view of neutrality as a necessary condition of constitutionality under the Establishment Clause to a view of neutrality—again, in the sense of equal treatment or evenhandedness—as a sufficient condition of constitutionality.[73]

[70] *Rosenberger v. Rector,* 515 U.S. 819 (1995), at 839.

[71] *Mitchell et al. v. Helms et al.*, 530 U.S. 793 (2000), at 878. He goes on to state at 883, "In sum, 'neutrality' originally entered this field of jurisprudence as a conclusory term, a label for the required relationship between the government and religion as a state of equipoise between government as ally and government as adversary. Reexamining *Everson*'s paradigm cases to derive a prescriptive guideline, we first determined that 'neutral' aid was secular, nonideological, or unrelated to religious education. Our subsequent reexamination of *Everson* and *Allen*, beginning in *Nyquist* and culminating in *Mueller* and most recently in *Agostini*, recast neutrality as a concept of 'evenhandedness.'" Souter's discussion deserves more examination than I can give it here.

[72] *Mitchell*, at 809.

[73] He writes in *Mitchell*, at 883–84, "This kind of neutrality is relevant in judging

The significance of this conceptual move is that it constitutes an inversion of the broad conception of neutrality. Whereas that conception holds that government may neither favor nor disfavor religion and may neither favor nor disfavor nonreligion, the conception of neutrality as equal treatment requires that government do for religion whatever it does for nonreligion. Steven V. Monsma explains this in his introduction to a volume of essays on the *Mitchell* case:

> The legal standard that is rising to challenge strict separation is usually called neutrality or equal treatment. In simplest terms, it is based on the premise that there is neither a constitutional nor a fairness problem in government recognizing, accommodating, or even in some degree aiding religion, as long as religion is being recognized, accommodated, or aided in the same manner as similar, but non-religious, entities. Religion is being treated equally or neutrally.[74]

The equal-treatment conception of neutrality, according to Monsma, rests on the idea of formal neutrality, which "says simply that government should not use religion as a category either to confer special benefits or to withhold benefits generally available. Under formal neutrality the key question in judging the constitutionality of an action of government is whether the action singles out religion either for special benefits or

---

whether a benefit scheme so characterized should be seen as aiding a sectarian school's religious mission, but this neutrality is not alone sufficient to qualify the aid as constitutional. It is to be considered only along with other characteristics of aid, its administration, its recipients, or its potential that have been emphasized over the years as indicators of just how religious the intent and effect of a given aid scheme really is." Earlier, at 877 in his *Rosenberger* dissent, he stated, "[The Court points to] the fact that the University's funding scheme is 'neutral,' in the formal sense that it makes funds available on an evenhanded basis to secular and sectarian applicants alike. While this is indeed true and relevant under our cases, it does not alone satisfy the requirements of the Establishment Clause, as the Court recognizes when it says that evenhandedness is only a 'significant factor' in certain Establishment Clause analysis, not a dispositive one" (internal references omitted). Additionally, "Evenhandedness as one element of a permissibly attenuated benefit is, of course, a far cry from evenhandedness as a sufficient condition of constitutionality for direct financial support of religious proselytization, and our cases have unsurprisingly repudiated any such attempt to cut the Establishment Clause down to a mere prohibition against unequal direct aid" (*Rosenberger*, at 882). Souter's position, by contrast is based upon what he considers two general rules: "that whenever affirmative government aid ultimately benefits religion, the Establishment Clause requires some justification beyond evenhandedness on the government's part; and that direct public funding of core sectarian activities, even if accomplished pursuant to an evenhanded program, would be entirely inconsistent with the Establishment Clause and would strike at the very heart of the Clause's protection" (*Rosenberger*, at 878).

74 Stephen V. Monsma, ed., *Church-State Relations in Crisis: Debating Neutrality* (Lanham, Md.: Rowman & Littlefield, 2002), at 1.

special liabilities."[75] By contrast, he writes, positive of substantive neutrality "says it is inadequate to look only at the formal neutrality of a law or governmental action—that is, to look at whether or not a law or action is neutral in a technical, legal sense—but it is also essential to look at whether its *effects* are neutral."[76] Whereas the broader conception of neutrality, consistent with traditional separationist principle, has been that government may not directly support or subsidize religious institutions or programs, the equal-treatment conception of neutrality is that government must support or subsidize religious institutions or programs if it supports or subsidizes secular institutions or programs.

The general difficulty with the equal-treatment conception of neutrality, I suggest, is that its mandate to treat religion equally flies in the face of the constitutional principle that religion is different. We can, for example, be required to contribute tax money to a defense policy, a foreign policy, a welfare policy, and so on, with which we disagree, but we cannot be required to contribute tax money to a religion with which we disagree. Similarly, government may legitimately sponsor a billboard that urges us to quit smoking, but it cannot legitimately sponsor a billboard that urges us to be Christian or to attend church—or, for that matter, sponsor a billboard that announces that religion is the opiate of the masses. Why not? Government may act in the one but not the other way because religion is constitutionally different if not sui generis. The equal-treatment conception of neutrality may argue that religion should not be treated differently from secular matters, but very existence of the religion clauses in their precise textual form mandates that government must treat religion differently from secular matters. Religion is constitutionally special, carrying with it certain advantages (free exercise) and certain disadvantages (prohibition on establishment). The existence of the religion clauses in the First Amendment singles out religion for special treatment, not equal treatment; there is no guaranteed free exercise of worldviews, philosophies, or moral perspectives.

Thus, religion is constitutionally special, if not unique. Government may take a position on smoking, proper diet, seat belts, public safety, and so on. Government may—apologies to libertarians—take the position and legally enforce the position that the use of illicit drugs is bad for us, and thus that the prohibition of such use is good for us. We would never, by contrast, accept that government may take the position that belief in and practice of all religions but religion X are bad for us, and

[75] Stephen V. Monsma, "Concluding Observations," chap. 13 in his *Church-State Relations*, 265–66, footnote omitted.

[76] Monsma, "Concluding Observations," 266, footnote omitted (emphasis in original). See Laycock, "Formal, Substantive, and Disaggregated Neutrality."

that government may legitimately act to recommend and enforce that we should believe in and practice religion X because religion X is good for us. If someone objects that this then is treating religion differently, not neutrally or equally, the response would seem to be that *the Establishment Clause and the Free Exercise Clause constitutionally mandate treating religion differently*. In its present usage, the concept of neutrality or equal treatment obscures this fundamental constitutional principle.

Moreover, the equal-treatment conception of neutrality, at least in its nonpreferentialist form, puts government into an arguably nasty constitutional position, for it leads to the need for government to decide what counts as a religion and thus creates precisely the governmental entanglement with religion that it is supposed to eliminate. If we say that government may aid or support religion (1) equally with nonreligion and (2) as long as it aids or supports all religions equally, the government will have to make the judgment that religions A, B, C, and so on are worthy of aid and support, and, more important, the judgment that religion A, B, or C is actually a religion (e.g., fire worshippers, or even a hypothetical First Church of the Blessed Weed). Regarding funding of religious activities, for example, Gregory Hamilton writes,

> To assume that the government—federal, state, and local—is capable of funding all groups evenly on a per-capita basis is to assume the improbable and, even more likely, the impossible. Some religious organizations, by their limited size and influence, would potentially receive less favored treatment than others, and even be ignored, despite the nonpreferential basis that a per-capita-aid program promises to administer. In violation of the establishment clause, it would also place the government in the awkward position of defining which are legitimate religious and religious organizations and which are not.[77]

The nonpreferentialist approach of the accommodationists suggests that government can support religion generally as long as it does so equally among religions. Could the government, federal or state, pass a bill and provide people with money or tax credit if they manage to show through some validation that they go to religious services each weekend? In other words, government is not tax-supporting religion directly, but rather simply wants to encourage religion (analogous to the way students get their "ticket punched" in some universities if they go to certain arts or cultural events as part of their education). We have a gut sense that this would not pass constitutional muster, but does nonpreferentialism have a coherent way around validating this practice? What about such support for pagan

[77] Gregory W. Hamilton, "The O'Connor Concurring Opinion: Interpretive Determinism and Neutrality's Pitfalls," in Stephen V. Monsma, *Church-State Relations*, 107.

rituals? Does government get into the position of deciding what is a religion and what is not, in order to decide what to support and what not to support?

Recall, however, the Court's holding regarding the solicitation statute in *Cantwell v. Connecticut*, which determined that it is not the function of government, on this holding, to determine what counts as a religion and what does not.[78] Even the IRS does not make such a judgment when evaluating a religious institution's application for a tax exemption: the central question is not whether the institution is religious, but whether it is charitable.[79] The IRS, in other words, makes an institutional rather than theological judgment. Were government to determine what counts as a religion and what does not, it would fall into precisely the entanglement with religion that the Establishment Clause—irrespective of the validity and viability of the *Lemon* test—is supposed to eliminate. Additionally, what does treating all religions equally mean? Is it a matter of providing funds on a per capita basis, thus benefiting majority religious over minority religions, or a matter of providing funds on a denominational basis, thus giving the same dollar amount to all religious denominations regardless of size? Either way, we still find government having to determine what is a legitimate religious denomination.

Finally, the concept of neutrality is problematic in that, as its contested nature indicates, it is not self-defining. Consider a classic formulation of neutrality:

> Government in our democracy, state and national, must be neutral in matters of religious theory, doctrine, and practice. It may not be hostile to any religion or to the advocacy of no-religion; and it may not aid, foster, or promote one religion or religious theory against another or even against the militant opposite. The First Amendment mandates governmental neutrality between religion and religion, and between religion and nonreligion.[80]

To say that government must be neutral between religion X and religion Y, and between religion and nonreligion, does not say what "being neutral" means or entails. My non-position-taking principle is, I suggest, the best way to make sense of the concept of neutrality. What does it mean to "be neutral in matters of religious theory, doctrine, and practice"? It

[78] See n. 30 and accompanying text *supra*.

[79] See the Court's ruling on tax exemptions for religious institutions in *Walz v. Tax Commission*, 397 U.S. 664 (1970): New York "has not singled out one particular church or religious group or even churches as such; rather, it has granted exemption to all houses of religious worship within a broad class of property owned by nonprofit, quasi-public corporations which include hospitals, libraries, playgrounds, scientific, professional, historical, and patriotic groups" (*Walz*, at 673).

[80] *Epperson v. Arkansas*, at 104.

means to refrain from taking a position or acting in a way that amounts to taking a position on the truth or worth of any religion, religious beliefs or values, or religious practice.[81] In fact, in her concurring opinion in *Wallace v. Jaffree*, Justice O'Connor writes, "It is difficult to square any notion of 'complete neutrality,' ante, at 60, with the mandate of the Free Exercise Clause that government must sometimes exempt a religious observer from an otherwise generally applicable obligation. A government that confers a benefit on an explicitly religious basis is not neutral toward religion."[82] The non-position-taking principle solves this problem with its contention that the Constitution takes the position that religion is so important to people that government must refrain from position taking.

The concept of neutrality, then, has always been highly contested, and in its contemporary, post-*Mitchell* conception, it is actually inconsistent with the uniqueness and special position of religion recognized textually in the First Amendment. For that reason, calling the principle I have advanced—government may not take a position, or do anything that amounts to taking a position, on the truth or worth of religion, religious beliefs or values, or religious practices—a neutrality principle obscures this variation among the possible conceptions of neutrality. Additionally, however, the awkwardness of a term like "the non-position-taking principle" itself points to the fundamental nature of the nonestablishment principle stated in the Establishment Clause, and it is to that issue that, at last, we now turn.

[81] This concept of position taking also makes sense as the principle that underlies the free-speech prohibition on content-based regulation—i.e., the principle that government may regulate time, place, and matter of expression but not regulate content or regulate based on content. That's saying that government may not take a position on the truth or worth of the content of speech.

[82] *Wallace v. Jaffree*, at 82–83.

Chapter 7

The Theoretical Core of the Establishment Clause *The Secularity Principle*

The burden of the previous chapter was to argue that the best understanding of the principle that underlies various concepts like neutrality, separation of church and state, and endorsement, concepts we find operating both in Supreme Court Establishment Clause cases and in the critical literature on religious freedom under the Constitution, is what I have inelegantly but expressively called the non-position-taking principle. The Constitution takes the position that, as history shows us, religion is of such intellectual and emotional importance to people, so fundamentally central to one's personal and social identity, that government shall not take a position, nor do anything that amounts to taking a position, on the truth or worth of religion, religious beliefs and values, and religious practices. Given the argument I have tried to make here that the principle I advance is distinct from both Justice O'Connor's endorsement test and the concept of neutrality (at least in its equal-treatment conception), I suggest, with some trepidation for reasons obvious immediately, that the non-position-taking principle I advance is conceived best as what we might call a secularity principle. My contention, in other words, is that the general, overarching principle expressed by the prohibitory text of the Establishment Clause is a secularity principle. I cannot fend off the reader's likelihood of already having thought, "Aha! I knew it," but in this chapter I shall try to specify precisely what might be the nature of a secularity principle and, of particular importance, how it might be something other than the same old secularism many people oppose, as well as precisely how a violation of the secularity principle may be understood as a form of coercion that violates the right to religious freedom.

To invoke a secularity principle as the core meaning of the Establishment Clause is to contend that government in the United States is an essentially secular institution. The principle is a claim about institutional competence: government is not a theological institution with a theological function, but rather a secular institution with a secular function. That is what it means to refrain from taking a position, or doing anything that amounts to taking a position, on the truth or worth of religion, religious beliefs and values, and religious practices. What does it mean to be "secular"? As we saw in chapter 3, the *Oxford English Dictionary* states that "secular" means "of or pertaining to the world," or "of or belonging to the present or visible world as distinguished from the eternal or spiritual world; temporal, worldly." More broadly, "secular" means "belonging to the world and its affairs as distinguished from the church and religion; civil, lay, temporal. Chiefly used as a negative term, with the meaning non-ecclesiastical, non-religious, or non-sacred."[1] The key distinction here is between that which belongs and pertains to the world and that which belongs and pertains to the church. This distinction is especially clear when we see the entry for "secularity": "secular or non-sacred character; absence of connexion with religion," or having to do with "worldly possessions or pursuits."[2] Interestingly enough, the biblical admonition to render unto Caesar what is Caesar's and unto God what is God's is itself grounded in the distinction the terms "secular" and "secularity" attempt to conceptualize.

By contrast, the concept of secularism is not equivalent to the foregoing idea of the secular and secularity. It is vitally important to be clear that I distinguish the term "secularity" from the more common idea of secularism. The latter I take to mean, among other things, a belief system that only things of this world are real or are important. The concept of secularity, by contrast, means in this context that government is not to take a position on the truth or falsity or worth of such a claim. Secularism, again referring to the *OED*, is, "[t]he doctrine that morality should be based solely on regard to the well-being of mankind in the present life, to the exclusion of all considerations drawn from belief in God or in a future state." Despite the fact that many people consider "secular," "secularity," and "secularism" to be variants of the same concept, my contention is that the former two terms refer to a formal distinction while the latter refers to a substantive philosophy, worldview, or belief system.[3] Put differently,

[1] "Secular," defs. I, 2a, and 3a, the *Oxford English Dictionary*, 2nd ed. (New York: Oxford University Press, 1989–).

[2] "Secularity," defs. 2c and 3, *OED*.

[3] The most common substantive usage of any of the variants of "secularism," of course, is "secular humanism," "a term, often pejorative, used to describe the belief

"secular" and "secularity" are terms of topography, describing a place; "secularism" is an *-ism*—a belief system. "Secular" and "secularity" are in essence descriptive terms; "secularism" is a prescriptive term.

Against this background, consider again my secularity principle: government may not take a position, or do anything that amounts to taking a position, on the truth or worth of religion, religious beliefs or values, or religious practices. According to this principle government must restrict itself to secular matters. On one view of that point, secularity is the disinterested "neutral zone" amid the wide variety of interested religious parties; on the other view, secularity is equivalent to secularism and secularism is simply one more interested religious party. Thus, according to Stephen Monsma,

> I suspect that most no-aid strict separationists, when they view the conflicts and disagreements among various religions and their beliefs, assume that when one removes all religious references or commitments, one has moved into neutral territory. After all, if one wishes not to take sides among the religious differences that make up a religiously pluralistic society such as the United States—if one wishes to occupy religiously neutral territory—one simply moves to religion-free territory. On the other hand, I suspect supporters of neutrality theory start out from a quite different mindset. They see religious systems of belief in their various manifestations and nonreligious or secular systems of belief in their various manifestations as competing worldviews in modern American society. . . . Those whose mindset is rooted in this assumption point out that for the government to run educational programs in which history, human origins, human sexuality, social obligations, environmental ethics, and more are all taught with no reference to the Divine, and, perhaps, to financially support private educational programs that are equally devoid of religious perspectives on life, values, and social issues, is implicitly to support a thoroughly secular worldview. Thus they feel that such programs discriminate against religion.[4]

"This latter mindset," he concludes, "is rooted in the assumption that 'secular' does not equal 'neutral.' Instead it says that secular understandings of life and the world are themselves competing alternatives to religious understandings of life and the world."[5]

---

that ultimate values reside solely in the human individual and possess no supernatural origin or grounding." *HarperCollins Dictionary of Religion*, ed. Jonathan Z. Smith (San Francisco: HarperSanFrancisco, 1995), 970. Given what I claim to be the non-position-taking core of secularity, the secularity principle prohibits government from supporting or opposing secularism and "secular humanism" just as much as it prohibits government from supporting or opposing religion.

[4] Monsma, "Concluding Observations," 268.

[5] Monsma, "Concluding Observations," 268.

Yet saying that government may act only with regard to secular matters is to say that government may not take a position on the truth or worth of religion, religious beliefs or values, or religious practices; it is *not* the same as saying that government is taking a position on the matter of secularism as a philosophy or worldview. Secularism, to reemphasize the *OED* definition a moment ago, is, "[t]he doctrine that morality should be based solely on regard to the well-being of mankind in the present life, to the exclusion of all considerations drawn from belief in God or in a future state." Indeed, if government were to support secularism as a philosophy, then it would violate the secularity principle, because it would take a position, albeit a negative one, on the truth or worth of religion. More important, if government were required to be neutral between secular and religious matters, there would be no need for the religion clauses because their distinctive character and special status would disappear. Inversely, the presence of the religion clauses in the Constitution indicates that government is required not to be neutral between secular and religious matters but rather to restrict itself to secular affairs and to leave religious matters alone. Thus, along these same lines Justice Blackmun, as we have seen in his criticism of Justice Kennedy's dissent in *Allegheny County*, writes, "A secular state, it must be remembered, is not the same as an atheistic or antireligious state. A secular state establishes neither atheism nor religion as its official creed."[6] If neutrality means treating religion no differently from the way we treat any kind of nonreligious matters, it clashes with the fact that the very existence of the religion clause is evidence that from the standpoint of the Constitution religion *is* different—indeed, unique—and should be treated differently.

Understood in this way, the concept of secularity explains why we cannot, as I formerly did, use the term "agnostic" to describe the position of government. It can be tempting to say that government must be agnostic regarding the truth claims of all the various religions, but "agnostic" and its variants actually represent a substantive philosophical perspective. Returning once more to the *OED*, we find that an agnostic is "[o]ne who holds that the existence of anything beyond and behind material phenomena is unknown and (so far as can be judged) unknowable, and especially that a First Cause and an unseen world are subjects of which we know nothing." These are normative or prescriptive claims: we do not know nor can we know anything beyond and behind material phenomena. To make such a claim, however, is to take a position on the truth of religious beliefs and values, and that is precisely what the

[6] *Allegheny County v. Greater Pittsburgh ACLU*, 492 U.S. 573 (1989), at 610. The Soviet Union, we might recall, was officially an atheist state. No serious commentator has ever maintained that the United States is an atheist state.

secularity principle forbids government to do.[7] Government is therefore

[7] In a 2008 article titled "Our Agnostic Constitution," *New York University Law Review* 83 (2008): 120, Steven Smith takes "agnostic" in its ordinary sense to reach a surprising conclusion. He writes, "Though philosophers and others worry (both when speaking generally and when speaking about their own beliefs) about how to draw the lines of demarcation, the term 'agnostic' was invented to denominate a middle ground between theism and atheism and, in popular usage, it maintains this meaning. The theist affirmatively asserts that God exists, and the atheist confidently contends that God does not exist, but the agnostic refrains from adopting either view. On epistemological grounds, or perhaps for more pragmatic reasons, the agnostic concludes that the preferred course is to suspend judgment—to take no position one way or the other on the existence of God." Smith, "Our Agnostic Constitution," at 128–29, footnotes omitted. The Constitution, in his view, is therefore agnostic in the sense that it takes no position either way on the existence of God, a view that is very close to my concept of non-position taking.

What is surprising is Smith's claim that the implication of the Constitution's agnosticism is that government is free to engage in religious expression. "It is the Constitution that is agnostic, in other words, not politics or government. Indeed, it is precisely the Constitution's agnosticism that permits governments, at different levels and in different ways, to sponsor the sorts of religious expression that American governments have traditionally engaged in, and that may well be important in securing the loyalty of citizens, while not making such affirmation constitutive of the political community." Smith, "Our Agnostic Constitution," at 164. This is a remarkable claim, for it seems to ignore the very presence and wording of the Constitution's religion clauses themselves.

Addressing the concept of community, Smith properly notes that a community "is more than just a collection of individuals who happen to occupy the same geographical space. Rather, a community is composed of people who understand themselves—or imagine themselves—to be bound together in some sense by common ties or commitments." Smith, "Our Agnostic Constitution," at 141, footnote omitted. And, he also properly notes, "Communities may coalesce around a common language, a shared history, common symbols, or loyalty to some ruling person or family. One frequent element in community, however, is the existence of shared beliefs or mutually supported affirmations on matters of importance to the members of the community." Smith, "Our Agnostic Constitution," at 142, footnotes omitted.

Yet Smith leaps immediately from the idea that a central constitutive element of community is a set of shared beliefs about fundamental matters to the idea of theology: "And for many people, the beliefs of utmost importance will be those that pertain to ultimate matters such as the existence and character of a deity." Smith, "Our Agnostic Constitution," 142. This leap, made without argument regarding whether liberal democracy in the United States involves or excludes some religious affirmation or commitment, therefore amounts to the claim, discussed earlier in this book, that the American political order is at the least a soft theocracy. Smith argues that because the Constitution is agnostic the government does not have to be, whereas the argument of this book has been that the Constitution takes the position that religion is so important to people that government may do nothing that amounts to taking a position on its truth or worth.

In Smith's telling, "Modern scholars and Justices . . . have interpreted the document in ways that have worked to subvert its momentous contribution to the problem of maintaining community under conditions of creedal diversity." Smith, "Our Agnostic Constitution," at 164–65. Contrast his idea of "maintaining community under

a secular institution not in that it is committed or may be committed to some substantive religious judgment, but rather in that it simply is not a theological institution with any theological function. At bottom, the secularity principle expresses Locke's argument in *A Letter Concerning Toleration* that "[t]he Commonwealth seems to me to be a Society of Men constituted only for the procuring, preserving, and advancing their own *Civil Interests*," that "all the Power of Civil Government relates only to Mens Civil Interests, is confined to the care of the things of this World, and hath nothing to do with the World to come."[8] Government is properly concerned with safety, property, and liberty in this world; it is the church that is properly concerned with our souls and the next world.[9] Government, that is, is properly concerned with security, not with Truth.[10]

---

conditions of creedal diversity" to Steven Gey's argument that "[c]ontrary to the theoretical claim at the heart of the integrationist paradigm, collective assertions of eternal social ideals and beliefs, attempts to formulate a uniform set of public values, and even the very concept of civic virtue itself are all deeply incompatible with the basic proposition that our system exists to accommodate a range of different, and even conflicting concepts of ultimate goods." Steven G. Gey, "Vestiges of the Establishment Clause," *First Amendment Law Review* 5 (2006): 1, at 19.

[8] John Locke, *A Letter Concerning Toleration*, ed. James H. Tully (Indianapolis: Hackett, 1983), 26 and 28. "Civil Interests I call Life, Liberty, Health, and Indolency of Body; and the Possession of outward things, such as Money, Lands, Houses, Furniture, and the like." Locke, *Letter*.

[9] "For the Political Society is instituted for no other end but only to secure every mans Possession of the things of this life. The care of each mans Soul, and of the things of Heaven, which neither does belong to the Commonwealth, nor can be subjected to it, is left entirely to every mans self. Thus the safeguard of mens lives, and of the things that belong unto this life, is the business of the Commonwealth; and the preserving of those things unto their Owners is the Duty of the Magistrate." Locke, *Letter*, 48. Nevertheless, Locke does contend, I should note, that toleration does not extend to atheists: "Those are not at all to be tolerated who deny the Being of a God. Promises, Covenants, and Oaths, which are the Bonds of Humane Society, can have no hold upon an Atheist. The taking away of God, tho but even in thought, dissolves all. Besides also, those that by their Atheism undermine and destroy all Religion, can have no pretence of Religion whereupon to challenge the Privilege of a Toleration" (Locke, *Letter*, 51). While not full dispositive, my argument here would be that by the evidence of this passage Locke rejects toleration for atheists for civil and political rather than religious or theological reasons—civil society would not be possible without an ultimate sanction for those who fail to honor promises, covenants, and oaths.

[10] This argument about Locke's view does raise a question I cannot explore here: does allowing for a political rather than theological justification for refusing tolerance to atheists end up opening a door that the secularity principle seeks to close? Locke's refusal to tolerate atheism suggests that government may legitimately employ religious means in pursuit of secular ends. As Justice Brennan contended in *Walz v. Tax Commission*, 397 U.S. 664 (1970), "What the Framers meant to foreclose, and what our decisions under the Establishment Clause have forbidden, are those involvements of religious with secular institutions which (a) serve the essentially religious activities of

All of this is to say, then, that what I call the secularity principle means nothing more and nothing less than that American government is a secular institution, not a theological institution along the lines of the Roman Catholic Congregation for the Doctrine of the Faith. To say that the Establishment Clause mandates that government be a secular institution is definitely not to say that it mandates secularism. Government, in other words, does not legitimately have the role of advancing "[t]he doctrine that morality should be based solely on regard to the well-being of mankind in the present life, to the exclusion of all considerations drawn from belief in God or in a future state."[11] To do so would contravene the secularity principle, for in so doing government would in fact be advancing a doctrine and thus taking a position on the truth or worth of religion, religious beliefs and values, and religious practices. Under the Establishment Clause, government is secular in that it does not take a position on the truth or worth of religion or even secularism itself.[12] This means, therefore, that democratic majorities may not exercise their *religious* values in and through the institutions and instrumentalities of the government. (Indeed, what could the Establishment Clause possibly mean if

---

religious institutions; (b) employ the organs of government for essentially religious purposes; or (c) use essentially religious means to serve governmental ends, where secular means would suffice. When the secular and religious institutions become involved in such a manner, there inhere in the relationship precisely those dangers—as much to church as to state—which the Framers feared would subvert religious liberty and the strength of a system of secular government" (*Walz*, at 681). Suppose one said that on the assumption that religious training helps to make people moral, or at least less immoral than they would be otherwise, government ought to foster the teaching of Christianity in the public schools in order to serve the secular goal of preventing or mitigating the incidence of criminal activity. By prohibiting government from selecting Christianity, or selecting an "approved" range of religions, the secularity principle denies the legitimacy of using religious means to achieve secular ends, a legitimacy that Locke's argument appears to affirm.

[11] "Secularism," def. 1, *OED*.

[12] Andrew Koppelman reaffirms this secularity principle more recently in "The Troublesome Religious Roots of Religious Neutrality," *Notre Dame Law Review* 84 (2009): 865, stating at 865, "The Supreme Court has repeatedly said that neither it nor any other branch of the state can decide matters that relate to the interpretation of religious practice or belief." However, at 882 he blurs this point somewhat by writing, "The Establishment Clause permits the state to favor religion so long as 'religion' is understood very broadly, forbidding any discrimination or preference among religions or religious propositions. This understanding makes it possible to defend accommodations without running into the free exercise/establishment dilemma. The state is recognizing the value of religion, but it is making no claims about religious truth. It is the making of such claims that violates the Establishment Clause." For government to recognize the value of religion is to violate the secularity principle, but for government to recognize that citizens value religion, and do so intensely, is not such a violation. It is, rather, a legitimate recognition and support of religious freedom.

democratic majorities could do so?) Private—i.e., nongovernmental—religious individuals and institutions have every right under the Free Exercise Clause to express their religious values; I am completely free to put whatever religious symbol I wish on my lawn in front of my house. The government officials and institutions, on the other hand, are not free to do so on or with government property, because the government in a democratic political order represents everyone equally, independently of the religious affiliations and commitments of anyone.

To be sure, as Chief Justice Burger was correct to note, "There is an unbroken history of official acknowledgment by all three branches of government of the role of religion in American life from at least 1789."[13] Leaving aside the details of what the Court might mean by its various references over the years to acknowledging or recognizing religion, the secularity principle distinguishes between acknowledging the importance to the individual of religious freedom and acknowledging the importance of religion as an institution and a belief system. The principle, manifesting the initial claim that the purpose of the religion clauses is to protect not religion but religious freedom, affirms the former. Yes, the Constitution does single out religion from almost every other human concern; the religion clauses do not say, "Congress shall make no law respecting an establishment of a political or moral philosophy." In a sense, the Constitution does take a position on the worth of religion, apparently contradicting the secularity principle, but it does so in a very special way that resolves any contradiction. The Constitution takes the position that religion is so fundamentally important to people that government should not take a position, nor do anything that amounts to taking a position, on the truth or worth of religion, religious beliefs and values, and religious practices.

By the secularity principle, then, the American political order is, contrary to the notion of a "sacred enterprise" championed most prominently by Richard John Neuhaus in *The Naked Public Square*,[14] not a religious community. We are a country, not a congregation. To say this is not (just) a personal political or constitutional preference, not an example of normative constitutional theory. Rather, my argument here is one of descriptive constitutional theory. The secularity principle and concomitant claim that the American political order is not a religious community, I suggest, are at the core of any coherent explanation of the existence and meaning of the religion clauses. Only a secular political order can accommodate religious freedom—and, in particular, an equal

[13] *Lynch v. Donnelly*, 465 U.S. 668 (1984), at 674.

[14] Richard John Neuhaus, *The Naked Public Square: Religion and Democracy in America*, 2nd ed. (Grand Rapids: Eerdmans, 1986), 7.

right to religious freedom—in a society of tremendously diverse religious belief and practice. That political order is constituted as secular not in an act of hostility toward religion but in an institutionalized recognition of the fundamental and intense importance of religion to individuals and groups who subscribe to a remarkable diversity of religious belief and practice. The central idea of the American concept of religious freedom is that the individual has the right to make his or her own decisions as to religious matters. More fundamentally, at the core of this idea is the equality factor: everyone has an equal right to religious freedom. As Martha Nussbaum has written,

> Liberty of conscience is not equal, however, if government announces a religious orthodoxy, saying that this, and not that, is the religious view that defines us as a nation. Even if such an orthodoxy is not coercively imposed, it is a statement that creates an in-group and an out-group. It says that we do not all enter the public square on the same basis: one religion is the American religion and others are not. It means, in effect, that minorities have religious liberty at the sufferance of the majority and must acknowledge that their views are subordinate, in the public square, to majority views.[15]

The only way to respect and institutionalize that equal right to religious freedom is to prevent anything approaching—"respecting"—an establishment of religion.[16] Whatever the religious environment in other countries

[15] Martha C. Nussbaum, *Liberty of Conscience: In Defense of America's Tradition of Religious Equality* (New York: Basic Books, 2008), 2.

[16] In this regard the website of the Center for Public Justice (http://cpjustice.org, retrieved 6-20-11) illustrates both the argument I make here and also the difficulties in keeping intact some necessary distinctions. On the one hand, the six basic points the website makes about religious freedom are consistent with the argument I make in this book. In particular, based upon the statements that "the constitution, or basic law, of a political community should recognize and protect the religious freedom of citizens" and that "government does not have the authority to define true religion and thus must protect the religious freedom of all citizens," the website concludes, "Government therefore does not have the authority to establish an official religion. If all citizens should be free to practice their religions, then government's establishment of one religion or one kind of religion would contradict the principle of equal treatment of all citizens" (http://cpjustice.org/content/religious-freedom, retrieved 6-20-11). CPJ thus argues for an equal right to religious freedom along with equal treatment of believers and nonbelievers alike.

However, a problem arises in the website's statements about political community (http://www.cpjustice.org/content/political-community, retrieved 6-20-11). The first of its basic points about religious freedom—"Created in the image of God, humans bear ultimate responsibility to their Creator. No human authority can stand in the position of God or otherwise establish the terms of human responsibility to God"—leads on my analysis to the argument that while "humans may bear ultimate responsibility to their Creator," that responsibility under our religion clauses must be ascribed to individuals and the religious organizations of their choosing, and not to

might be, the chief danger to religious freedom in the United States is not secularists or atheists, but religion itself. The most fundamental protection of religious freedom in the American political order is the fact that the religion clauses do not constitute us as a religious community, but rather as a political order in which government has no religious identity or responsibility.

Government, then, violates the secularity principle when it takes a position, or does anything that amounts to taking a position, on the truth or worth of religion, religious beliefs and values, or religious practices. Justice O'Connor's concept of endorsement—more specifically, her argument that the Establishment Clause prohibits governmental endorsement (or disapproval) of religion—comes close to the secularity principle I have suggested. Government under the Establishment Clause cannot endorse religion not just because someone may feel bad or disfavored but

---

government. In other words, the religion clauses as I understand them provide that for those who are religiously oriented, individuals, not government, may bear ultimate responsibility to their Creator.

Yet, at the same time, the organization's view of political community holds that "[t]he mutual obligation of citizens and public officials exhibits a covenantal character, pointing us to the accountability of government and citizens to God." Then again, what the website calls the second implication of the principles of political community states, "A political community should not be fashioned as a community of faith, whether of Christian faith, secularist faith, or a general civil-religious faith. Rather, our republic should be constituted as a community of citizens that does not discriminate against anyone for reasons of faith." My argument is concerned to uphold this latter point against what I see as the probably inconsistent claim of the former point, as well as the claim elsewhere on the website (at http://www.cpjustice.org/content/government) that "[w]hile government and citizens hold one another accountable under the law and to the law, the ultimate accountability of both is to God." This is precisely the point raised by Justice Scalia's reference in *McCreary* to the desire of the American people to give thanks to God *as a people*, which I have challenged by arguing that the claim that basic decisions as to religious orientation rest with the individual and not the majority requires that the U.S. as a corporate body, as a political order, have itself neither a religious identity nor a religious mission.

Finally, what the website calls the first implication of its points about religious freedom is that "neither a particular religion nor secularism may be established in public life. Instead, government should uphold public pluralism." I agree fully, but to make this claim successfully one must refute the counterclaim that it is possible *not* to establish either a particular religion or secularism. That is the burden of my distinction between "secularism" and "secularity," and it is the primary reason why in chapter 3 I addressed the claim of Christian Reconstructionists like Rushdoony that any political order involves an establishment of religion. Neuhaus, a tremendously humane, cultured, and sympathetic individual sensitive to concerns like that of his rabbi friend who said, "When I hear the term 'Christian America,' I see barbed wire" (*Naked Public Square*, 145), at the same time argued that the public square can never be naked, for without "conventional religion" there would be "ersatz religion." This is a position that, on my analysis, is a softer version of Rushdoony.

also, more important, because any such endorsement (1) makes religious identification an aspect of American citizenship and (2) thereby actually impinges upon religious freedom.

Yet how does endorsement actually impinge upon religious freedom? If government violates what I call the secularity principle and takes a position on the truth or worth of religion, religious beliefs or values, or religious practice, then how does it coerce me and thus infringe upon my religious freedom if it nevertheless allows me the free exercise of my own religious beliefs? The fundamental question that remains is, in what sense is it plausible to say that a violation of the secularity principle through governmental position taking creates a coercive situation?

Here is where in the secularity principle we join the concepts of coercion and position taking developed in the previous two chapters. My argument is that when government takes a position on the truth or worth of religion, religious beliefs or values, or religious practices, it creates the structure of implicit coercion by forcing us to choose between what I call our civic identity and our religious identity. Our civic identity is our self-identification as Americans (and, as such, it is, in the United States, a universal category), with the corollary that the government is our government, that the government's acts are our—*my*—acts. Our religious identity is our self-identification as a member or follower or adherent of a particular faith tradition or secular belief system, and thus, in a religiously pluralistic country like the United States, is a particularistic category. Consider for example, such terms as Catholic-American or Jewish-American. One's religious identity is to the left of the hyphen; one's civic identity is to the right. In this formulation, which represents the perspective of our political order, civic identity is what is primary (as it should be from the government's standpoint), modified by religious identity; one is an American who happens to be Catholic or Jewish. (The reverse occurs when we say American Catholic or American Jew, whereby then the religious identity is primary, modified by the nationality or citizenship; one is a Catholic or a Jew who happens to be an American. This formulation, however, is inconsistent with the individualism of the American political tradition.) Indeed, the central premise of the religion clauses in general and the Establishment Clause in particular is that our civic identity and our religious identity are two different things; otherwise, we would have no need of the protections provided by the Establishment Clause or the Free Exercise Clause. Were our civic identity and our religious identity fully and completely the same, the inclusion of these clauses in the First Amendment would be at best redundant if not simply inexplicable. Thus, the religion clauses presuppose, and give constitutional protection to, a distinction between civic identity and religious identity.[17]

Now, my argument is that coercion occurs in its implicit form when we confront a case of government's having taken a position on the truth or worth of religion, religious belief, or religious practice—say, by erecting a cross outside the legislature or some such action—because this position taking puts us in the position of having to choose between our civic identity and our religious identity. Laycock, for example, hints at this richer concept of coercion:

> The coercive powers of government include its powers to allocate money, licenses, privileges, and the like in discriminatory ways. The principle that government should not coerce religious beliefs or behaviors necessarily entails the proposition that *government should not create incentives to change religious beliefs or behaviors*—that government should be neutral with respect to religion in all its regulation, taxation, and spending.[18]

While Laycock refers here to standard, overt forms of coercion, his reference to a government-created incentive structure points to the implicit dimension of coercion.[19] Making us choose between our religious identity

[17] Recall our reference in the introduction to Newt Gingrich's idea of "an America in which a belief in the Creator is once again at the center of being an American." Cited in Isaac Kramnick and R. Laurence Moore, *The Godless Constitution: The Case against Religious Correctness*, 2nd ed. (New York: Norton, 1997), at 196. Such an idea fuses civic and religious identity, as opposed to the distinction I seek to draw here. An individual's identity is of course an amalgam of all sorts of things, but it is the relation between these two fundamental elements of identity that is at issue here.

[18] Douglas Laycock, "Religious Liberty as Liberty," *Journal of Contemporary Legal Issues* 7 (1996): 313 at 319, emphasis added. He does, however, retreat to a thinner concept of coercion when he writes at 320, "Government should be entirely neutral in matters of religion even when it coerces no one," and refers at 321 to "noncoercive government influence."

[19] When Michael McConnell talks about how to assess the legitimacy of the impact of a government law or act on religious freedom, he contends that any such assessment should take as a baseline "the hypothetical world in which individuals make decisions about religion on the basis of their own religious conscience, without the influence of government. The underlying principle is that governmental action should have the minimum possible effect on religion, consistent with achievement of the government's legitimate purposes." Michael McConnell, "Religious Freedom at a Crossroads," *University of Chicago Law Review* 59 (1992): 115, at 169. My idea of structure is what is important here. Note also that, without necessarily approaching the concept of coercion as I do, Cynthia Ward, cited much earlier here, writes that the Court's opinions in such cases as *Lee v. Weisman*, 505 U.S. 577 (1992) and *Santa Fe Independent School District v. Doe*, 530 U.S. 290 (2000) suggest that "the state has been 'coercive' under the Establishment Clause not only when it expressly penalizes citizens for refusing to engage in state-sponsored religious activity, but also when it presents citizens with a choice between religious and nonreligious activity and the choice is one

and our civic identity is, I submit, creating just such an incentive. We are not denied our right to our own religion when we confront a crèche or a cross or a menorah, or when we object to an officially sponsored prayer, but we are forced publicly to reject someone else's religion as a condition of maintaining our own, or to accept someone else's religion as a condition of participating in a civic function.[20] There is of course no threat of violence or legal penalty in such a situation, but the government's act of position taking forces us to make a choice and is thus, implicitly, coercive. To be sure, if a celebrity endorses a particular product, he or she is not coercing me to buy it, nor is he or she putting me into any kind of awkward position; I am free simply to ignore that endorsement. So, too, if my neighbor displays a religious symbol not my own, or contributes money to religious groups or practices not my own, I am free to ignore those actions because they do not speak for me. They are not *my* actions.

Yet if the government, which in a liberal-democratic society is *my* government and speaks for me no less than for anyone else, violates the secularity principle and engages in an act of position taking by sponsoring a particular religious display, holiday, value, or practice contrary to my own, it is thereby not *my* government and does *not* speak for me; it forces me to choose between my civic identity and my religious identity even if it does not coerce me overtly to join in those things.[21] Still, what does it mean to say that government makes us choose between our civic identity and our religious identity? In what sense am I being made to choose? Is that purely mental or emotional or subjective, having to do with my self-image and identity? Yes, but, after all, the government does want to shape my self-image and identity by stirring patriotic sentiments, by getting me to identify with the government or the Constitution or the country. If the government does attempt to shape my self-understanding and identity in this latter sense of cultivating patriotism, it does put me in

---

that the citizen would not be required to make in the absence of the challenged state-sponsored activity." Ward, "Coercion and Choice under the Establishment Clause," *University of California-Davis Law Review* 39 (2006): 1621, at 1637.

[20] In the *Engel* case on school prayer, Justice Douglas, arguing that "[s]tudents can stand mute or even leave the classroom, if they desire," *Engel*, at 438, obviously did not see this structuring of choice as coercive in any sense.

[21] In Justice Souter's dissent in *Van Orden* he expresses this conflict between one's civic identity and one's religious identity: "There is something significant in the common term 'statehouse' to refer to a state capitol building: it is the civic home of every one of the State's citizens. If neutrality in religion means something, any citizen should be able to visit that civic home without having to confront religious expressions clearly meant to convey an official religious position that may be at odds with his own religion, or with rejection of rejection of religion." *Van Orden v. Perry*, 545 U.S. 677 (2005), at 745.

a bind when it pushes a religious orthodoxy not my own. In fact, precisely to avoid putting someone into a situation where he or she is forced to make a choice, government, in the days of the military draft, traditionally allowed a pacifist to opt for conscientious-objector status in order not to have to choose between God and the government, and for years school districts in many states have designated Wednesday evenings as "church night" in order that students not be forced to choose between school activities and church activities. Such practices, I suggest, manifest a recognition that forcing someone to choose—thus not allowing him or her not to choose, not to take a position—is a case of coercion no less than forcing him or her to take a particular position. In overt coercion, government makes a choice for us; in implicit coercion, government makes us make a choice; the latter is still coercion.

Consider two examples of this point that we can draw from the discussion in the Introduction. First, if Drake were a religious institution with a religious mission, then, like many though not all religiously affiliated universities, it could say that students, faculty, and staff of all religious backgrounds are welcome, but on the condition that they respect the religious identity and mission of the university. This means that people who do not share or subscribe to that religious identity and mission are not quite in an equal position in the Drake community with those who do. Yet Drake is not a religiously defined institution, which means that everyone is welcome regardless of religious orientation and that one's religious orientation is completely irrelevant to one's standing in the university community. In a second example, suppose, as everyone outside a university fears, a professor were quite vocal about his political views, but said that students were certainly free to hold their own views and would not be penalized or otherwise disadvantaged for doing so. Many if not most students do not feel quite comfortable in this situation; they might be reticent to stand up for their own views, because the professor has authority over them and controls rewards and sanctions. Students can drop a class, but that means that they must choose between their academic interest and their personal political views. In both cases, at Drake University faculty, staff, and students are certainly free *as individuals* or even in certain groups to take a variety of positions on political matters, but that is quite different from what it means for the university as the university to take a position on such matters, or the professor as professor.

The parallel is that if the United States itself endorses or otherwise privileges a particular religious orientation, there is much more of an authority that people cannot "drop" with any ease and without much sacrifice. There is certainly a difference between persuasion and coercion, but persuasion, when done by government, can shade into coercion. I am free to ignore my neighbor's attempts to persuade me to adopt his or her religious beliefs, but how free am I to ignore the government's attempts at such persuasion? Formally, I am indeed free to ignore the government, but, as in the classroom case immediately above, there is a "one had better think twice" component to doing so. Indeed, this bind becomes clearer if we consider the opposite example of government position taking. Imagine that government takes the position that religion in general or a particular religion is wrong or bad, and it buys public-service announcements in print and broadcast media like those we see saying that cigarette smoking is bad for us, or posts signs saying "religion is the opiate of the masses." Although no one would be forbidden to hold and practice religious beliefs in this example, just as no one of legal age is forbidden to smoke cigarettes, it would be hard to argue that the government has not put one in the position of conflict between one's civic identity ("this is my government") and one's religious identity.

Thus, using the thicker concept of coercion (without the theoretical underpinnings I have attempted to elucidate), Justice Kennedy argues in the *Lee v. Weisman* case of school-sponsored graduation prayer that not to find a violation "would place objectors in the dilemma of participating, with all that implies, or protesting."[22] The government here took a position on the worth of religion and religious practice, and that act forced some students to choose between their civic and religious identities. Students ordinarily are not overtly coerced into participating in graduation prayers of football game prayers, but those events make dissenting students choose between attending the graduation or the game at the cost of seeming to affirm beliefs contrary to their own, or staying away. Participating in the religious rituals thus becomes a condition of participating in the event in this significant circumstance: participating in an official, government-sponsored event on the basis of its being open to all citizens equally becomes contingent upon participating in a religious ritual that is not a religious ritual of all citizens equally. Perhaps Kennedy concluded in those circumstances that there was too much accommodation of religion, but we recall that he defended accommodation earlier in *Allegheny*, where he wrote, "Government policies of accommodation, acknowledgment, and support for religion are an accepted part of our political and cultural heritage."[23] However, while we know what "accommodation" is—technically, it is a matter of lifting a government-imposed burden on the free exercise of religion[24]—it is less clear what "acknowledgment" and

[22] *Lee v. Weisman*, at 593.

[23] *Allegheny*, at 657.

[24] At footnote 59 of his opinion in *Allegheny*, Blackmun writes that an accommodation of religion, in order to be permitted under the Establishment Clause, must lift

"support" could be other than a matter of position taking. For example, also in *Allegheny*, Blackmun writes,

> Celebrating Christmas as a religious, as opposed to a secular, holiday, necessarily entails professing, proclaiming, or believing that Jesus of Nazareth, born in a manager in Bethlehem, is the Christ, the Messiah. If the government celebrates Christmas as a religious holiday (for example, by issuing an official proclamation saying: "We rejoice in the glory of Christ's birth!"), it means that the government really is declaring Jesus to be the Messiah, a specifically Christian belief. In contrast, confining the government's own celebration of Christmas to the holiday's secular aspects does not favor the religious beliefs of non-Christians over those of Christians. Rather, it simply permits the government to acknowledge the holiday without expressing an allegiance to Christian beliefs, an allegiance that would truly favor Christians over non-Christians.[25]

He appears alert to what I have called the inadmissibility of governmental position taking, but what is it to "acknowledge" the holiday if not for government to take a position?[26] Government (if memory serves me) does not, after all, officially "endorse" or "acknowledge" the Super Bowl or the World Series; these are events that interest millions of people who themselves are free to endorse and acknowledge them, but there would seem to be no compelling need for government to do so. Why, then, does

---

"an identifiable burden on the exercise of religion" (internal citations omitted). In *Lee v. Weisman*, at 627–68, Justice David Souter states, "The State may 'accommodate' the free exercise of religion by relieving people from generally applicable rules that interfere with their religious callings. . . . Contrary to the views of some, such accommodation does not necessarily signify an official endorsement of religious observance over disbelief" (internal citations omitted). Accommodation thus has constitutional meaning, in terms of free exercise, but "acknowledgment" does not. Indeed, Souter suggests that accommodation does not involve what I have called position taking: "In everyday life, we routinely accommodate religious beliefs that we do not share. A Christian inviting an Orthodox Jew to lunch might take pains to choose a kosher restaurant; an atheist in a hurry might yield the right of way to an Amish man steering a horse-drawn carriage. In so acting, we express respect for, but not endorsement of, the fundamental values of others. We act without expressing a position on the theological merit of those values or of religious belief in general, and no one perceives us to have taken such a position." *Lee v. Weisman*, at 628, emphasis added.

[25] *Allegheny*, at 611–12. O'Connor, too, states, "Clearly, the government can acknowledge the role of religion in our society in numerous ways that do not amount to an endorsement." *Allegheny*, at 631.

[26] As we saw in the text at n 18 in cha. 2, the *OED* defines "acknowledge" as "to own the knowledge of; to confess; to recognize or admit as true," or "to own as genuine, or of legal force or validity; to own, avow, or assent, in legal form, to (an act, document, etc.) so as to give it validity." To recognize the existence of a holiday might be all right, but to recognize or admit it as true would be a matter of government's making a religious or theological statement.

government need to acknowledge a religious holiday? If government may "acknowledge" a religious event, then whose religious event is to receive such acknowledgment—that of some religious majority? Yet the concern that renders the religion clauses intelligible can be nothing other than the rights of religious minorities to their own beliefs, values, and practices.[27]

Perhaps "acknowledge" functions with regard to religion the same equivocal way "recognition" functions in foreign relations and diplomacy when one government "recognizes" another: diplomatic "recognition" can be factual judgment that, yes, a given government is indeed the government of a country, or it can be a normative judgment about the worth of the government of another country. Thus, when Kennedy in *Allegheny* wanted to allow "government's attempts to recognize the religious underpinnings of the holiday" and talked of allowing government "to participate in its citizens' celebration of a holiday," he appears to allow government to take a position—i.e., to make a normative judgment—as to the truth or worth of religion, religious beliefs and values, or religious practices, and that act forces an individual into having to choose between his or her civic identity and his or her religious identity.[28] Indeed, this

[27] The school prayer cases and the arguments for school prayer encapsulate what is essential about the whole idea of nonestablishment. When people complain about "throwing God out of the schools" or talk about wanting "voluntary" prayer in the schools, the key of course is that there is voluntary prayer in the schools: students may meet with each other outside of class, join hands, etc. This, however, is not enough for the advocates of returning voluntary prayer to the schools. What they want actually is some sort of official, organized, collective dimension to prayer. That at bottom is what the Establishment Clause is supposed to prohibit.

[28] In "Religious Freedom Deserves More Than Neutrality: The Constitutional Argument for Nonpreferential Favoritism of Religion," *Florida Law Review* 57 (2005): 1, Patrick Garry argues that the Establishment Clause, rightly understood, calls for not just allowing accommodation, in the sense of lifting government-imposed burdens, but nonpreferentialism, which I interpret as a kind of affirmative action for religion (see his comments at 40). "Contrary to the neutrality doctrine," he writes at 3, "which seeks to prevent the government from showing any favoritism at all to religion in general, the Establishment Clause model presented in this Article does not forbid the government from conferring special aid or benefits upon religion in general, as long as the aid or benefits are given without preference to any religious denominations" (footnote omitted). On this argument, however, government has to engage in position taking, for it necessarily gets government into the job of deciding what counts as a religion if government is going to confer special aid or benefits. Garry opposes the neutrality doctrine because he maintains it rests on "the assumption that the First Amendment protects secularism as much as religion; that atheism is protected as much as religion. Neutrality ignores the special value of religion, a value that prompted the framers to specify religious freedom as the first liberty articulated in the Bill of Rights" (at 33, footnote omitted). Yet if secularism is not religion (i.e., a set of answers to the ultimate questions of human existence), then it is a neutral standpoint vis-à-vis religion where government takes no position; whereas if secularism is religion, then it would qualify

becomes clearer if we consider once again the opposite example of government position taking suggested earlier. If government takes the position that religion in general, or a particular religion, is wrong or bad, and it publicizes that position analogously to its occasional campaigns against smoking that nevertheless do not outlaw smoking, we would be hard put to argue that the government has not put one in the position of conflict between one's civic identity ("this is my government") and one's religious identity (this is my religion) even if no one would be forbidden to hold and practice religious beliefs.

Still, one remains tempted to ask, is this situation really coercive? After all, as Scalia insists, there is no sanction here. Recall his idea of "coercion of religious orthodoxy and of financial support by force of law and threat of penalty."[29] By defining "sanction" narrowly—force of law and threat of penalty—Scalia quite logically conceptualizes coercion quite narrowly and thereby leaves almost all of what government might do regarding religion in the twentieth and twenty-first centuries immune to challenge under the Establishment Clause. Can there be coercion without a sanction? Scalia argues that there cannot be, saying that there is no sanction for choosing to remain seated during a graduation prayer or choosing not to attend one's graduation ceremony. On the other hand, one surely suffers something unpleasant when one is forced into the position of having to choose between the lesser of two evils—listening to a prayer from another religion or not attending one's graduation ceremony—as opposed to not having to make such a choice at all. What is coercive here is my having to opt for one of two evils, even if the lesser, neither of which I would ever choose to choose, so to speak. The result is that I am pushed into accepting an evil that I would not have chosen otherwise.

Nevertheless, recall Scalia's opposition to what he considers mushy psychology in his claim in *Lee*, cited earlier, that "[t]he Court's argument that state officials have 'coerced' students to take part in the invocation and benediction at graduation ceremonies is, not to put too fine a point on it, incoherent."[30] Surely, however, Scalia is familiar with Alexis de Tocqueville's classic concern in *Democracy in America* with what he labeled the tyranny of the majority. That tyranny can appear in the force of law, according to de Tocqueville, but it also can appear in the force of public opinion:

---

for the special aid and benefits Garry wants for all religions under his nonpreferentialism standard. When he argues that "the beneficiaries of the [Establishment] clause are not the nonreligious but the religious" (at 51), therefore, he calls upon government to take the position that religion is worth more or is truer than nonreligion.

[29] *Lee v. Weisman*, at 640.

[30] *Lee v. Weisman*, at 636.

> In America the majority raises formidable barriers around the liberty of opinion; within these barriers an author may write what he pleases, but woe to him if he goes beyond them. Not that he is in danger of an auto-da-fe, but he is exposed to continued obloquy and persecution. His political career is closed forever, since he has offended the only authority that is able to open it. Every sort of compensation, even that of celebrity, is refused to him. Before making public his opinions he thought he had sympathizers; now it seems to him that he has none any more since he has revealed himself to everyone; then those who blame him criticize loudly and those who think as he does keep quiet and move away without courage. He yields at length, overcome by the daily effort which he has to make, and subsides into silence, as if he felt remorse for having spoken the truth.[31]

This is a tyranny, de Tocqueville writes, that is not physical:

> Monarchs had, so to speak, materialized oppression; the democratic republics of the present day have rendered it as entirely an affair of the mind as the will which it is intended to coerce. Under the absolute sway of one man the body was attacked in order to subdue the soul; but the soul escaped the blows which were directed against it and rose proudly superior. Such is not the course adopted by tyranny in democratic republics; there the body is left free, and the soul is enslaved. The master no longer says: "You shall think as I do or you shall die"; but he says: "You are free to think differently from me and to retain your life, your property, and all that you possess; but you are henceforth a stranger among your people. You may retain your civil rights, but they will be useless to you, for you will never be chosen by your fellow citizens if you solicit their votes; and they will affect to scorn you if you ask for their esteem. You will remain among men, but you will be deprived of the rights of mankind. Your fellow creatures will shun you like an impure being; and even those who believe in your innocence will abandon you, lest they should be shunned in their turn. Go in peace! I have given you your life, but it is an existence worse than death."[32]

The point of de Tocqueville's analysis here is clearly that there can be, especially in democratic polities, forms of coercion without the force of law and threat of penalty.[33] As Samuel Cook argues, "Coercion takes a

[31] Alexis de Tocqueville, *Democracy in America*, vol. 1 (New York: Vintage, 1990), 264.

[32] de Tocqueville, *Democracy in America*, 264. I doubt that Justice Scalia rejects de Tocqueville's analysis, but in places he is so oriented toward a majoritarian position that he appears not to care. See, e.g., his opinion in *Employment Division, Oregon Department of Human Resources v. Smith*, 494 U.S. 872 (1990), discussed earlier.

[33] For her part, Ward seems to recognize this form of coercion without the de Tocqueville connection: "Under the Court's conception of indirect coercion, a state-mandated choice between religion and nonreligion may be unconstitutionally coercive even though the state has expressed no preference as to how the choice should

variety of forms. The tendency to identify it with purely physical force—violence, physical sanctions and rewards—is not only misleading but profoundly dangerous. Nonphysical forms are as significant and far-reaching as physical manifestations."[34]

My argument, then, is that coercion—in its broader rather than narrower sense—is at the core of an Establishment Clause violation when government takes a position on the truth or worth of religion, religious beliefs and values, or religious practices, because by doing so government forces us to choose between our civic identity and our religious identity.[35] The choice we are forced to make is whether to take our civic identity as Americans as primary, thus subordinating our personal religious identity to the religious orientation supported by the government, or to take our religious identity, whether that of a particular religion or that of an atheist or secularist belief system, as primary, thus subordinating our civic identity. Instead of allowing us to consider ourselves constituted equally by, or otherwise to reconcile, our civic and our religious identities, government's violation of the secularity principle by taking a position on the truth or worth of religion, religious beliefs and values, and religious practices forces us to choose and thereby becomes the exercise of coercion

---

be made, it has not intentionally weighted the choice with a legal penalty, and the source of any negative sanction is not the state but the behavior of private citizens who may seek to pressure or ostracize a religious dissenter into complying with the majority religious view. In such cases, however, according to the best reading of the Court's coercion test as applied in *Lee v. Weisman* and *Santa Fe Independent School District v. Doe*, the state has behaved coercively only when the negative social sanction is a reasonably foreseeable consequence of requiring religious dissenters to make the choice in question. In *Lee* and *Santa Fe*, the potential for social ostracism of dissenters was both foreseeable and substantial, since both cases occurred in school settings and involved the potentially great influence of social pressure on vulnerable teenaged students." Ward, "Coercion and Choice," at 1660, footnotes omitted.

[34] Samuel DuBois Cook, "Coercion and Social Change," in *Coercion*, ed. J. Roland Pennock and John W. Chapman (Chicago: Aldine-Atherton, 1972), 107–43, at 116. Cook, at 116, continues, "Coercion may be physical or nonphysical (psychological, spiritual, intellectual, aesthetic), violent or nonviolent, public (official) or private, individual or collective, overt or covert, legitimate or illegitimate, positive (rewards or promise of benefits) or negative (punishment, threat of deprivation), formal or informal, etc."

[35] Winnifred Fallers Sullivan writes that religious freedom involves, affirmatively, a right of what we call free exercise, but also that "religious freedom can be understood to have a negative meaning as well, a rejection both of religious foundations for government and of governmental support for religion. At the time of the founding, Americans of all sorts arguably committed themselves to a secular national government that claimed, perhaps for the first time in human history, no authority in matters religious." *The Impossibility of Religious Freedom* (Princeton, N.J.: Princeton University Press, 2005), 156.

in the implicit dimension of the concept.[36] Indeed, if people are free to erect whatever kinds of religious symbols on their own lawns or to meet on their own time to express religious beliefs of their own choosing, for example, then what is the purpose of having government make a religious statement? What does having government engage in religious symbolism by sponsoring a religious practice add to what individuals already may do in private? The whole point of using government to affirm a religious belief or engage in a religious practice is to make the belief or practice "official" in some sense, which is to put the power and authority of the state on the side of religion in general if not the side of some particular religion. This the Establishment Clause forbids.

Finally, my argument helps us understand the coherence of the two religion clauses. If the purpose of those clauses is to guarantee and protect the freedom of religion, then their duality implies that religious liberty can be infringed in two ways: government can infringe the freedom of religion by prohibiting certain religions, religious beliefs, or religious practices, and government can infringe the freedom of religion by establishing certain religions, religious beliefs, or religious practices. Consequently, an establishment violation infringes the freedom of religion and thereby must be understood in some sense as having created a coercive situation, since the opposite of freedom is coercion.[37] I have advanced what I take to be the central principle of nonestablishment in an attempt to explain how an establishment violation infringes the freedom of religion, and I have advanced a two-dimensional concept of coercion in an attempt to explain how an establishment violation creates a coercive situation. My argument, I hope, makes such a case intelligible and thus contributes to a comprehensive theory of religious freedom in the American constitutional system.

[36] If the purpose of the religion clauses is to guarantee religious freedom, particularly to prevent people from becoming caught between alternative systems of authority and obligation—between conscience and the law, between God and Caesar—then the sense of being caught between two competing and inconsistent systems of obligation is what is at stake when I am having to choose between my civic identity and my religious identity. This is precisely what the religion clauses are designed to prevent.

[37] The apparent absence of a sanction in establishment claims as opposed to free-exercise claims may be what leads to the notion that coercion is not a necessary element of establishment violations. Justice O'Connor's concept endorsement gets at the absence of a sanction by saying that where there is no sanction government still makes you choose between your civic identity and your religious identity. That sense of having to make a choice is not a formal, but rather a Tocquevillian, sanction, and that is what makes us feel coerced.

Conclusion

One Nation under Whose God?

The religion clauses in the First Amendment to the American Constitution are the focus of extensive litigation regarding such matters as school prayer, government aid to religious institutions, religious exemptions from otherwise generally applicable laws, and so on, but the broader question, beyond simply legal matters but underlying such legal matters, is, what is the political meaning of the religion clauses regarding the character of the American political order? The United States is not constituted as a religious order itself, but rather as a political order that protects the religious freedom of individuals and groups, that guarantees them a space to make their own choices regarding religious beliefs, values, and practices. Culminating in what I think is our best understanding of the meaning of the religion clauses in general and of the Establishment Clause in particular, the goal of this book has been to argue that the purpose of the religion clauses of the American Constitution is to protect not religion, but religious freedom. These clauses constitute not a religious community, but a political order that protects religious freedom. There is a difference between religion "in the public square," wherein people as private individuals and groups publicly affirm and engage in the religious beliefs, values, and practices they hold dear, and religion "as the public square," wherein the public square is itself an essentially religious community. The master premise of the American political order is that the United States is a liberal-democratic polity in which all citizens have an equal right to their liberties, including their religious liberty. Consequently, any attempt on the part of citizen A to use the machinery of the government to impose his or her religious beliefs and practices on citizen B is in fact a rejection of that fundamental commitment to an equal right to our liberties.

The first principle of the religion clauses is that their purpose is to secure religious liberty, freedom of religion. Assuming that the people who wrote and ratified these clauses knew what they were doing, the question arises, as we have seen, as to why there are two clauses. As a matter of logic, it would seem to be the case that this is because they each deal with opposite threats to religious liberty: in one case, the threat is that government might forbid or penalize the free exercise of religion; government may not make rejection of some religion, religious belief, or religious practice the precondition of full participation in American citizenship. Of course we know that government does prohibit certain kinds of religious practice (human sacrifice, polygamy). The Establishment Clause comprises the other side of that coin; in other words, the assumption is that government can threaten religious liberty not only when it requires you to reject or deny your religious beliefs or values, but also when it requires you to affirm the religious beliefs or practices that are not your own. That is a denial of religious liberty as well. Religious liberty is protected, in other words, when the Constitution prohibits government from requiring that you deny or reject religious belief or practice, and when the Constitution prohibits government from requiring that you affirm or subscribe to a religious belief or practice. What this means, therefore, is that an establishment of religion can amount to a denial of religious liberty; a denial of religious liberty is a form of coercion; so an establishment of religion is a form of coercion.

There are those, however, who argue that, as I have used the terms here, religion is more fundamental than religious freedom, and that it is with this fundamental proposition in mind that anyone must understand the meaning and significance of the religion clauses. The argument is that self-government depends upon a certain quality of moral virtue among the citizens of a republic, that moral virtue depends upon religion, and, thus, that self-government depends upon religion. Consider this passage, though lengthy, from Justice Story's *Commentaries*:

> How far any government has a right to interfere in matters touching religion, has been a subject much discussed by writers upon public and political law. The right and the duty of the interference of government, in matters of religion, have been maintained by many distinguished authors, as well those, who were the warmest advocates of free government, as those, who were attached to governments of a more arbitrary character. Indeed, the right of a society or government to interfere in matters of religion will hardly be contested by any persons, who believe that piety, religion, and morality are intimately connected with the well being of the state, and indispensable to the administration of civil justice. The promulgation of the great doctrines of religion, the being, and attributes, and providence of one Almighty God;

> the responsibility to him for all our actions, founded upon moral freedom and accountability; a future state of rewards and punishments; the cultivation of all the personal, social, and benevolent virtues;—these never can be a matter of indifference in any well ordered community. It is, indeed, difficult to conceive, how any civilized society can well exist without them. And at all events, it is impossible for those, who believe in the truth of Christianity, as a divine revelation, to doubt, that it is the especial duty of government to foster, and encourage it among all the citizens and subjects. This is a point wholly distinct from that of the right of private judgment in matters of religion, and of the freedom of public worship according to the dictates of one's conscience.[1]

The heart of this passage exemplifies the view that a nation is, must be, essentially a religious community. A nation certainly involves a commitment to a common set of ideals and values, but does such a commitment necessarily imply a commitment to a common religious identity? The question is whether a commitment to a common set of ideals and values can be independent of a commitment to a common religious identity. If not, if a nation must be an essentially religious community, such that a nation cannot not be an essentially religious community, then (1) whose religion, and (2) what meaning is left to the religion clauses of the First Amendment? Perhaps we would have simply the establishment of one set of religious values, if not that of an institutional church, with, at best, toleration of other faiths.[2] This seems to be the burden of the last sentence in Story's passage cited here. Yet a regime of religious toleration is different from a regime of religious freedom.[3]

However, Prof. Steven Gey, for one, argues—rightly, I believe—that religion cannot provide the basis for the broad sense of national unity that some find missing in American society. "Proponents of religious unity,"

[1] Joseph Story, "Commentaries on the Constitution 3:§1865," in *The Founders' Constitution* (http://press-pubs.uchicago.edu/founders/documents/amendI_religions69.html, retrieved 3-23-08).

[2] Thus, regarding the rights of citizens who do not adhere to a monotheistic religion, Scalia writes in *McCreary County, Kentucky, et al. v. American Civil Liberties Union of Kentucky, et al.*, 545 U.S. 844 (2005), "The beliefs of those citizens are entirely protected by the Free Exercise Clause, and by those aspects of the Establishment Clause that do not relate to government acknowledgment of the Creator."

[3] A regime of toleration would be one in which there is a de jure or de facto established religion but also the free exercise of other religious beliefs. A regime of religious freedom, by contrast, would be one with free exercise and no establishment. On this schema, Great Britain, with the established Church of England, would be a regime of toleration, while the United States would be one of religious freedom. Just to finish the possible combinations, we can say that the conjunction of establishment without free exercise would be a religious polity, or even a theocracy, and the conjunction of no establishment and no free exercise would be a secular tyranny.

he writes, contend "that in the absence of religion and other mediating institutions, the framework of democratic government will be nothing but an empty shell, devoid of the moral center needed to keep the entire machine running properly."[4] But religion, Gey argues, cannot fill the gap:

> National unity will not occur within a religious framework. In fact, the religious framework is peculiarly unsuited to the quest for unity because the very design of that framework is configured around notions of inclusion and exclusion. The religious framework is designed to thwart efforts at unity by making demands on believers that are specifically intended to ensure their inclusion into the holy precincts of the faith. But those same standards for inclusion are also standards for exclusion of nonadherents, and any religion of substance will define itself in part by reference to those who do not meet the standards of the creed.[5]

Protecting religion, therefore—even those (especially those?) with universalistic claims—means protecting institutions, beliefs, and practices that define themselves both in terms of who and what they are *and in terms of who and what they are not.* A religion defines itself partly be drawing and policing a line between those who are adherents and those who are nonbelievers. It is only religious freedom that can provide the inclusiveness that religion cannot.

When Gey argues more recently that "the new majority on the Supreme Court is about to embark on a wholesale reinterpretation of the entire constitutional approach toward the relationship between church and state"—that, more specifically, "[t]he Court's new majority is prepared, in other words, to exchange the old separationist Establishment Clause paradigm for the new integrationist paradigm"—he is pointing, in my terms, to a shift from the protection of religious freedom to the protection of religion itself.[6] There are, he writes, five themes or elements in the separationist paradigm:

> These themes are: (1) the Establishment Clause creates an American political structure that is essentially secular in nature; (2) the religious majority cannot use its political dominance to enlist the government to endorse or otherwise advance the majority's sectarian views; (3) a citizen's religious views (or lack of religious views) are irrelevant to that citizen's political status; (4) the rules regarding religious establishments are national rules, which prohibit overwhelmingly dominant local religious majorities from exercising

[4] Steven G. Gey, "Unity of the Graveyard and the Attack on Constitutional Secularism," *Brigham Young University Law Review* (2004): 1005, at 1010.

[5] Gey, "Unity of the Graveyard," at 1011.

[6] Steven G. Gey, "Life after the Establishment Clause," *West Virginia Law Review* 110 (2007): 1, at 2 and 8.

> their dominance over even extremely small and unpopular local religious minorities; and (5) the Establishment Clause is a subset of the unifying First Amendment premise that it is presumptively impermissible for the government to enforce any collective assertion of ultimate value.[7]

Similarly, there are five parts to the integrationist paradigm:

> These integrationist counter-themes include the following premises: (1) United States is a religious country, and the United States government is and always has been defined by and structured around the culture's religious principles and precepts; (2) in the American political system the religious majority should be allowed to exercise its political influence on the government; (3) religion is a relevant factor in political decision-making; (4) local religious majorities have a legitimate interest in infusing their community with the dominant religious perspective; and (5) moral and theological relativism is not a constitutional command, and in fact is deleterious to the commonweal; therefore, the government is not required to shy away from incorporating moral absolutes into its legal mandates.[8]

It is unclear whether Gey considers accommodationism, as usually understood, to be a middle position between separationism and integrationism, or whether he considers integrationism to be the necessary, logical outcome of any accommodationist position. In either case, what Gey calls integrationism represents the idea broached above that any nation is and must be an essentially religious community. Not only does a polity make religious claims, but a religion makes political claims.[9]

Further discussion of Gey's argument is beyond our analysis here, but his distinction between the separationist paradigm and integrationist paradigm suggests that the fundamental question—If the existence of a nation necessarily involves a commitment to a common set of ideals and values, does such a commitment necessarily imply a commitment to a common religious identity?—is one of political and constitutional theory rather than a narrower one of legal doctrine. As I have argued, to say that any political system is committed to a certain set of values—an orthodoxy—is not to say, without the premise that all values are essentially

[7] Gey, "Life," at 9.

[8] Gey, "Life," at 9.

[9] "In light of the growing confluence of religion and politics, it is clear that at the most basic level, church/state integrationists disagree comprehensively with the separationist perspective that religion is at heart a private, individual matter that is best left to each individual believer and that person's faith community. In contrast to the separationist approach to religion as quintessentially a private matter, integrationists view religion as in many important respects a collective enterprise. To integrationists, religious faith can only be fully realized if it is celebrated and appreciated in public by groups of believers or, indeed, by society as a whole." Gey, "Life," at 16.

religious in nature, that it is committed to a certain set of religious beliefs. A liberal political system certainly has a set of value commitments, most centrally the value of freedom. The argument of this book has been that secularity, in the special, careful sense explained in the previous two chapters, is not itself a religious position; it abstains from religious positions. Anyone who finds that claim problematic must find problematic the First Amendment itself. Even if one were to contend that the religion clauses are purely jurisdictional in nature, that argument presupposes the substantive claim that it is possible for government not to take a religious position. The very intelligibility of the religion clauses in singling out religion necessarily presupposes that some things are not religion or not of religious concern. To argue that the secular itself is religious is to undermine the intelligibility of the religion clauses.

What is clear at this point, I hope, is that there is a distinction between religion and religious freedom, and that the placement of the religion clauses in the First Amendment—thus taking any political or legal dimension of religious matters out of the hands of a popular majority—indicates that their purpose is to protect religious freedom rather than religion. *Protecting religious freedom means protecting your right to believe in and belong to a religion or belief system different from my own; protecting religion does not necessarily mean protecting your right to believe differently.* To understand the religion clauses properly, we have to disentangle the ideas of religion and religious freedom, and doing so disarms the issue of hostility to religion that appears so often in critiques of the idea of separation of church and state.

Perhaps the ultimate constitutional paradox is that we protect religion best not by protecting religion directly, but by protecting religious freedom.[10] For this reason, Madison cautioned that "[a] religious sect may degenerate into a political faction," and that is why, as an institutionalized agreement to disagree, a liberal-democratic political order purports to

[10] See Gey, "Life," at 11–12 (footnote omitted): "At the end of the day, the single most important consequence of the separation principle is the creation of a secular government, free of religious dominance, control, or manipulation. The state is not beholden to religious authorities and is structurally independent from religious institutions. The paradox is that this actually benefits religion and religious practitioners. Contrary to the usual criticism of separation principle, the separation of church and state does not entail institutionalized governmental hostility to religion. The reality under a separationist Establishment Clause is exactly the opposite of the picture usually painted by opponents of separationism: A separationist Establishment Clause works in conjunction with other parts of the First Amendment (including the Speech and the Free Exercise Clauses) to create a vibrant and dynamic private sector, in which religion is immunized from political interference or control. Religion becomes stronger under such a system because it does not have to defend itself constantly from the state."

enable diverse people to live together by excluding absolutes from public life. As Bernard Crick writes in his classic *In Defence of Politics*, politics "is simply not concerned, as politics, with absolute ends."[11] Politics is the activity in which we negotiate our differences, an activity that necessitates compromise. Since a compromised absolute is no longer an absolute, politics as the domain of compromise is incompatible with absolutes. The special problem for liberal democracy posed by religion is that religion's very nature is frequently to assert and deal with absolute and ultimate truth. Religion may well have to do with Truth, but politics has to do with the problem of finding some way for us to live in an environment of competing and often conflicting truths. To return to Locke, "[T]he business of Laws is not to provide for the Truth of Opinions, but for the Safety and Security of the Commonwealth, and of every particular mans Goods and Person."[12]

Consider the difference between a mathematics class and a political science class. If I am teaching math, and you want to claim that 2 plus 2 in a base-ten system equals 5, you are wrong. You do not have the right to be wrong, and I legitimately may fail you for the course. Error has no rights. On the other hand, if I am teaching American politics, and you happen to have a political or moral or even religious view different from my own—not that I ever am going to announce my own views—we all agree that I cannot legitimately fail you for the course. Given whatever I might think is right, I have to respect your right to be what in my own view I think is wrong.[13]

A liberal-democratic political order takes that latter position on political questions. Differences must be respected, and that is why there is a danger to a liberal-democratic political order if we "religify" politics, that is, turn politics into a matter of Truth. Recall the famous speech of Pat Buchanan at the 1992 Republican National Convention that we noted earlier:

[11] Bernard Crick, *In Defence of Politics*, 2nd ed. (Chicago: University of Chicago Press, 1972), 159.

[12] John Locke, *A Letter Concerning Toleration*, ed. James H. Tully (Indianapolis: Hackett, 1983), 46. Prefacing the argument he will make in the *Letter*, 26, he writes, "that the whole Jurisdiction of the Magistrate reaches only to these Civil Concernments; and that all Civil Power, Right and Dominion, is bounded and confined to the only care of promoting these things; and that it neither can nor ought in any manner to be extended to the Salvation of Souls, these following considerations seem unto me abundantly to demonstrate."

[13] The claim that controversial moral, political, or religious matters must be understood along the lines of "2 + 2 = 4; anything else is wrong" suggests what we might call a lack of intellectual empathy, the capacity to see one's own point of view from another, outside perspective, as a point of view.

> My friends, this election is about much more than who gets what. It is about who we are. It is about what we believe. It is about what we stand for as Americans. There is a religious war going on in our country for the soul of America. It is a cultural war, as critical to the kind of nation we will one day be as was the Cold War itself.[14]

With such sentiments we come perilously close to reversing the famous saying of von Clausewitz, "War is the continuation of politics by other means":[15] Politics becomes the continuation of (religious) war by other means. Moreover, beyond impairing the willingness to negotiate and compromise that is the essential precondition of a liberal-democratic political order, religifying politics also poses the danger of politicizing religion. There were people in the 2004 presidential election who advocated voting *for* President Bush because he was a Christian, but that licenses someone else to argue that we should vote against a candidate because he is a Christian (or any other religious orientation). As noted earlier in our discussion here, during the 2008 Iowa caucus season, a devout Southern Baptist said of Mitt Romney, "I couldn't vote for him. His cross is not my cross."[16] And, as a perceptive student of mine once said, "If you combine religion and politics, you get politics."

From the standpoint of American political and constitutional theory, therefore, the purpose of the religion clauses of the First Amendment—"Congress shall make no law respecting an establishment of religion, or prohibiting the free exercise thereof"—is to enable us to agree to disagree about religious matters by taking them out of the domain of majority rule and placing them in the domain of individual rights. To be sure, the clauses are an admonition to Congress rather than the states, but, despite criticism from Justice Thomas and others, it is now settled doctrine that their mandates apply to state governments as well.[17] Regarding government, the religion clauses stand for the proposition, as we have seen Justice Jackson put it, that "[i]f there is any fixed star in our constitutional constellation, it is that no official, high or petty, can prescribe what shall be orthodox in politics, nationalism, religion, or other matters

[14] Pat Buchanan, 1992 Republican National Convention Speech (http://www.buchanan.org/pa-92-0817-rnc.html).

[15] Carl von Clausewitz, *On War*: "War Is Only a Continuation of State Policy by Other Means" (*der Krieg nichts ist als die fortgesetzte Staatspolitik mit anderen Mittell*) (http://www.gutenberg.org/files/1946/1946-h/1946-h.htm#2HCH0001, retrieved 7-21-08).

[16] Personal discussion with the author.

[17] See *Cantwell v. Connecticut*, 310 U.S. 296 (1940) for the Free Exercise Clause and *Everson v. Board of Education*, 330 U.S. 1 (1947) for the Establishment Clause. For Justice Thomas' critique, see *Van Orden v. Perry*, 545 U.S. 677 (2005).

of opinion or force citizens to confess by word or act their faith therein."[18] Regarding the individual, the religion clauses stand for the proposition that the affirmation of a particular religion, religious belief, or religious practice cannot be a condition of full participation in American citizenship (Establishment Clause), and the rejection of a particular religion, religious belief, or religious practice cannot be a condition of full participation in American citizenship (Free Exercise Clause).

My argument, then, is that the religion clauses in general and the Establishment Clause in particular negotiate the tension between the American value of religious freedom and the American fact of religious diversity by standing for the secularity principle: government may not take a position, nor do anything that amounts to taking a position, on the truth or worth of religion, religious beliefs and values, or religious practices. Paradoxically, the Constitution takes the position that religion and religious matters are so intensely important to people that government may not take a position on them. Government may not "put its finger on the scale," so to speak, the way the state of Alabama tried to do when it amended a state statute authorizing a period of silence in the public schools "for meditation or voluntary prayer," instead of the original language, "for meditation." The state government, the Supreme Court said, "intended to characterize prayer as a favored practice."[19] The political meaning of the religion clauses in general, and of the Establishment Clause in particular, is that while the individual is certainly free to talk to people about his or her religious beliefs and even try to convince them to accept those beliefs, he or she must respect their decision to reject his or her views; he or she is *not* free to attempt to use government, the machinery of the state, to assist him or her in either a coercive or even a noncoercive way. One cannot use government to support and advance one's own religious beliefs (Establishment Clause), and one cannot use government to oppose and undermine the religious beliefs of others (Free Exercise Clause).[20] Whatever the appropriateness of laissez-faire as an economic policy, certainly

[18] *West Virginia v. Barnette*, 319 U.S. 624 (1943), at 642.

[19] *Wallace v. Jaffree*, 472 U.S. 38 (1985), at 60.

[20] Put differently, the Free Exercise Clause means that you are free to believe as you please, to practice and worship (within limits) as you please, to proselytize as you please; the Establishment Clause means that you are not allowed to use the machinery of the state to endorse or advance or affirm or proselytize for your beliefs. We thus have a constitutional bargain in the United States regarding the question of religion: on the one hand, you are free to believe in and practice what you wish (within certain limits) and to attempt to encourage, persuade, and convince other people that your religion is the right religion for them; but, on the other hand, your freedom to do the former hinges on your agreement that you may not attempt to use government in any way to pursue your religious goals.

the existence of the religion clauses amounts to a constitutional mandate for a religious laissez-faire.

The religious clauses determine this character of the American political order by the fact that they protect not religion but religious freedom, and only this allows for the possibility of our living together with people with whom we have significant differences. Therefore, the function of the religion clauses of the Constitution is to constitute us as a political order in which the locus of religious identity is the individual and not the political order itself. It follows that politics, particularly in a liberal democracy, is simply not about God. If it were, then we would face the impossible task of finding a way to live together with people with whom we have not just significant, but fundamental, absolute differences. An attempt to make politics about God, then, is an attempt, witting or unwitting, to change radically the character of the American constitutional order. A true constitutional conservative, a position the overwhelming majority of the American people in fact affirm, would seek to preserve the character of the American constitutional order, and thus to reject any attempt to religify politics.

As we have seen, therefore, the phrase, "One Nation under God" leads immediately and necessarily to the question, "One Nation under Whose God?" The answer to that question must be, one nation under no one's God. To say that is to say nothing less, but also nothing more, than that the meaning of the religion clauses is that the Constitution does not constitute the United States as a religious community. The American political order, in terms of the three possibilities we saw in the Introduction, is constituted neither as a community with an institutional religious identity and mission that a diverse citizenry must respect but not necessarily affirm and endorse, nor as a community with an institutional religious identity and mission that a diverse citizenry must not only respect but also affirm and endorse as a condition of membership, but as a community with a civic identity and mission but no religious identity and mission. The American political order allows for and encourages the existence of individuals and groups with their own religious identities, but does not and—due to the religion clauses of the Constitution—cannot have a religious identity of its own. This is not an official endorsement of atheism or opposition to religion, but rather the constitutional means of ensuring everyone's freedom to stand as one individual under whatever he or she conceives to be his or her God.

In the end, readers may disagree with the argument in this book as to the place of religion in our constitutional order, and they certainly would reject any attempt on my part to use government to support my point of view. Yet readers' very freedom to reject my argument as to the place of religion in our constitutional order in effect confirms my argument, for readers are exemplifying precisely what I will call the point of the religion clauses: to enable us, however imperfectly, to agree to disagree about religious matters in a civil and respectful manner. By keeping government out of these issues—by making the locus of religious identity private individuals and groups instead of the nation—the religion clauses enable us to live together equally as Americans despite our religious differences.

Cases Cited

Abington School District v. Schempp, 374 U.S. 203 (1963).
Allegheny County v. Greater Pittsburgh ACLU, 492 U.S. 573 (1989).
Braunfeld v. Brown, 366 U.S. 599 (1961).
Cantwell v. Connecticut, 310 U.S. 296 (1940).
Church of the Holy Trinity v. United States, 143 U.S. 457 (1892).
Church of Lukumi Babalu Aye v. City of Hialeah, 508 U.S. 520 (1993).
Davis v. Beason, 133 U.S. 333 (1890).
Edwards v. Aguillard, 482 U.S. 578 (1987).
Elk Grove Unified Sch. Dist. v. Newdow, 542 U.S. 1 (2004).
Employment Division, Oregon Department of Human Resources v. Smith, 494 U.S. 872 (1990).
Engel v. Vitale, 370 U.S. 421 (1962).
Epperson v. Arkansas, 393 U.S. 97 (1968).
Everson v. Board of Education, 330 U.S. 1 (1947).
Freedom from Religion Foundation et al. v. Obama, U.S. (2010).
Goldman v. Weinberger, 475 U.S. 503 (1986).
Grove City College v. Bell, 465 U.S. 555 (1984).
Jacobellis v. Ohio, 378 U.S. 184 (1964).
Kiryas Joel v. Grumet, 512 U.S. 687 (1994).
Lee v. Weisman, 505 U.S. 577 (1992).
Lemon v. Kurtzman, 403 U.S. 602 (1971).
Lynch v. Donnelly, 465 U.S. 668 (1984).
Marsh v. Chambers, 463 U.S. 783 (1983).
McCollum v. Board of Education, 333 U.S. 203 (1948).
McCreary County, Kentucky, et al. v. American Civil Liberties Union of Kentucky, et al., 545 U.S. 844 (2005).
McGowan v. Maryland, 366 U.S. 420 (1961).

Minersville School District v. Gobitis, 310 U.S. 586 (1940).
Mitchell et al. v. Helms et al., 530 U.S. 793 (2000).
Mozert v. Hawkins City Board of Education, 827 F.2d 1058 (1987).
Murdock v. Pennsylvania, 319 U.S. 105 (1943).
Palko v. Connecticut, 302 U.S. 319 (1937).
People v. Ruggles, 8 Johns. 290 (1811).
Presbyterian Church v. Hull Church, 393 U.S. 440 (1969).
Reynolds v. United States, 98 U.S. 145 (1878).
Rosenberger v. Rector, 515 U.S. 819 (1995).
Santa Fe Independent School District v. Doe, 530 U.S. 290 (2000).
Sherbert v. Verner, 374 U.S. 398 (1963).
Snyder v. Massachusetts, 291 U.S. 97 (1934).
Texas Monthly, Inc. v. Bullock, 489 U.S. 1 (1989).
Thomas v. Collins, 323 U.S. 516 (1945).
Torcaso v. Watkins, 367 U.S. 488 (1961).
United States v. Ballard, 322 U.S. 78 (1944).
United States v. Carolene Products Company, 304 U.S. 144 (1938).
United States v. Seeger, 380 U.S. 163 (1965).
Van Orden v. Perry, 545 U.S. 677 (2005).
Varnum v. Brien, No. 07-1499 (April 3, 2009).
Wallace v. Jaffree, 472 U.S. 38 (1985).
Walz v. Tax Commission, 397 U.S. 664 (1970).
Watson v. Jones, 13 Wall. 679 (1871).
West Virginia v. Barnette, 319 U.S. 624 (1943).
Zorach v. Clauson, 343 U.S. 306 (1952).

Selected Bibliography

Anton, Thomas J. "Power, Pluralism, and Local Politics." *Administrative Science Quarterly* 7, no. 4 (1963): 425–57.

Augustine. *The City of God Against the Pagans.* New York: Cambridge University Press, 1998.

Bachrach, Peter, and Morton S. Baratz. "Two Faces of Power." *American Political Science Review* 56 (1962): 947–52.

Baker, Peter, and Susan Saulny. "At Notre Dame, Obama Calls for Civil Tone in Abortion Debate." *The New York Times*, May 17, 2009. http://www.nytimes.com/2009/05/18/us/politics/18obama.html.

Banerjee, Neela. "Families Challenging Religious Influence in Delaware Schools." *The New York Times*, July 29, 2006. http://www.nytimes.com/2006/07/29/us/29delaware.html?_r=1&scp=2&sq=Dobrich&st=nyt&oref=slogin.

Bayles, Michael D. "A Concept of Coercion." In J. Roland Pennock and John W. Chapman, *Coercion*, 16–29.

Beal, Timothy. "Among the Evangelicals: Inside a Fractured Movement." *The Chronicle of Higher Education*, December 12, 2010. http://chronicle.com/article/Among-the-Evangelicals/125647/.

Berg, Thomas C. "Religion Clause Anti-Theories." *Notre Dame Law Review* 72 (1997): 603.

Blumenthal, Max. *Republican Gomorrah: Inside the Movement That Shattered the Party.* New York: Nation Books, 2009.

Bork, Robert H. *The Tempting of America: The Political Seduction of the Law.* New York: Simon & Schuster, 1990.

Bottum, Joseph. "The Death of Protestant America: A Political Theory of the Protestant Mainline." *First Things* (August–September 2008). http://www.firstthings.com/article/2008/08/001-the-death-of-protestant-america-a-political-theory-of-the-protestant-mainline-19.

Bradley, Gerard V. "Religion at a Public University." *William and Mary Law Review* 49 (2008): 2217.

Brettschneider, Corey. "A Transformative Theory of Religious Freedom: Promoting the Reasons for Rights." *Political Theory* 38, no. 2 (2010): 187–213.

Brint, Steven, and Jean Reith Schroedel, eds. *Evangelicals and Democracy in America*. Vol. 2: *Religion and Politics*. New York: Russell Sage, 2009.

Broadway, Bill. "The Limits of Religious Unity: Interfaith Services for Terrorism Victims Raise Questions for Clergy." *Washington Post*, November 24, 2001. http://www.washingtonpost.com/ac2/wp-dyn?pagename=article&node=&contentId=A7821-2001Nov23, retrieved 9-6-11.

Buchanan, Patrick J. 1992. Republican National Convention Speech. http://buchanan.org/blog/1992-republican-national-convention-speech-148.

Burhani, Ahmad Najib. "Religious Orthodoxy and the Blasphemy Law." *Jakarta Post*, April 17, 2010. http://www.thejakartapost.com/news/2010/03/18/religious-orthodoxy-and-blasphemy-law.html.

Burke, Edmund. *Reflections on the Revolution in France*. Indianapolis: Hackett Publishing, 1987.

Cavanaugh, William T. *The Myth of Religious Violence: Secular Ideology and the Roots of Modern Conflict*. New York: Oxford University Press, 2009.

Center for Public Justice. http://cpjustice.org.

Clarkson, Frederick. "Christian Reconstructionism." *Public Eye Magazine* 8 (March–June 1994). http://www.publiceye.org/magazine/v08n1/chrisrec.html.

Cohen, Arthur A. *The Myth of the Judeo-Christian Tradition*. New York: Harper & Row, 1970.

Colby, Thomas B. "A Constitutional Hierarchy of Religions? Justice Scalia, the Ten Commandments, and the Future of the Establishment Clause." *Northwestern University Law Review* 100 (2006): 1097.

"Columnist Ann Coulter Shocks Cable TV Show, Declaring 'Jews Need to Be Perfected by Becoming Christians.'" *Fox News*, October 11, 2007. http://www.foxnews.com/story/0,2933,301216,00.html.

The Concise Oxford Dictionary of World Religions, 1997. http://www.encyclopedia.com/doc/1O101-Cuiusregio.html.

Conkle, Daniel O. "Toward a General Theory of the Establishment Clause." *Northwestern University Law Review* 82 (1988): 1115.

Cook, Samuel DuBois. "Coercion and Social Change." In J. Roland Pennock and John W. Chapman, *Coercion*, 107–43.

Crick, Bernard. *In Defence of Politics*. 2nd ed. Chicago: University of Chicago Press, 1972.

Dierenfield, Bruce J. *The Battle over School Prayer: How* Engel v. Vitale *Changed America.* Lawrence: University Press of Kansas, 2007.

Digeser, Peter. "The Fourth Face of Power." *The Journal of Politics* 54, no. 4 (November 1992): 977–1007.

Donahue, William. "Catholic League for Religious and Civil Rights." http://www.catholicleague.org/about.php.

Dostoevsky, Fyodor. *The Brothers Karamazov.* http://www.online-literature.com/dostoevsky/brothers_karamazov/73/.

Drakeman, Donald L. *Church, State, and Original Intent.* New York: Cambridge University Press, 2010.

Dunn, Charles W., ed. *The Future of Religion in American Politics.* Lexington: University Press of Kentucky, 2009.

Eichel, Larry. "'Values Voters': Credit and More." *Philadelphia Inquirer,* November 7, 2004. http://philly.newspaperdirect.com/epaper/viewer.aspx.

Eisgruber, Christopher L., and Lawrence G. Sager. *Religious Freedom and the Constitution.* Cambridge, Mass.: Harvard University Press, 2007.

———. "The Supreme Court's Hands-Off Approach to Religious Doctrine: Does It Matter What Religion Is?" *Notre Dame Law Review* 84 (2009): 807.

Esbeck, Carl H. "A Restatement of the Supreme Court's Law of Religious Freedom: Coherence, Conflict, or Chaos?" *Notre Dame Law Review* 70 (1995): 581.

"Evangelist Says He Was Misled in Giving Up PTL." *The New York Times,* May 27, 1987. http://www.nytimes.com/1987/05/27/us/evangelist-says-he-was-misled-in-giving-up-ptl.html?scp=3&sq=fundamentalists%20vs.%20pentecostals%20ptl%20scandal&st=cse.

Feldman, Noah. *Divided by God: America's Church-State Problem—and What We Should Do about It.* New York: Farrar, Straus & Giroux, 2005.

———. "From Liberty to Equality: The Transformation of the Establishment Clause." *California Law Review* 90 (2002): 673.

Feldman, Stephen M. *Please Don't Wish Me a Merry Christmas.* New York: New York University Press, 1997.

Finkelman, Paul. "The Ten Commandments on the Courthouse Lawn and Elsewhere." *Fordham Law Review* 73 (2005): 1477.

Fisher, Louis. *Religious Liberty in America: Political Safeguards.* Lawrence: University Press of Kansas, 2002.

Fowler, Robert Booth, Allen D. Hertzke, Laura R. Olson, and Kevin R. den Dulk. *Religion and Politics in America: Faith, Culture, and Strategic Choices.* 4th ed. Boulder, Colo.: Westview, 2010.

Galston, William A. *Liberal Purposes: Goods, Virtues, and Diversity in the Liberal State.* New York: Cambridge University Press, 1991.

Gamwell, Franklin I. "The Question of Democracy." *DePaul Law Review* 57 (2008): 997.

Garry, Patrick M. "The Democratic Aspect of the Establishment Clause: A Refutation of the Argument That the Clause Serves to Protect Religious or Nonreligious Minorities." *Mercer Law Review* 59 (2008): 595.

———. "Religious Freedom Deserves More Than Neutrality: The Constitutional Argument for Nonpreferential Favoritism of Religion." *Florida Law Review* 57 (2005): 1.

Gedicks, Frederick Mark. *The Rhetoric of Church and State: A Critical Analysis of Religion Clause Jurisprudence*. Durham, N.C.: Duke University Press, 1995.

Gedicks, Frederick Mark, and Roger Hendrix. "Uncivil Religion: Judeo-Christianity and the Ten Commandments." *West Virginia Law Review* 110 (2007): 275.

Gert, Bernard. "Coercion and Freedom." In J. Roland Pennock and John W. Chapman, *Coercion*, 30–48.

Gey, Steven G. "Life after the Establishment Clause." *West Virginia Law Review* 110 (2007): 1.

———. "Reconciling the Supreme Court's Four Establishment Clauses." *University of Pennsylvania Journal of Constitutional Law* 8 (2006): 725.

———. "Religious Coercion and the Establishment Clause." *University of Illinois Law Review* (1994): 463.

———. "Unity of the Graveyard and the Attack on Constitutional Secularism." *Brigham Young University Law Review* (2004): 1005.

———. "Vestiges of the Establishment Clause." *First Amendment Law Review* 5 (2006): 1.

Goldberg, Michelle. "Bachmann's Unrivaled Extremism." *The Daily Beast*, June 14, 2011. http://www.thedailybeast.com/articles/2011/06/14/michele-bachmanns-unrivaled-extremism-gay-rights-to-religion.html.

Goldford, Dennis J. *The American Constitution and the Debate over Originalism*. New York: Cambridge University Press, 2005.

Green, Steven K. "Locke v. Davey and the Limits to Neutrality Theory." *Temple Law Review* 77 (2004): 913.

Greenawalt, Kent. *Religion and the Constitution*, Vol. 1: *Free Exercise and Fairness*. Princeton, N.J.: Princeton University Press, 2006.

———. *Religion and the Constitution*, Vol. 2: *Establishment and Fairness*. Princeton, N.J.: Princeton University Press, 2008.

Hamburger, Philip. *Separation of Church and State*. Cambridge, Mass.: Harvard University Press, 2002.

Hamilton, Alexander, James Madison, and John Jay. *The Federalist Papers*. Edited by Clinton Rossiter, with a new introduction and notes by Charles R. Kesler. New York: New American Library, 1961 and 1999.

Hamilton, Gregory W. "The O'Connor Concurring Opinion: Interpretive Determinism and Neutrality's Pitfalls." In Stephen V. Monsma, *Church-State Relations in Crisis*, 103–26.

Hamilton, Marci A., and Rachel Steamer. "The Religious Origins of Disestablishment Principles." *Notre Dame Law Review* 81 (2006): 1755.

Hart, H. L. A. *The Concept of Law*. 2nd ed. Oxford: Oxford University Press, 1997.

Hertzke, Allen D. "The Supreme Court and Religious Liberty." *Weekly Standard* 16, no. 5 (October 18, 2010): 22–28.

Hobbes, Thomas. *Hobbes's Leviathan*. Oxford: Oxford University Press, 1967.

Hughes, Richard T. *Christian America and the Kingdom of God*. Urbana and Chicago: University of Illinois Press, 2009.

Hunter, James Davison. *Culture Wars: The Struggle to Control the Family, Art, Education, Law, and Politics in America*. New York: Basic Books, 1992.

Hyer, Marjorie. "Evangelist Reverses Position on God's Hearing Jews." *Washington Post*, October 11, 1980. http://www.washingtonpost.com/wp-dyn/content/article/2007/05/15/AR2007051501197_pf.html.

Ingersoll, Julie. "Mobilizing Evangelicals: Christian Reconstructionism and the Roots of the Religious Right." In Steven Brint and Jean Reith Schroedel, *Evangelicals and Democracy in America*, 179–208.

Iowa Family PAC. "We Will Keep Our Word, Because the Alternative Is Unacceptable." Press release, June 14, 2010. http://www.iowapolitics.com/index.iml?Article=199768.

Issenberg, Sasha. "Faith Still Sticky Issue as Romney Mulls Run: Mormonism Remains Hard Sell for Evangelicals." *Boston Globe*, July 3, 2010. http://www.boston.com/news/nation/washington/articles/2010/07/03/faith_still_sticky_issue_as_romney_mulls_run/.

Jefferson, Thomas. Letter to General Alexander Smyth, January 17, 1825. http://www.city-data.com/forum/religion-philosophy/188445-th-jeffersons-opinion-bibles-book-revelation.html.

Just, Felix, S. J. "Jewish and Christian Bibles: A Comparative Chart." http:/catholic-resources.org/Bible/Heb-Xn-Bibles.htm.

Kendall, Willmoore. *The Conservative Affirmation*. Chicago: Regnery Gateway, 1985.

———. "Three on the Line." *National Review*, August 31, 1956, 179–81, 191.

Kinsley, Michael. "Gaffes to the Rescue." *Time*, February 8, 2007. http://www.time.com/time/magazine/article/0,9171,1587283,00.html.

Kommers, Donald P., and Michael J. Wahoske, eds. *Freedom and Education:* Pierce v. Society of Sisters *Reconsidered*. South Bend, Ind.: Center for Civil Rights, University of Notre Dame Law School, 1978.

Koppelman, Andrew. “Secular Purpose.” *Virginia Law Review* 88 (2002): 87.

———. “The Troublesome Religious Roots of Religious Neutrality.” *Notre Dame Law Review* 84 (2009): 865.

Kramnick, Isaac, and R. Laurence Moore. *The Godless Constitution: The Case against Religious Correctness*. 2nd ed. New York: Norton, 1997.

Kurland, Philip B., and Ralph Lerner, eds. *The Founders' Constitution*. Vol. 5. Chicago: University of Chicago Press, 1987.

Kurtz, Stanley. “Scary Stuff.” *National Review Online*, April 28, 2005. http://www.nationalreview.com/kurtz/kurtz200504280758.asp.

Lafferty, Andrea. “Who Says Anti-Christian Bigotry Is Not on the Rise?” April 21, 2009. http://www.andrealafferty.org/2009/04/who-says-anti-christian-bigotry-is-not.html.

Laser, Rachel, Nikki Yamashiro, Jim Kessler, Robert P. Jones, and Daniel Cox. “Beyond the God Gap: A New Roadmap for Reaching Religious Americans on Public Policy Issues.” The Culture Program, Third Way, and Public Religion Research. http://www.publicreligion.org/objects/uploads/fck/file/Third%20Way-PRR%20Report%20-%20Beyond%20the%20God%20Gap.pdf.

Laycock, Douglas. “Formal, Substantive, and Disaggregated Neutrality toward Religion.” *DePaul Law Review* 39 (1990): 993.

———. “Religious Liberty as Liberty.” *Journal of Contemporary Legal Issues* 7 (1996): 313.

Leip, Dave. “Atlas of U.S. Presidential Elections.” http://uselectionatlas.org/RESULTS/.

Levy, Leonard W. *The Establishment Clause: Religion and the First Amendment*. 2nd ed., revised. Chapel Hill: University of North Carolina Press, 1994.

Locke, John. *A Letter Concerning Toleration*. Edited by James H. Tully. Indianapolis: Hackett, 1983.

Lukes, Steven. *Power: A Radical View*. 2nd ed. Houndmills, U.K.: Palgrave Macmillan, 2005.

Madison, James. *Memorial and Remonstrance against Religious Assessments*. http://press-pubs.uchicago.edu/founders/documents/amendI_religions43.html.

Mann, David. “Religious Billboards along I-65 Pulled after Protests.” *Evening News and Tribune*, Jeffersonville, Ind., February 8, 2007. http://newsandtribune.com/local/x519362641/Religious-billboards-along-I-65-pulled-after-protests.

“Marriage Activists Back Vander Plaats.” *Cedar Rapids Gazette*, January 13, 2010. http://gazetteonline.com/local-news/2010/01/13/marriage-activists-back-vander-plaats.

Marshall, William P. "What Is the Matter with Equality? An Assessment of the Equal Treatment of Religion and Nonreligion in First Amendment Jurisprudence." *Indiana Law Journal* 75 (2000): 193.

Martin, Gary. "The Myth of the Separation of Church and State: American's [*sic*] Founding Fathers: Deists or Christians." The Young Earth Creation Club. http://www.creationists.org/myth-of-the-seperation-of-church-and-state.html.

Marty, Martin E. "A Judeo-Christian Looks at the Judeo-Christian Tradition." *Christian Century* (October 5, 1986): 858–60. http://www.religion-online.org/showarticle.asp?title=188.

McConnell, Michael W. "Coercion: The Lost Element of Establishment." *William and Mary Law Review* 27 (1986): 933.

———. "Religious Freedom at a Crossroads." *University of Chicago Law Review* 59 (1992): 115.

McMullen, Cary. "Atheist Group Sues Lakeland for Prayers." *The Ledger.com*, July 12, 2010. http://www.theledger.com/apps/pbcs.dll/article?AID=/20100712/NEWS/7125028&template=printart.

Milbank, Dana. "With Pawlenty's Iowa Speech, a Side of Syrup." *Washington Post*, March 9, 2011. http://www.washingtonpost.com/wp-dyn/content/article/2011/03/08/AR2011030805530.html?wpisrc=nl_politics.

Miller, Lisa. "Saint Sarah." *Newsweek*, June 11, 2010. http://www.newsweek.com/2010/06/11/saint-sarah.html.

Monsma, Stephen V., ed. *Church-State Relations in Crisis: Debating Neutrality*. Lanham, Md.: Rowman & Littlefield, 2002.

———. "Concluding Observations." In Monsma, *Church-State Relations in Crisis*, 261–71.

Moore, Roy S. "Religion in the Public Square." *Cumberland Law Review* 29 (1998): 347.

Muñoz, Vincent Phillip. *God and the Founders: Madison, Washington, and Jefferson*. New York: Cambridge University Press, 2009.

———. "The Original Meaning of the Establishment Clause and the Impossibility of Its Incorporation." *University of Pennsylvania Journal of Constitutional Law* 8 (2006): 585.

Neuhaus, Richard John. *The Naked Public Square: Religion and Democracy in America*. 2nd ed. Grand Rapids: Eerdmans, 1986.

Nussbaum, Martha C. *Liberty of Conscience: In Defense of America's Tradition of Religious Equality*. New York: Basic Books, 2008.

Nylen, Leah. "DOJ to Appeal in National Day of Prayer Case." *Main Justice*, April 22, 2010. http://www.mainjustice.com/2010/04/22/doj-to-appeal-in-national-day-of-prayer-case/.

The Oxford English Dictionary, 2nd ed., prepared by J. A. Simpson and E. S. C. Weiner. Oxford: Clarendon, 1989.

Pennock, J. Roland, and John W. Chapman, eds. *Coercion*. Chicago: Aldine-Atherton, 1972.

Perry, Michael J. "Freedom of Religion in the United States: Fin de Siecle Sketches." *Indiana Law Journal* 75 (2000): 295.

———. *Religion in Politics: Constitutional and Moral Perspectives*. New York: Oxford University Press, 1997.

Pew Forum on Religion & Public Life. "Growing Number of Americans Say Obama Is a Muslim." http://pewforum.org/Politics-and-Elections/Growing-Number-of-Americans-Say-Obama-is-a-Muslim.aspx.

———. "2008 U.S. Religious Landscape Survey." http://religions.pewforum.org/.

Pew Research Center for the People and the Press. "Republican Candidates Stir Little Enthusiasm." http://people-press.org/2011/06/02/section-2-candidate-traits-and-experience/#mormon.

Powell, H. Jefferson. "Rules for Originalists." *Virginia Law Review* 73 (1987): 659.

Putnam, Robert D., and David E. Campbell. *American Grace: How Religion Divides and Unites Us*. New York: Simon & Schuster, 2010.

Rawls, John. *Political Liberalism*. Expanded ed. New York: Columbia University Press, 2005.

Rhodes, Michael R. "The Nature of Coercion." *Journal of Value Inquiry* 34 (2000): 369–81.

Romney, Mitt. "Faith in America." *The New York Times*, December 6, 2007. http://www.nytimes.com/2007/12/06/us/politics/06text-romney.html.

Rousseau, Jean-Jacques. *The Social Contract*. Translated by G. D. H. Cole. http://www.constitution.org/jjr/socon_01.htm#007.

Rushdoony, Rousas John. *The Institutes of Biblical Law*. Phillipsburg, N.J.: Presbyterian and Reformed Publishing, 1973.

———. "The State as an Establishment of Religion." In Kommers and Wahoske, *Freedom and Education*, 37–46.

Scalia, Antonin. "Originalism: The Lesser Evil." *University of Cincinnati Law Review* 57 (1989): 849.

Schaeffer, Franky. *A Time for Anger: The Myth of Neutrality*. Westchester, Ill.: Crossway Books, 1982.

Sedler, Robert A. "Understanding the Establishment Clause: The Perspective of Constitutional Litigation." *Wayne Law Review* 43 (1997): 1317.

Sen, Amartya. "Rights, Words, and Laws: Constitutions and Their Motivation." *The New Republic*, October 28, 2010, 24–29.

"Senate Confirmation Hearings for Joseph A. Alito. Day 2." *The New York Times*, January 10, 2006. http://www.nytimes.com/2006/01/10/politics/politicsspecial1/text-day2.html?pagewanted=all.

"Sexes: Women's War on Porn." *Time*, August 27, 1979. http://www.time.com/time/magazine/article/0,9171,920580,00.html.

Smith, Gina. "Will Religion Become a Weapon?" *The State*, June 16, 2010.

Smith, Steven D. *Foreordained Failure: The Quest for a Constitutional Principle of Religious Freedom*. New York: Oxford University Press, 1995.

———. "Our Agnostic Constitution." *New York University Law Review* 83 (2008): 120.

Stone, Geoffrey R., and Richard A. Epstein, eds. *The Bill of Rights in the Modern State*. Chicago: University of Chicago Press, 1992.

Story, Joseph L. *Commentaries on the Constitution of the United States*. http://www.lonang.com/exlibris/story/sto-305.htm.

———. "Commentaries on the Constitution 3: §§1865–73." In *The Founders' Constitution*. http://press-pubs.uchicago.edu/founders/documents/amendI_religions69.html.

Sullivan, Kathleen M. "Religion and Democracy." In *The Bill of Rights in the Modern State*, edited by Geoffrey R. Stone and Richard A. Epstein, 195–223. Chicago: University of Chicago Press, 1992.

Sullivan, Winnifred Fallers. *The Impossibility of Religious Freedom*. Princeton, N.J.: Princeton University Press, 2005.

Tocqueville, Alexis de. *Democracy in America*. Vol. 1. New York: Vintage, 1990.

Underkuffler, Laura S. "Through a Glass Darkly: Van Orden, McCreary, and the Dangers of Transparency in Establishment Clause Jurisprudence." *First Amendment Law Review* 5 (2006): 59.

Viteritti, Joseph P. *The Last Freedom: Religion from the Public School to the Public Square*. Princeton, N.J.: Princeton University Press, 2007.

von Clausewitz, Carl. *On War*. http://www.gutenberg.org/files/1946/1946-h/1946-h.htm#2HCH0001.

Wald, Kenneth D., and Allison Calhoun-Brown. *Religion and Politics in the United States*. 6th ed. Lanham, Md.: Rowman & Littlefield, 2010.

Waldman, Paul. "The God Squad. The Republican Frontrunners: Christian Superstars." *The American Prospect*, June 14, 2011. http://prospect.org/cs/articles?article=the_god_squad3.

Ward, Cynthia V. "Coercion and Choice under the Establishment Clause." *University of California-Davis Law Review* 39 (2006): 1621.

Washington, George. "The Farewell Address." The Papers of George Washington. http://gwpapers.virginia.edu/documents/farewell/transcript.html.

Whitehead, John W. *The Second American Revolution*. Elgin, Ill.: David C. Cook, 1982.

Whitehead, John W., and John Conlan. "The Establishment of the Religion of Secular Humanism and Its First Amendment Implications." *Texas Tech Law Review* 10 (1978): 1.

Wilcox, Clyde. *Onward Christian Soldiers? The Religious Right in American Politics*. 4th ed. Boulder, Colo.: Westview, 2010.

Wilhelmsen, Frederick D. "My Doxy Is Orthodoxy." *National Review*, May 22, 1962, 365–66.

Witte, John, Jr. *Religion and the American Constitutional Experiment*. 2nd ed. Boulder, Colo.: Westview, 2005.

Index